Letters From a
Fainthearted Feminist
and
More From Martha

Jill Tweedie

Illustrated by Merrily Harpur

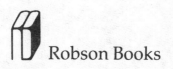

Robson Books

Grateful thanks to the *Guardian*,
where these letters first appeared

Letters From a Fainthearted Feminist first published in Great Britain in 1982 by Robson Books Ltd, Bolsover House, 5-6 Clipstone Street, London W1P 7EB.
Copyright © 1982 Jill Tweedie

More From Martha first published in Great Britain in 1983 by Robson Books Ltd, Bolsover House, 5-6 Clipstone Street, London W1P 7EB.
Copyright © 1983 Jill Tweedie

First published in Great Britain as a single volume in 1994 by Robson Books Ltd.
Copyright © 1994 Jill Tweedie

British Library Cataloguing in Publication Data
A catalogue record for this title is available from the British Library

ISBN 0 86051 914 7

Printed by The Guernsey Press Company Limited, Guernsey, Channel Islands.

Letters From a Fainthearted Feminist

Introduction

Martha and Mary have been soul mates of mine for more years than I can count. Well, I can count them actually – I'm not daft you know – but I do not choose to at this moment in time. All three of us are deeply committed to the principles of the Women's Movement. That is to say, Martha's committed, Mary's committed and I'm committed, though none of us is entirely convinced of the ideological correctness of the others' commitment. Not that we make a thing about it, obviously, being Sisters. We just talk occasionally among ourselves. For instance, Martha might say to me that it's all very admirable, she's sure, Mary carrying on like she's Boadicea, but she (Martha) cannot help noticing that she (Mary) keeps a very low profile when it comes to the question of men, children and families generally, which is a bit odd since that's where feminism's front line is, if you come right down to it, right?

Whereas Mary might point out to me that if Martha really rejected housework and the patriarchal society as completely as she (Mary) has, she (Martha) would have downed brooms and booted out a certain patriarch who shall be nameless long ago, not to mention the fact that it's no good calling yourself a feminist without having a political dimension. Also, I happen to know that both of them get together behind my back now and then and point out to each other that me being a wage slave and a paid-up wife and houseperson means I've capitulated to the Superwoman put-down, which is hardly the royal road to women's liberation, is it?

Mary once mentioned that the seminal influence on her feminism was Valerie Solanas, the woman who shot Andy Warhol in the sixties, wrote the S.C.U.M. Manifesto (Society for Cutting Up Men) and advocated women's total separatism. And Martha once told me that her seminal influence was Betty Freidan, author of *The Feminine Mystique*, who is rather keen on women in the family, all things being equal. Personally, I think that says something about the level of both their consciousnesses – how can two feminists talk about seminal influences when the word is clearly 'ovarian'? My own ovarian influences are Valerie Solanas and Betty Freidan, which is why I am forced to retire, once or twice a year, to quiet cottage hospitals in country surroundings.

I first came across Martha's letters when I was staying for a few days with Mary at Sebastopol Terrace. They were being used to prop up Mary's kitchen table at the time because it only had three and a half legs. I unwedged and read them in between meals, which gave me plenty of time to absorb them because Mary doesn't go in a whole lot for what are generally called meals. And I thought, when I'd finished them, that other women in Martha's situation might like to read them too, if only to check out their feelings *vis-à-vis* hers. So, with Martha's permission, I suggested their publication and this is them. These are they. Mary's letters to Martha, in case you were wondering, ended up in Martha's cat's litter tray.

Before I close, I should like to make my own position clear. I have often been irritated by Martha's fainthearted approach to feminism (I am not at all like that, myself) and I must say I often deplore Mary's blinkered fundamentalism (I am not at all like that, myself). I'm sure that sensible readers will agree with me that the way ahead for women is an amalgam of the two. A faintheartedness tempered with fundamentalism. Or is it a fundamental faintheartedness? You pays your money and you takes your choice. Women's liberation is, after all, about choice.

1982   Jill Tweedie

Dear Mary

Sorry I haven't written for a while, but back here in Persil Country the festive season lasts from November 1 (make plum pudding) to January 31 (lose hope and write husband's thank-you letters). I got some lovely presents. A useful Spare Rib Diary. A book called The Implications of Urban Women's Image in Early American Literature. A Marks and Sparks rape alarm. A canvas Backa-Pak so that the baby can come with me wherever I go – a sort of DIY rape alarm. And, of course, your bracing notelets, which will be boomeranging back to you for the rest of the year. Things I did not get for Christmas: a Janet Reger nightie, a feather boa, a pair of glittery tights.

Looking back, what with God Rest Ye Merry Gentlemen, Good King Wenceslas, Unto Us a Son is Born, We Three Kings, Father Christmas ho-hoing all over the place and the house full of tired and emotional males, I feel like I'm just tidying up after a marathon stag party. Our Lady popped up now and again but who remembers the words to her songs once they've left school? We learnt them but, then, ours was an all-girl school, in the business of turning out Virgin Mother replicas. If I ever get to heaven, I'll be stuck making manna in the Holy Kitchens and putti-sitting fat feathered babies quicker than I can say Saint Peter. Josh, on the other hand, will get a celestial club chair and a stiff drink. If God is a woman, why is She so short of thunderbolts?

I went to a fair number of parties dressed up as Wife of Josh but, to tell you the shameful truth, it was my Women's Collective beanfeast that finally broke my nerve. One wouldn't think one could work up a cold sweat about going as oneself to an all-woman party, would one? One can. I had six acute panic attacks about what to wear, for a start. Half my clothes are sackcloth, due to what Josh still calls my menopausal baby (come to me, my menopausal baby) and the other half are ashes, cold embers of the woman I once was. Fashion may well be a tool of women's oppression but having to guess is worse. In the end I went makeup-less in old flared jeans and saw, too late, that Liberation equals Calvin Klein and Lip Gloss or Swanky Modes and Toyah hair but not, repeat not, Conservative Association jumble. Misery brought on tunnel vision, I swooned like a Victorian lady and had to be woman-handled into a taxi home. Quelle fiasco.

That same evening, the blood back in my cheeks, I complained to Josh that I was cooking the three hundred and sixtieth meal of 1980 and he said move aside, I'll take over. Coming to, I found myself, family and carry-cot in a taxi driving to a posh restaurant. Very nice, too, but Josh was so smug afterwards that I felt it incumbent upon me, in the name of Wages for Housework, to point out that his solution to the domestic chore-sharing problem had just cost us fifty quid, and if he intended to keep that up, he'd have to apply for funding to the IMF. Bickered for the rest of the evening, Josh wittily intoning his Battle of Britain speech – you can please some of the women all of the time and all of the women . . . but you know the rest, ha ha.

I had hardly recovered from these two blows to the system when Mother arrived to administer her weekly dose of alarm and despondency. How can I *think*, she said 18 times, of letting my Daughter drive van, alone, to Spain? Do I *want* her to be raped, mutilated and left for dead in foreign parts? It is my duty to insist that a *man* goes with her. I point out that Jane is a large, tough, 20-year-old rather more competent than me, Mother and Mother's Husband put together and Mother leaves room in huff. I then had a panic attack about Jane being raped, mutilated and left for dead in foreign parts and insisted she took a man with her. Like the Yorkshire Ripper, you mean, shouted Jane and left room in huff.

Myself, I blame British Rail. Does Sir Peter Parker realize the mayhem caused to family units all over Britain by pound-a-trip Grans intent on injecting overdue guilt into long-unvisited daughters? Josh's Ma trained over, too, apparently to make sure I wouldn't grass on Josh if he turned out to be the Yorkshire Ripper. Ma, I said, what alternative would I have? Even the sacred marriage bonds might snap, given that one's spouse was a mass murderer. Marriage bonds maybe, she said, but I am his Mother. Then she said would I inform on Ben, I said what else could I do and she said you could stop his pocket money. She did. Ben, I said, glaring at the stick of celery that is my son, if I hear you've murdered *one more woman*, no sixpence for you next Friday. Well, now they've arrested someone who's got a wife and a mother.

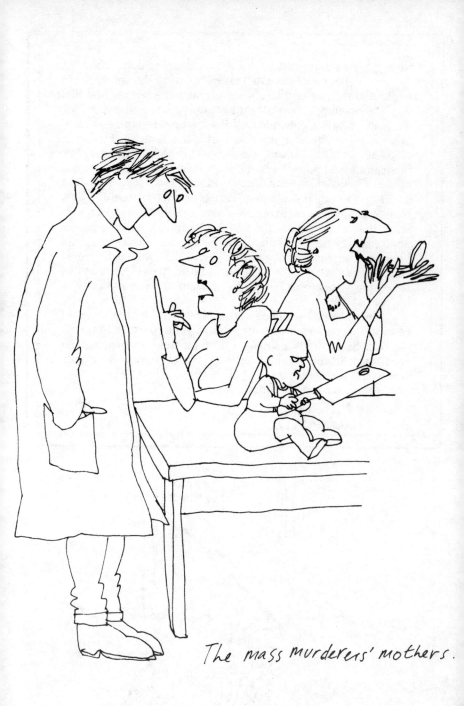

The mass murderers' mothers.

Keep your ears pinned back for the feminine connection.

Ben's friend Flanagan stayed most of the holiday. He explained that he had left home because his mother had this new boyfriend. How difficult it must be, I thought, for adolescent boys in the midst of the Oedipal Dilemma to have alien males vying for their love-object's favours. Flanagan said he couldn't stand the way his Mum bullied her boyfriends and now she had chucked them both out because of her women's meetings. You're as bad as the NFers, he told her. I can't help being a boy, can I, any more than if I was black? But you *are* black, Flanagan, I said, and Black is Beautiful. Yeah, except I'm white, he said. Flanagan's Dad is white, said Ben, so why shouldn't Flanagan choose? What am I, anyway, a racist or something? With that, they both pulled on jackets covered with swastikas and went out. At times like this, I am so grateful for the baby. Dear thing, he's hardly a boy yet at all.

You probably won't read this letter until mid-January – I read in the papers that your lot had gone to Rome to picket Nativity Scenes. My goings-on here on the home front must seem very trivial to you. Ah well, we also serve who only stand and whine.

Yours, from a hot stove,

Martha

hardly a boy...

Dear Mary

So it's Arrivaderci Roma and now you're in Berlin. Lucky old you, I'm so housebound these days I have to take Kwells to get to the greengrocers. Fascinated to hear how you all burst into that German lawyer's office, debagged him and sprayed his naughty bits with blue paint. Frosted, yet. What larks, eh? Though not, I suppose, for the lawyer, who was obviously terrified you were going to perform an emergency dingalingectomy. Read out the details to Josh at breakfast and he couldn't finish his kipper. When his voice was back to normal he got very pompous about lawyers' rights to defend rapists and rapists' rights to be defended and now he knew why Justice was a woman and blind. She may be a woman, I said, burning the toast, but she is not a Sister. The law is made by the men for the men of the men and I never heard you complain about its bias against us over the last two thousand years. He stormed out in the end, saying he'd be sleeping in the spare room from now on because he wasn't having his personal plumbing redecorated by power-mad libbers. By the way, I suppose he's all right now, is he? The lawyer, I mean.

Anyway, sweet of you to say you'll get me a duty-free goodie on the boat back. In a sort of way I wouldn't say no to a bottle of scent. There, I've got it out. No, I don't want to be a sex object and I do know scent is pushy, getting up people's noses without their permission, and I don't want expensive French ooo-la-la but English Rose can't be all bad? It's natural enough, though mainly of course, on roses. There are the herby scents, too. Is one considered a sex object if one smells of coq au vin? Oh dear, that even *sounds* wrong – buy what you think best.

Goodness knows why I've got this yen for scent lately. Josh says women exhibit some very odd symptoms years before anything happens or, rather, doesn't happen. Our next-door neighbour's wife started laughing. It upset her husband no end, he says she's never been one for laughing before and now it's chronic. It's not as if she has much to

11

laugh at, poor dear, what with looking after her husband's senile Mum and her boy in trouble and working nights at the Kentucky Fried. Personally, I wonder she can raise a smile. Perhaps she's read that book I picked up at the library. It said The Change was nothing to worry about because most women only got shrinking breasts, swelling hips, hot flushes and facial hair. Looking forward to being a fat red-faced flat-chested bearded lady is enough to give anyone terminal laughter.

The baby's fine, since you ask, and ever so good, even if he is a trifle permanent. I thought I'd have the babysitting problem licked, this time round, but silly me. Jane explodes if I ask her more than once a month, accuses me of chromosome exploitation, gender fascism, daughter colonization and other crimes I've never heard of, though I expect she's right. What she won't understand is that boys are so bad at it. I know I ought to persevere and prepare Ben for being a house-husband and a truly involved father in later life but should I use the baby as a teaching machine? Last time he baby-sat we couldn't find the poor wee thing for half-an-hour, though it's true he was only sitting under Ben's dismantled record player chewing a bit off Adam and the Ants. You *see*, Ben kept saying, there's nothing the *matter* with him, is there? What's all the *fuss* about? The episode hasn't done a thing for his vestigial fathering instincts, either. Now he says he'll never have kids, if everyone makes such a *fuss* about it. Bess and May at the Women's Centre have offered to come but the last time I called they were out demonstrating for 24-hour nurseries.

I'm sure all this bores you concrete, what with your very sensible decision not to have children because of men being the way they are and the world being what it is. They are and it is, I do so agree, but there he is. I don't think any of my friends have quite forgiven me for having him, especially since he's a boy, the misguided sausage. And he was premature, due to that long walk from Hyde Park Corner on the last Every Child a Wanted Child March. Is that a sort of excuse? Am enclosing snap of him. It's blurred because he has a rash and a tooth coming through and is howling.

Chalked up two bad boo-boos last week. First, we were invited by the Department to meet Josh's new boss. There were masses of people and Josh didn't introduce me to a soul, just shot off into a corner to talk shop with the pin-stripes. I felt I ought to make an effort so I said to this woman wasn't the Department a mysterious place and could she understand a word her husband told her about it? She slid off sharpish, looking like she'd just swallowed glass. Turned out she was Josh's new boss, quite good-looking in a bureaucratic way, brilliant double first, breakthrough for womankind trala. I drank rather a lot after that one.

Then, at the launderette, I got chatting with another woman, recounted the aforementioned story and said didn't she hate being asked what she did at parties and having to say she was a housewife? Quick as a flash, she turned into a militant houseperson, gave me a lecture about some women *choosing* to stay at home with the children and if women's lib wasn't about *choosing* what was it about and she couldn't stand the view that you weren't liberated until you were pinned behind a typewriter from nine to five. People like you, she said, won't be happy till you've made women robots just like men and she flounced off with her plastic bag and her three screaming kids.

Sometimes I think, Mary, that you don't quite grasp the complications we face, here at the grassroots.

Yours, covered with facial egg,

Martha

Dear Mary

Of course I understand your objection to rapists and rippers and robbers – in a word, men. But you have to understand my position. I have them in the house, Mary, three of them. Well, you can't quite count the baby yet, though he's already very demanding, wanting to be fed at inopportune moments and forcing me to drop everything and retire to the bedroom. Jane and Ben had the nerve, the other night, to ask why I couldn't breastfeed him naturally? I told them I was under the impression I was doing just that and they said they meant in *front of them*. I was shocked. Certainly *not*, I said in a Lady Bracknell voice. Then they both delivered a diatribe about Mother Nature that included references to dogs and puppies, the women of Africa and the women in Parliament who did it in front of MPs.

As coolly as I could, I pointed out to the kids that even women in Parliament tucked themselves under the Woolsack or somewhere and pretty watercolours of breastfeeding women with rosy toddlers gathered round their knees were one thing but doing it with two great yawks like them gaping down their Mother's hitherto unrevealed assets – and the possibility of Flanagan & Co. joining the merry throng – was quite another. Besides, it could wreak havoc with Ben's Oedipal Dilemma, if he had one, which I doubt. And if, Mary, you are thinking of taking their side, I would remind you that the only helpless member of God's creation you've ever fed in public was that baby guinea pig of yours and it died.

But I digress. What I meant to say was that living with men makes you realize they suffer too. This morning, Ben's face had all gone to pieces and he kept jumping suddenly, like a flea-ridden cat. Asked the matter, he said his jaw was fractured, his molars ached, his gums had gangrene, and he might quite possibly die, all because he'd spent last evening grinding his teeth at a party. But why, I said. So's to look like this, he said, clenching his teeth, sucking in his cheeks and allowing an expression of psychopathic blankness to flatten his features. But *why*, I said. At which he groaned and gibbered and smirked until I got it. He was being *High Noon* and *Gunfight at the OK Corral* and Jack Palance in anything, for the sole purpose of attracting the girls and to hell with his jawbones, his dentures, and endemic facial dystrophy. I think that's rather touching, don't you?

No, you don't. Ah well, I'll try you with a larger ethical problem – President Reagan. It took me a longish while to realize that he didn't have two heads like Zaphod Beeblebrox, one talking and the other doing the noddies. Ah *ha*, I said to myself of a sudden. So that's Mrs Reagan, the head with the hat, just like Mrs Carter before her.

Now, as you know, I'm all in favour of wives being rewarded for the unpaid labour they put in on behalf of their husbands' careers. The place is awash with the wives of vicars and doctors and diplomats and lord mayors and corporate gents (I include myself modestly in here) all flogging our guts out, gratis, for the sake of our husbands' companies, practices, parishes, towns, countries and so on. We are charming hostesses, delightful dinner-givers, caring telephone voices, judicious flatterers and soft shoulders for people to cry on so they don't wet the men's suits.

And is there a penny in it for us? There is not. Are there even thanks? Usually they go to the husband, as if he were the one who whisked up the soufflé, coped with Mrs Hoo-Ha's nasty turn and rubbed up against the boss. Though we might get a surreptitious pinch on the bottom for services rendered. I've been there, Mary.

But at the other extreme, why should the Americans get a Presidentess they never voted for? Whispering away in the President's ear without the say-so of a single ballot paper? That's power without responsibility if you like. A woman who wears red from top to toe at her husband's inauguration is not about to back out of the limelight and those who think Ron used the movies to get to be President might ask themselves if Madam Reagan isn't using the Presidency to get back into movies? Her and her bedside revolver. Who does she think is going to break in on her White House slumbers? A flying Ayatollah? That one is a bigger sabre-rattler than her Ron and it worries me. Imagine what it will do for women's image when survivors of a nuclear holocaust scuttle up from their underground caves, take a look round the ruined planet and say, 'Of course, I blame *her*.'

A friend of mine wrote from America that she never saw so many dead animals on so many women's backs as at Ron's inaugural ball – she said it looked like the biggest ecological disaster since the Raj. She mentioned this to some man standing near her and he said look at it this way, it's a triumph of biodegradability, which is more than you can say for punks and their plastic. Yes, Mary, I am aware that I possess a beaver coat but it is a very old coat and the beaver passed away yonks ago.

That's all for now except to say I do think you ought to stop harassing Shirley Williams. She is not the most hopeless female since Bo Peep nor the worst little madame since Shirley Temple and if the Chinese can suspend Mrs Mao's death sentence, surely you should follow suit? Mrs Williams has done a lot for women that I can't immediately recall and it will do no one any good to keep shouting abuse through her letter-box. At the moment she is simply a distressed gentlewoman of insecure means who needs all the sleep she can get.

Yours, from the middle of the right of centre,

Martha

President Reagan's Inaugural Ball

Dear Mary

It was lovely to see you so unexpectedly last Saturday and such a pity the visit was so short. Did you get the stain out of those super Fiorucci jeans? The trouble is, babies with nappy rash can't wear plastic pants because the ammonia in the urine gets trapped and irritates the . . . well, you don't want all the details, do you? I'm afraid Mother wasn't at her best, either. She's been over-excited ever since the Labour Conference, though why that should concern her I don't know – in Mother's political spectrum Mrs Thatcher is dripping wet. I think it was that Labour MP that set her temples throbbing again, the one who chairs the Mobilizing Committee for what she always calls the Rank and Vile but that's only her little joke and I don't honestly think she would shoot quite all the Lefties she says she'd shoot. Not dead, anyway.

And then, of course, there was Josh. It's a funny thing that when he and I are alone together, I am permitted to dig over the garden, tar the roof and clean the chimney, all without a murmur of protest from him. But you come on the scene and suddenly Josh can only just restrain his chivalrous urges out of respect for your feminism. He *would* pull out your chair but he knows you'd disapprove. He *would* uncork the wine except you'd think him an mcp. He *would* carve the roast but that might seem sexist. He *would* say how well you're looking but he doesn't want to be hit over the head with your handbag, what, what? I'm perspiring lightly, Mary, just writing this.

Repeat to yourself, over and over, that Josh is fifty. Half a century old. Women can change, whatever their age (except Mother, that is) but leave men in peace for a minute and they set like cement and spend the rest of their lives repelling the faintest whiff of a new idea as if it were a bulldozer come to hack out their foundations. Josh, let's face it, is the original unreconstructed male but he can be very sweet sometimes, in his own way. Last time I told you that, you said some people thought gorillas were cute but that's very unfair. Friends must accept friends, warts and all, particularly if they're joined to their warts in holy matrimony, as I am.

Actually, I'm sure Josh secretly admires you and is only afraid you'll subvert me and, one of these days, I'll follow you out through the front door like the Pied Piper's children, leaving him to live on boiled eggs for the rest of his life, which wouldn't be long considering what boiled eggs do for the cholesterol level. As it happens, we had the most almighty row after you'd gone (Josh says we always have the most almighty row after you've gone *and* after I've read Marilyn French *and* after I've been to my women's collective). Ask yourself *why*, I shouted at him, pourquoi, perchè, warum? Because women never know when they're well off, he said. At the time, I was down on my knees scrubbing the kitchen floor and he was spreadeagled on the sofa sipping a Scotch, though he did lift up his feet as I scrubbed by.

But enough of the squalid domestic front. Let us cast our eyes to the bracing outside world and give three cheers for another woman Prime Minister. That makes five by my count – Norway, India, Iceland, Bolivia and us. Well, Iceland is a President, not a PM, and India is more your Royalty than anything and I've got an uneasy feeling Bolivia has already hit the dust and our own Mrs. T. would be better hidden under a bushel, whatever that is.

But Norway is fair and square, a democratically elected mother of four and Labour, to boot. Odd that her husband is a leading member of the Conservative Opposition. What can it be like, to quarrel over the kitchen table *and* the front benches? or perhaps Norwegians, up to their knees in permafrost, can maintain a matrimonial *sang froid* unknown to the warm-blooded, volatile English.

Not that I think it's done our Cause much good, some of the women who've made the Top Job. Men have managed to live under male monsters – Hitler, Stalin, Caligula, Peter the Great, Attila the Hun – without drawing any derogatory conclusions about their own sex but let a woman add 2p to the cost of false teeth and all anti-feminist hell breaks loose. On the other hand, Josh voted for Mrs T. and still thinks this makes him an honorary founder member of the Women's Movement. Whenever I register an egalitarian complaint he says he voted for a woman Prime Minister didn't he, so how can anyone accuse him of being against women's liberation?

Two jokes that are making the school rounds now, just to keep you in touch with an adolescent world you will never, the Goddess willing, know at first hand: what did Elvis Presley get for Christmas? Answer, John Lennon. And what do Paul McCartney and John Lennon have in common? Answer, Wings. Well, at least they're non-sexist. A Chinese friend who came from Hong Kong last week adds an inscrutable Chinese quip. She says whenever the Chinese criticize the Gang of Four, they hold up five fingers, thus indicating the silent presence of Mr Mao among their souvenirs. She maintains that if Jiang Qing were to appear on Peking pavements, in two seconds there wouldn't be a shred of her left unlynched. Oh dear.

How, I often worry, are we going to prevent these token women turning the tide against us for good? And talking of token women, I've spend the last two days getting Josh's wardrobe washed and ironed for his trip next week to Brussels for the Department. He's accompanying his new boss who is, if you remember, this summa cum laude trollop who thinks I am just a Wife and will soon be sending me memos in triplicate on where to buy Josh's ties. Josh is in a state of most unJoshlike nerves. Is it permitted for Sisters to burst into other Sisters' offices and hit them hard across their lipsticked chops?

Yours, with a fist clenched,

Martha

18 February

Dear Mary

Well, well. What a lot of plots are being hatched chez vous. Is your friend Mo the one with the purple scalp? Fancy her starting a new Party and already having the support of every squatter on her block. 'Women Against Everything Against Women!' is certainly a very comprehensive name but had you thought that its initials make WAEAW, which isn't the easiest acronym I've ever heard. A cry for help, really. Is that what Mo had in mind?

Obviously, all real feminists must be disillusioned with the three existing parties – four, probably, by the time you read this. As you say, all of them are male, never mind what female fairy they've stuck on the top of the tree. What with the closet Right and the butch Left and the spayed Centre, where do women come in?

The Right do their male-bonding (which is to say female-unbonding) in prep schools, public schools and ghastly clubs and call themselves Monetarists, which is just a Tory word for Muggers; they don't actually hit women over the head and snatch our handbags, they just make sure no money gets into the handbags in the first place.

The Left pinch your bottom while you make the tea, propose snide anti-women motions at trade union meetings (like the one you sent me about 'pets' being their owners' responsibility, when they meant 'children') and shout 'take it off' at strippers in their working men's clubs.

As for the Liberal Democratic Council for Being Jolly D. to Everybody, we know they have no visible means of support and will therefore instantly require all female members to spend their entire time making jam and organizing jumble sales. At most we can only expect a prize for the woman who knits the best party policy without using a pattern.

I expect you're right when you say Foot and Benn the Flowerpot Men aren't really interested in women's equality or they'd get their pronouns sorted out but it is unkind of you to add that Foot is, anyway, overdue for his meeting with the Great Chiropodist in the Sky.

So when I read about your idea, I thought it was brill, as Ben would say. Better than Mo's, in the long run. A Feminist Tendency that infiltrates the Tories as sleepers (ho ho) and then erupts, at designated times, against particularly repulsive policies. I've always felt that this kind of subversion would be far more effective than constantly scratching away at those who believe more or less as you do – people take more notice of you if you've got a sterling anti-Them pedigree and then suddenly come down on Their side.

Is it possible that there are men doing it at this very moment? Viz Very-Right-Wing Tory John Gorst proclaiming that he's got his reservations about telephone-tapping? Or the Right-Wing MPs against Murdoch? Don't you feel an awful temptation to forgive them all their past sins and love them? Whereas boring old Labour MPs who've been against everything since Runnymede merely make you yawn? Well, not you, perhaps. Me.

The only flaw in your idea that I can see is that infiltration is a slow business and you won't have that much time if the Duke of Edinburgh has his way. Should I start a campaign naming him as HRH Nuclear Waste personified? Next thing we know, he'll be blasting the grouse off Scottish moors with a Cruise missile. Personally, I don't believe he'd even qualify as a Third-Class British citizen unless the Tories have in mind a special loophole for itinerant Royals.

And I bet he's got a nuclear shelter built under Buck House where the Royals can breed through 5,000 years of radiation half-life. But with them, who would notice?

Anyway, count me in as a founder member of the Feminist Tendency and the WAEAW, but *don't tell Josh*. It's Department policy that none of its staff 'or their wives' should be members of any political party. A detached overview, says Josh, must be seen to be held. Rather than actually held, he means, since no one in the Department, including friend husband, would dream of voting anything but Tory.

Chez moi, unlike toi, all is stasis. Josh left yesterday, rising like a pin-striped waistcoated Phoenix from the ashes of his home to fly Sandy or Debbie or Whoever to Brussels. It transpires that his boss lives not far away, so she collected him in her white Porsche 924 de luxe, sun roof, tinted glass, at 8 am. I'd been packing his suitcase since seven and was still in my dressing-gown so I couldn't emerge to meet her, like Mr Rochester's wife. Josh just shouted goodbye up the stairs, doubtless leaving Ms Boss with a cockle-warming impression of wifely sluttishness and neglect.

I peered out of the bedroom window and saw her wearing, I swear, a Jean Muir original, with hair so sprayed it didn't budge in the force nine gale. And get this, Josh opened the car door for her. That could have been me in there, Mary, if I hadn't sacrificed everything for love.

And what has love got me? A Marks and Sparks candlewick unoriginal and a fortnight's family camping in France. Men, I feel, are like wine – before buying, a real connoisseur takes a small sip and spits them out. If only I could spit Josh far enough away that he would have to look back and see me as more than a bunch of electricity bills chewed to the shape of a woman. It was St. Valentine's Day last Saturday, but all I got was a card from a plumber, saying he'd fix my pipes.

Yours, with a leaking heart,

Martha

Dear Mary

I've got an old bone to pick with you. No, I'd better re-word that. I should like to discuss my spouse with you, one Josh. Look, when you moan to me about some hitch in one of your campaigns or an ideological spat or something, do I ever write back and just say, flatly, give it up then? I do not. I scratch about in the dim folds of my grey matter in order to come up with some constructive solution or subtle circumnavigation. I do not blow even metaphorical raspberries. But when I complain to you about Josh, you more or less imply that if I haven't dumped, executed or otherwise dispatched him by return of post I will be drummed out of the women's movement and forcibly enrolled in my local chapter of the Mother's Union. This is unhelpful.

Why is it that you're perfectly happy battling men in the abstract – the patriarchal society, the male ethos, the masculine principle blah blah – and say you're a champion of Womankind, yet if one woman complains about one man you don't want to know? I've noticed that about some feminists. They'll devote their lives to the struggle of the sexes but any individual manifestation of that struggle and they go into spasms of boredom and contempt. Unless, of course, the man is a really big concrete nasty, a rapist or a batterer of his wife, in which case she'll get all the support she can use.

But the sort of problems I have, representing as they do ordinary women's lives in the patriarchal society, like packing Josh's suitcase and washing his socks and not flying anywhere because of the baby, dry up even your crocodile tears. The ties between a man and a woman, Mary, are a mite too complex to be completely solved by shouting *stuff 'im*. There's sex for a start and I don't fancy women, even if that is the result of masculine conditioning, like Adrienne Rich says. I'm too old to get de-conditioned now. Besides, how many women are going to get turned on by me in my candlewick dressing-gown, tastefully spotted by the baby's second thoughts? With all the conditioning on their side, I don't notice *men* battering down my door for the chance to possess my middle-aged spread, never mind two delinquent teenagers and a blotchy sort of baby, and I haven't had the glad-eye from a woman since I was Miss Shaw's favourite goal-keeper back in the Upper Fifth. I'm not sure they make 'em like Miss Shaw any more.

The truth is, Mary, that many women defect or never get involved with feminism in the first place because they see all too clearly that Achilles is their Heel and they can't afford to start from there, especially if they've already given birth to little Achilleses. Do try thinking of me as, say, a subsistence tenant farmer and Josh as the wicked landowner. You'd hardly give the tenant farmer a ticking-off for not having upped stakes, would you? Sometimes I'd *like* to walk out but what's the point of disappearing into a feminist sunset hand in hand with nothing?

Depressing, isn't it, that the only triumph for women last week was Princess Anne winning over Nelson Mandela and Jack Jones as Chancellor of London University? Still, it must be a majority of men that put her there and I imagine men suffer more from Mummy dreams about the Royal ladies than we do. It made me feel Princess Anne was only too right when she said higher education was an over-rated pastime. If it gets her into office over a man who's spent 20 years in prison for fighting injustice, it certainly is. I don't think I'll take that Open University course, after all. It might give me weak knees, a symptom of what we doctors call the Curtseying Syndrome.

By the way, when I said I'd help your friend Mo's 'Women Against Everything Against Women" party, I didn't mean I was yearning to spend the next fortnight licking envelopes. Mo's envelopes have a particularly disgusting taste and will probably pollute my maternal milk and poison the baby. Why can't Mo's male supporters lick them for a change and give us women the space to go power mad? Tell her I'll do this lot now they're here but one of the Things Against Women is definitely envelope-licking. Mixed bag of names she's come up with, hasn't she? Mrs Whitehouse only represents Women Against, Mrs Kennedy seems a trifle far-flung, I'm sure Leila Khaled gives all her money to the Golan Heights Home for Retired Hi-jackers and I think Anais Nin is dead.

You don't think Mo had anything to do with that lot who fired on the Greek Patriarch last week, do you? She did mention, in her note with the envelopes, that she was going to be in the Middle East shortly. Could the title 'Patriarch' have

overly inflamed her? I hope not. As a woman and mother of three I cannot condone violence, even against Patriarchs wearing funny hats and if Mo is, by any chance, fancying herself as the Baader-Meinhof of Sebastopol Terrace, I'm afraid I shall have no option but to withdraw my spit from her envelopes.

Meanwhile, back at the ranch, Ben has acquired four white mice. I was rather chuffed when I heard him call one of them Goethe. There are literary hopes for that boy I thought, until I realised he was only saying Gertie. Apparently, they're all Gerties, so they won't breed, though how Ben can tell I don't know. From their expressions, he says. I suppose they all look itsy-bitsy cute, said Jane crossly. No, just dumb, said Ben. They broke Josh's spare specs, fighting, *after that.*

I'd just had a phone call from Josh in Brussels. He said he was speaking from the office but, if so, they've just hired a 10-piece band on the ratepayers' money. He wanted to remind me to write to the Gas Board. It's wonderful to know I'm in his thoughts, even when he's over the water. I bet that Ms Boss of his with the sticky hair approves of open-ended marriages. I bet you do too. Even I might, if the open-end revealed anything more alluring than our eighty-year-old postman.

Yours, in a state of non-specific arousal,

Martha

Dear Mary

This week I've been slogging through a housewife's hell. Monday, the baby decided to recapture its youth and began waking at 6 am again, demanding milk, women and song. Ben, on the other hand, off for half-term, never appeared before noon. Pretty soon the household had split into different time zones – him having breakfast Down Under, me having a midnight snack in the Old Country. Then the fridge flipped its lid and started making ice like it had just bought shares in John Curry.

Twenty phone calls later I raised a sleeping beauty in the repair department who said she'd send a man but couldn't promise an a.m. or a p.m. You mean to say, I said, that I have to stay chained *chez moi* from nine to five to suit the whims of your repairman? If Doctor Finlay could make appointments, why can't you? Just wait, I said. One of these days it'll be you at home going bonkers, Miss Brook Street Bureau, and then you'll be sorry you didn't show solidarity with your female customers. Pardon? she said. I could *hear* her filing her nails.

So all day Tuesday I stayed in but I did, once, go to the loo. I have this weak bladder. When I got downstairs again, there was the card on the doormat. 'Your repairman called but could not get an answer.' Printed, it was, all ready for him to stuff, quick as a flash, through the letterbox and run off, chortling. Back on the phone to sleeping beauty, confined to barracks another whole day and the repairman finally cometh, regardeth the fridge and tutteth. Tut tut, he says. Nasty, that. Haven't got the tools in the van for *that*. Oh yes? I said. Has this fridge broken down in ways no fridge has ever broken down before? Is this a First for Fridgedom? A breakthrough for Fridgekind? Has Dutch Elm disease struck again, is there dry rot in its private parts? The repairman's eyes flicked from side to side, looking – I dare say – for the gents in white and I wouldn't have said no to a short interval in the funny farm myself.

I'm on the phone again, this time to some man called a

Customer Liaison Officer. That's a very strange story, madam, he says, very strange. Strange to you, maybe, I shout, but deeply familiar to me, mate, and I'll bet it's familiar to your wife, too. Shall I tell you why we never see appliances break down on Coronation Street or Crossroads or even Soap? No, madam, he says. Because you can't keep an audience on the edge of their seats by showing them women on the edge of *their* seats, waiting for repairmen. You can have women kissing the lodger or winning the pools or linging alongaMax but you can't have them sitting there twiddling their thumbs, waiting for repairmen. That isn't what is called good telly, but that's what half of England's wives are doing half of the time in what is called real life.

Sometimes, Mary, I think, stuff a liberated sex life and the Sexual Opportunities Bill. What we housewives want is the nitty gritty. In Mexico they've just permitted women to drink in men's bars but the women can't because Mexican barmen won't put in women's loos and a world traveller like you should know what tequila does to the system. Withholding loos is the way they always keep women out of where they want in. Storm any barricade and behind it there's the inevitable man with his hands up saying back, girls, no loo. So what we need is Super Repairwoman. At the clap of a housewife's hands, she'd zoom in with her kit and give the breath of life to any appliance. At another clap she'd streak across the sky with her portable Elsan, to the cheers of feminists everywhere. Here comes the Germaine Greer of the S-Bend, we'd yell. Hurrah!

Dreams, dreams. Meanwhile, Ben's been driving me mad fiddling with things. Yesterday, he wandered into my bedroom and absent-mindedly stuck a No Nukes badge in Latin I'd been saving for the car slap on the side of my walnut cupboard. His huge hands just went fiddle fiddle all by themselves and there it was, unpeeloffable. I threatened to go into his room and do something terrible to it, for revenge, and Jane said like what, Ma? Clean it? Now I can't find the Optrex that was in my bedroom and I know Ben's nicked it. Can you get high, sniffing Optrex?

Referring to yours of the ult. (yes, I know I'm being really self-centred this week) I can't agree that the plighting of the Royal troth removes the last excuse for any nubile girl in the Western hemisphere to say no. Nubile Jane, for instance, is so blank about royalty in general that when our neighbour mentioned the Prince of Wales' engagement she thought he was on about a gig at the local pub. And Jane *always* says no to men, anyway. *Yuk* no and *ugh* no and *aargh* no. Sometimes I worry about that girl. But at least we've seen the last of those caveman articles about Lady This and Princess von That not being suitable on account of their purple pasts. Marvellous, isn't it, that it's perfectly OK for anyone in skirts to be profoundly conversant with Prince C's nocturnal habits but too hideous to contemplate a male who's even *swum* over the future Q of E and lived to tattle-tale. And they say women are gossips?

Josh's secretary rang just now to pass on his home thoughts from abroad. Back at the weekend, bringing Ms Boss for a bite, would I get food in and please remember, this time, have ice ready for drinkies. Ice? The way that fridge is acting, I'll soon be engulfed in a glacial tide like the last of the dinosaurs, my youth preserved forever to mock Josh's greying hairs.

Yours, on the rocks,

Martha

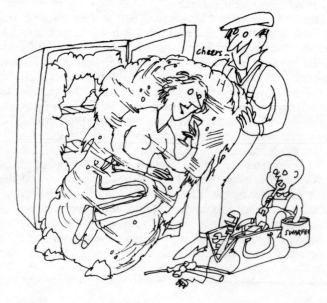

11 March

Dear Mary

How my heart raced when I read your last letter and learnt that your Women's Sub-Orgasmic Therapy Group has been discussing little me. Or rather, as you most discreetly put it, 'my type'. Such a relief you all concluded that 'my type' is not really neurotic *as such* but is merely 'an organism appropriately adapted to a restricted environment like a crossopterygian fish'. Well, ta ever so, Sisters. A man once told me his wife never cooked *as such* and another man confided that he didn't have sex *as such*. I couldn't bring myself to ask as such *what* in case the answer was too boggly but I do know I'm not at all like a crossopwhatsit fish, even as such.

Personally, since you're not asking, I think people who keep talking to cushions, as you say your group does, are already well on the road to the bin and no as such about it. And I'd be glad if you'd inform the next cushion you converse with that this particular organism will shortly leave its restricted environment and hit them all over the head with its appropriately adapted handbag unless they stop discussing it instanter. As for you, be warned. One of these days I may be forced to telephone the News of the Screws and reveal to a stunned public that behind Smash Video-Porn and Vegans Against Sexism and Lesbians for the Whale and Women Pavement Artists' Workshop and Wages Due Very Small Grannies in Hair Nets there is only you and Mo squatting on overdue library books at Sebastopol Terrace with an old Imperial you ripped-off back stage, the night you raided the Miss World contest. So watch it.

My friend in America sent me this really depressing article, all about how the whole country is awash with wonderfully warm, highly educated, deeply brilliant and purposefully independent women who come home from their executive jobs and spend the nights sobbing in their lonely beds because they can't find a single man who isn't either gay or being mobbed on all sides by hundreds of other wonderfully warm, highly educated etcetera women hungry for their annual quickie. At least I think the writer meant quickie but you never know with Americans – one came into the pub the other day and asked for a mushroom quickie, which was the cute way he pronounced quiche.

And the article went on that when these men do decide to marry, they 'marry down,' which means they get themselves hitched to dumb blondes well below them on the evolutionary ladder, which must take some doing. Of course, that's a typical mcp ploy, making sure you're top dog by picking a pussy cat of very few brains with whom to exchange vows of eternal domination-submission, but we have to remember that though American men are God's gift to no one, all those warm, wonderful women are also American. That means most of them spend most of their time verifying their perceptualizations, relating to their authentic selves, demanding positive ego-reinforcement, diagnosing their Irritable Bowel Syndrome (IBS), detailing their Pre-Menstrual Tension (PMT) and then telling everyone to have a good day. No wonder the sexes are drifting apart. Never mind. If things go on this way, Americans will shortly stop producing little Americans, the whole nation will vanish from the earth and we can all breathe a sigh of relief.

And another thing, Mary, before we bury the Gestalt hatchet. I'm sure it's very nice and unselfish of you to say you're working on your feelings with the aim of becoming a truly caring and accessible friend but, to tell you the honest truth, I prefer the old uncaring fairly inaccessible you I know and love. OK? As for me, I have been taking lessons from old Mother Nature who is all around me, especially in Ben's room. There, amongst the luxuriant flora and fauna – curls of dry orange peel, banana skins, stale jam crusts, half bottles of festering milk and cups containing tea leaves half as old as time – two of God's little creatures live and have their being. Ben won them three years ago on Hampstead Heath and brought them home, two goldfish in a plastic bag. Ever since, they have swum round and round in a green and slimy bowl, hardly ever cleaned, hardly ever fed. I have threatened to call in the Hunt Saboteurs to spray lemon in his eyes, I have vowed that the Animal Liberation Front will vivisect him in his bed but all to no avail. Yet do the wretched fish protest? They do not. His friends' goldfish, treated properly, have all given up their little goldfish souls a long time ago. His flourish. Their scales gleam, their fins waggle, they are clearly in the pink.

Same applies to the Gerties, Ben's white mice. Sunk in

Stygian gloom, their only pals the gaping goldfish, nothing to do all day but hide their heads in straw and they're happy as clams and what, for heaven's sake, have clams to be happy about? Plants are the same. Leave them in draughts over radiators, their earth as dry as Arizona and what do they do? Put out shy little shoots and coy buds. Start to care, bustle around them, give them doses of plant food, chat to them and they reward you by turning brown and passing away.

There's a lesson there for us all, Mary, and especially for me. Neglect is Good. Care kills. And that is my new life plan for Josh. He didn't come home at the weekend after all. No sooner had I transferred the contents of Sainsburys to my pantry and the fridge had produced enough ice to sink the *Titanic* than I got his cable. Can only make it back Thursday, bringing Irene. So Ms Boss is now Irene, is she? Well, this is my new scenario. Hullo Irene. Hullo Josh. Have some green slime? A little stale fishmeal? I'm off to beddy-byes. Goodnight Irene.

Yours, from a whole new space,

Martha

A Whole New Space

Dear Mary

I knew I'd get the fall-out from your new caring self. So I was mean about America, was I? What do you think that'll do? Sink our Special Relationship in mid-Atlantic? Blow the San Andreas Fault? Mary, I'm just a slightly overweight London housewife writing to a friend and I know you're into cosmic responsibility but this is ridiculous. As for what I said about the women, well, I had one of my heads at the time. I do realize that Sisters in their little nests should agree and that being warm, wonderful and deeply human isn't a capital crime.

It's just that American women make me feel inferior and superior at the same time and that's an uneasy mix. How can they whip up batches of brownies while being Executive Directors of Computer Software (Far East) Inc. while writing world best-sellers while raising four Junior Citizens on fluoride toothpaste and shots of vitamin B12 when I come over a bit queer just getting the milk bottles in from the doorstep? Nevertheless, they are also silly. I can't explain how, they just are.

And so will you be if you insist on training yourself in Caring. You've got it wrong Mary. Women should care a bit less so that men are made to care a bit more. Daily, I conduct my own one-woman in-home classes. Martha, I say to myself, today you will not care that the floor needs scrubbing, the sink is blocked and we're down to two fish fingers. You will not care that the roses are unpruned and the cats unwormed. You will ignore Ben demanding who's pinched his Biology Project, Jane moaning about how boring everything is and Mother just moaning. Don't care was made to care, my father used to say, but he meant me, not him.

Before my new leaf turned, I worried about everything. Starving Ethiopians, gulls in oil slicks, mugged old ladies, badgers, apartheid, Sri Lankan workers on tea plantations and the bits that fall off Suffolk villages when juggernauts drive by. You name it, I've cared about it. My cheeks have fallen in, my teeth are falling out, I've got white flecks on my nails and a twitchy sciatic nerve and still Ethiopians starve, gulls get oiled and bits fall off Suffolk villages. Whereas Josh, who only cares about the MLR and the state of his shirts, blooms.

Yes, Josh has finally returned. He and Ms Boss – or Irene, as I am now instructed to call her – zoomed back from Brussels on Thursday. They were high on travel, I was low on home sweet home. Irene must be at least my age but then so am I, so that's no advantage and as far as coiffures go, I'm still cantering up to the starting post. Josh remarked on how small and dark the kitchen looked, Irene said everything was delightful. Delightful home, delightful baby, delightful to meet delightful me. She said Ben was delightful too, and even I, who gave him birth, know that delightful he isn't.

I stuck three frozen pizzas in the oven and she said how delightful home cooking was, after hotels. When I said I could do with some hotel cooking myself, she gave me such an understanding chuckle, put her hand over mine and told me she knew I didn't mean that because home cooking and motherhood was the most rewarding career of all. What conversational exchange is left after that? Tisn't, tis, tisn't, tis? I wanted to say why waste your time then, rushing off to foreign parts with other people's husbands and getting four million pounds a year, if boiling nappies is your heart's desire, but Josh gave me one of his looks.

All through the meal they both chatted merrily on about macroeconomics and private equity investments and people called names like Hoofy van Winkle and Jay Bee. Mind you, Irene was most polite. She kept leaning over to include me. Hoofy, she'd say, is the MD of IBD International. Had I noticed, she'd say, the pre-Budget 5 per cent over base rate and oh and yes and would you believe it, I'd say. What stick do I have, Mary? All I hear about is the 10 per cent rise in brassicas and that's only the price of cabbages in fancy dress. If home-making is so deeply rewarding, how come no women who aren't doing it want to hear about it. You don't, do you? I just keep telling you because it's good for you.

I mean, take two of my aunties. Mother rang about them last week. So sad about Aunt May, she said. Always so neat, lived for the children and Uncle John. Now she's gone peculiar. Came to see Mother, stared at her for a while, said 'I want my tea', stuffed herself with scones and cake, said 'I want to go now,' and went; waddled off, says Mother, fat as a house, her hair all over the place. As for Aunt Myrtle, she spends all her waking hours packing. She packs, Uncle Eddie

Another Whole New Space

unpacks, she packs, Uncle Eddie unpacks. Mother puts on her compassionate voice and says it's senile dementia and they ought to be put in homes.

I say it's getting what you want at last, or trying.

Those two old ladies have looked after other people all their lives and now that they're looking after themselves, they're instantly called dotty and locked up. I said to Josh, the night he came back, would he put me in a home if I ate cake all day and packed, like Aunties May and Myrtle and he said (compassionately) that he supposed he'd have to. Still, he'd brought me a very pretty nightie edged with Brussels lace and we retired to have a good time in it. We might have done, if Ben hadn't knocked on the bedroom door in the middle, asking could he have £3 for an all-night movie and where were his Converse All-Stars and did I know the baby was crying? Good idea, your Sub-Orgasmic Group, Mary, but what happens once you are orgasmic? Ben is what happens. I'm sure he's already had sex himself but clearly it's never crossed his mind that Josh and I have too or why would he rattle the door and shout Mum, it's *locked*, in an informative sort of voice. Can he still think step-fathers are just step-*fathers*?

Which reminds me, I got a letter from Ben's father yesterday. He says he's writing a book entitled *The Flasher's Guide to Feminism*, but more of that in my next.

Yours, frustrated,

Martha

Dear Mary

Ask yourself this. If the Pill is a conspiracy against women, as you insist, who's conspiring with whom for whose benefit? I know it has nasty side effects but what doesn't? My life is filled with nasty side effects – blocked drains, cat's hairs on the sofa, pains around the heart. Come to that, the whole human race may be a side effect of some galactic spray for eradicating bugs on Betelgeuse Two. You complain the Pill is making you fat but pregnancy, Mary, is not an on-going slimming situation.

I am older and sadder than you and the things I've had to do with tubes of jelly in my time still return to haunt me on moonless nights. In those days, the sexual urge meant retiring to the bathroom with your armoury and emerging hours later, all precautions taken and all urges gone, in you and your partner, who was already snoring. And being forced to fiddle about like that before your loved one had even raised an eyebrow made you feel peculiarly pushy – the rude version of taking your harp to the party and having nobody ask you to play.

The Pill being only for women is a bore but what is the alternative? Suppose they'd invented a male-only Pill – then we'd really be in the conspiracy business. Imagine having to ask a man are you, you know, *on it*, and then, too late, finding out he wasn't on it and he'd dropped you in it. What would you say then? Naughty boy? Of course it's unfair, swallowing something that keeps your body in permanent hormonal upheaval but trusting men to see you all right would simply mean turning false pregnancies, abracadabra, into the real thing. On that principle, I'd have thirteen kids by now and feminism wouldn't be a twinkle in anyone's eye.

Anyway, the really crucial information you've coyly withheld is – why are you taking the Pill all of a sudden? I thought the only male you ever received, so to speak, was the bloke from the Electricity. Can you have experienced true love at last, crammed cheek to cheek with a Council Official in a cupboard under the stairs? But you don't go in for high-tech at Sebastopol Terrace, do you? I reckon it's all to do with your friend Mo being away. If she were there, she wouldn't let you take a wine gum, never mind a man-made, multi-national, pharmaceutical con-trick like the Pill.

By the way, where on earth *is* Mo and why? I got a card from her last week. It showed a scrubby sort of desert being pecked at by some large and sinister black birds, the stamp was obliterated by squiggly marks and all it said, in those scratchy red ink capitals Mo uses when she's about to flip her lid, was: 'We Know DisGracefully LiTTle abouT the KUrds; in Pan-ARabiC SisterHood, Mo.' Well, as it happens, I do know disgracefully little about the Kurds and I'll bet they know disgracefully little about me. D'you think she's using some kind of code? All that leaps to mind in the way of *double-entendres* is a dreary kind of cheese. Is she a prisoner in a factory farm? Please reveal all in your next or I shall have to table a question in the House.

After a refreshing bout of post-travel togetherness, Josh has lapsed back into male separatism and is presently slumped in front of the telly. Ludovic Kennedy has just said Patrick Moore will introduce Uranus and Josh has just said 'not mine, he won't.' But mostly he's been working late at the office. The awesome possibility occurs that the whole feminist struggle has only achieved the kind of role reversal that means male Secretaries have affairs with their female bosses. If so, I shall shortly collapse, stabbed to the heart with a cliché. They say power is an aphrodisiac – does that go for powerful women, too? Perhaps, after hours, Irene goes on the town arm-in-arm with Mrs T, both of them buying drinks all round, ogling young men in G-strings and telling Josh and Denis to stop sulking or they won't take them out any more. We may soon read all about it in the gutter press and when Josh appears, hands over face, trousers down, in a smeary snapshot on the front page, I shall fold my tent and stomp away. Again.

I told you Ben and Jane's father (Tom, if you remember that far back) wrote last week, first letter in a year, but I didn't tell you what he said. What he said was, he hoped I wasn't turning *his* son into a Mother's boy. That, after seeing *his* son exactly three times in eight years and never giving me a brass aduki bean towards his upbringing. Pause for my apoplectic fit. Then he asked for money, a float – as he put it – while he writes *The Flasher's Guide to Feminism* which, he assures me, will be a wild best-seller and enable him to shower me and *his* offspring with gold. The whole idea is

Reading Mo's card

repulsive and typical of my macho ex. I told Josh how revolting I found it. Josh said yes indeedy, and looked thoughtful.

Well, Mary my love, tomorrow we shall a have little stranger among us, a brand-new baby political Party. I must say, the run-up has been fascinating, rather like being told the facts of life for the first time. The other Parties have been around so long I never liked to ask how they got there in case the answer was rude. Now I feel I've been watching an educational documentary called Where Did I Come From? Are you sitting comfortably, kiddies? Then I'll begin.

First, we have a Mummy-lady and a Daddy-man. They like each other so they ask all their friends if they should get married and their friends say yes and so they do, with the Bride wearing something old, something new, a lot borrowed and most of it Blue. Oh what lovely telegrams and prezzies they get! Then they rent a little house, open a joint bank account and soon they're sending their friends cards saying they're expecting. Everyone is very excited and very supportive of the Mummy-lady because she has attacks of quite bad heartburn, which often happens when ladies are expecting. But at last, her ordeal is over, she's come out of Labour and there they are, the proud parents of a tiny, wrinkled SDP. Aaah.

Yours, winking back a tear,

Martha

1 April

Dear Mary

Describing the new man in your life to me, your bosomy chum, as 'this bloke in the next-door squat with a double-barrel name' hardly scales the Heights of Wuthering but is, nevertheless, revealing. You are ashamed of him, Mary, and so you should be, unless he's under sixteen, in which case you should be ashamed of yourself. Any man who hasn't lost his hyphen after that age is telling the world something that I, for one, don't wish to know. People called Pyddlington-Potty or whatever have no right to inhabit squats because it is a well-known fact that they always have Pyddlington-Potty relatives in large country houses where they could squat in the east wing without anyone ever noticing, instead of taking away valuable squatting room from those who need it. I dare say he goes down to Potty Hall at weekends and makes the house party *scream* with his stories of one's life in one's squat. Thank heavens for the Pill, then. Otherwise you'd soon be adding to the sum of Pyddlington-Pottys and one of the many things this country doesn't need is more of them.

You'll be telling me next that he's just down from Oxford, where he had one long hoot being unutterably silly in the Piers Gaveston Society or whatever that club is called where they all camp about pretending to be Evelyn Waugh. Even E. Waugh, by all accounts, tried not to be E. Waugh *all* the time. Really, I despair of women. The more liberated and independent we fancy ourselves, the more we dredge up our atavistic talent for flattening ourselves under the boots of moral idiots. At this very moment half my lovely women friends are squabbling like a pack of starlings over a drunken male named, believe it or not, Studs, who calls them all chicks and acts as if he had a bit-part in a 1930s B-movie. He wears a Jimmy Cagney hat and we all know Cagney only liked women if they were Mothers and then only if they were Irish Mothers and *then* only if they were *his* Irish Mother.

I shall have to make sure Jane doesn't hear about your passing weakness – you know how she admires you. Whenever she narrows her eyes at Josh, she's thinking *Mary* wouldn't put up with him, unlike her doormat Mum, though of course she doesn't know what she's been spared by not being better acquainted with her own father, Tom, the John Wayne of Mousehole.

My daughter is a sore trial to me at times, especially now that she's off from the LSE. She looms about looking as grim as Bernadette MacAliskey and at least Bernadette has a lot to look grim about. Just yesterday I was glooming on about all these newspapers being bought up by Diggers and Tinies and so on, trying to explain to Jane about millionaires and monopolies and the Freedom of the Press. All she does is shrug and say she couldn't give a tinker's because whoever buys them will still fill every page with articles calculated to bore her rigid. They'll keep on blathering about the War, for a start. Any War. Then they'll dig up a fifth diary about what one Cabinet Minister said to another Cabinet Minister before she was born. Then they'll discover sixteen million more letters in an old picnic hamper from a Woolf to a Bell, then they'll drivel on about ten crashing bores at Oxbridge in 1920 and then when she, Jane, is already catatonic, they'll start another ninety-part series on the memoirs of Mugg.

Who *is* Mugg, she says, making horrible faces. What on earth did he *do*? I think, I said with some dignity, he was editor of *Punch* once. *Oh*, says Jane. I *see*, says Jane. That *accounts* for it, says Jane, falling on the floor and writhing about in a very irritating fashion. Your stepfather admires him, I informed her, Josh frequently says Mr Muggeridge is the quintessential Man of his Time. Then give me Page Three any day, says Jane and flounces out, doing some rather vulgar body language as she goes.

Of course, that's par for Jane's present course. Nothing pleases her, Mugg included. She doesn't like men, she doesn't like children, she doesn't even like puppies. A neighbour's dog just had six of the sweetest little roly-poly things but Jane just said 'Yuk' when she saw them and announced that they gave her the creeps. She went babysitting last week to earn herself some pin-money and came back swearing she wouldn't go any more because they had this silly baby who argued all the time. How can a three-month-old argue?

Then I went out for the first time in months and bought myself a gorgeous pair of sort of bronze-coloured high-heel shoes and showed them to Jane. She practically had a convulsion on the spot, yukking and ughing till I almost hoped she'd choke. Call yourself liberated, she kept saying, and you're going to walk about propped up on top of *those*?

Teetering around like some ancient geisha girl with bound feet?

I said don't be so rude and then she got all serious and said no, really how could I? Didn't I realize that high heels were a male plot to make women look like silly twits, unable even to walk with any efficiency? Dear Josh came in just then and said the shoes were lovely and made my ankles look delectably fragile. He actually whistled at me as I paraded about.

I could hear Jane making sickey noises all the way up the stairs. Josh said take no notice and gave me a delicious kiss, first one for quite a while. Then he said he'd decided to give Tom the money he wanted to write *The Flasher's Guide to Feminism*. So I followed Jane up the stairs, making sickey noises, and twisted my ankle on the landing, due to the high-heel shoes.

Yours, in a no-win situation,

Martha

Dear Mary

No letter on my doormat this week. Either you and Pyddlington-Potty have sunk for good and all into your waterbed, leaving naught but plastic beakers and a faint oil slick to mark the final submergence or you're angry with me or both. Perhaps Potty has abandoned you for a girl with gold bits in her Gucci shoes called Cynthia Yeovil-Orne (pronounced Yawn) and you're shut in the broom cupboard, agrophobic with grief. I wish you had a telephone. It's an awfully useful device, you know. We could say hullo and guess who and you could shout the line is bad and all manner of interesting things. Without it, I worry about you. Who would look after you if you're ill? True, Josh only notices I'm laid low by the milk bottles piling up outside but you haven't anyone in the house, unless Mo has returned from desert parts.

Actually, I imagine you're quite all right, just off me for the moment because of my remarks about P-P having a name like P-P. Forgive me. I was intolerant, impolite and class-ridden. People cannot help what they are called. After all, Mr Benn was born hyphenated and though he's been doing his best to lose it ever since, half England still distrusts him because he once had it and the other half because he's dropped it. If you like Pyddlington-Potty, then so do I and I expect his real names are something perfectly acceptable like . . . er . . . Well, never mind. I'll tell you a gruesome secret about me and then we'll be quits. I still call my Mother Mummy. Yes, I know that's utterly pathetic. A shrink I went to when I was in that fearful state of indecision about whether to leave Tom for Josh (the shrink said don't) informed me that women who call their Mothers Mummy suffer from unresolved identity conflicts. He spent the whole hour going on about breast fixations and nipple substitutes and oral infantilism and all the time he was sucking away on this really giant pipe, slurp, slurp. Amazing.

I explained to him that I call Mother Mummy so as not to hurt her feelings but, apparently, not wanting to hurt one's

Luring back the Sun God

Mother's feelings is a serious psychic perversion. What am I supposed to do to signify maternal liberation, put the poor old bag through the Magimix? Speaking as a Mother myself (called Mum by Ben and Martha by Jane) I'd be only too glad to have my feelings spared but, as all good shrinks know, we Mothers devote our entire lives to deforming and stunting our offspring until such time as one of them smacks us round the chops and steams off into the sunset, adult at last. How unfair it all is. When I went into the local florists ('Bette's Nosegays – Love In Bloom') to order regressive roses for Mummy on Mummy's Day, the place was packed with huge, tatooed, boiler-suited blokes buying gladdies for their Mums and I bet their Mums made King Kong look cosy. One old bird I met on a bus said she had these three six-foot sons and she clouted them regularly across the earholes and they hadn't forgotten her on Mother's Day in 20 years. Whereas your sweet, kind, democratic Mother Martha, who could not raise a hand in anger against her kiddiewinks, has never had a Mother's Day card in all her permissive life. Not that I want one, you understand.

Talking of mothers, mine writes to say she's coming to stay for a week, to buy her spring wardrobe. Evans Outsizes, Prepare to Meet Thy Doom. Mother on the shop floor has been known to make entire departments come out on strike. She believes that what shop assistants are for is to assist her, shopping. She also believes they are fascinated by any pearl of information that drops from her lips about herself, her family and her world views and she thinks they all love her. They love me at Harrods, she says, smiling like the Queen Mum. And she always, but always, returns every purchase exactly one week later. In fact, she's staying a week just to give herself time for returns. Spring shopping is my Mother's version of luring back the Sun God and everything she buys is an exact replica of everything she's already bought. Thank heavens I shan't be able to go with her this year, because of the baby. Last year I had to stand there lightly sweating as she hooted across the counter, 'I'll have two of them, dear, in Nigger Brown'.

Yours, blushing Knicker Pink,

Martha

Dear Mary

Well, I got it all wrong. Your bloke doesn't have a double-barrel surname, he has a double-barrel *first* name. Bobby-Joe from the Lone Star State and I'm mighty glad to make his acquaintance, yessiree. Though you can't blame me for not guessing, can you? There hasn't been a male in this United Kingdom with a double first name since Christopher Robin finished saying his prayers, booted his Nanny downstairs and changed his name to Alf. What in the world is a Texan doing, squatting in Sebastopol Terrace? And he plays the guitar a treat, you say. Now, Mary, you'd better watch yourself. You know you have this weakness for men who play musical instruments. An uncle of mine suffered the same way and had four disastrous marriages as a result. First he was seduced by Auntie Louise tinkling on the piano, then by Auntie Ruth sawing away on the violin, then Auntie Gwen booped at him with her clarinet and he ended up with a Ukrainian on the harmonica, who led him a dog's life until he went stone deaf and lived happily ever after.

It's all childhood conditioning, I think. I've spent hours singing the baby to sleep, getting myself well lodged in his inner ear. I rather fancy myself in the role, bending sweetly over the cradle, warbling away. Two bars of carry the lad who's born to be *King* over the sea to *Skye* and his dear little eyelids droop. Unfortunately for my ego, Ben can do the same thing with his record player. Eek, scrawk, crash, bang go the Clash and the baby's dear little eyelids droop. Lord knows, I actively long to be dispensable most of the time but when I am, it puts me out no end. I just adore that baby. He's so yummy at the moment I could eat him, munch his pink fingernails, nibble his teeny ears, crunch every one of his crisp little curls. Which reminds me, I was on the telephone once and I turned round, talking, and there was our hamster with one of her new-born half-way down her throat. It's a thin line we mothers tread between desirable physical manifestations of bodily affections and plain old-fashioned cannibalism.

Ben came in yesterday and said one of his Gerties (the white mice) looked a bit dead. The poor rodent was lying with all four paws in the air. That's not a bit dead, I said to Ben, that's one stiff mouse you've got there and it looks like it's been murdered. See that other Gertie with gore on its whiskers? Ben denied all, said dead Gertie and gory Gertie were best friends. Just then, his best friend Flanagan came pounding up the stairs, leapt on Ben's back, chopped him on the neck and clobbered him to the ground. *Quod erat demonstrandum*, I said, and left them to it. What *is* it with boys? For what purpose is God readying them, apart from being cut–throats, footpads, commodity brokers and other social menaces?

I've devoted my life to eliminating every undesirable masculine trait from Ben's Y-chromosomes and what's the result? He hasn't a sensitive bone in his body and is absolutely enraptured by violence. He and Flanagan spend hours telling each other exactly how they'd poke people's eyes out if they were going to poke people's eyes out and then lean back with sated grins, saying oh wow, that's *bad* man, that's really *bad*.

I must do better with the baby. Perhaps, this time round, I should be a working mother but what work can I get nearby? My friend Lorna, opposite, is retraining at the local hospital as an autopsy technician. Corpses are OK on flexi-hours but it's a dead-end job, she says. I think Lorna's getting callous. There is a woman two roads away who runs a warehouse called Annie's Attic full of junk and I mean junk. Singer sewing machines without the sewing machines, chairs without seats, lamps that lack all standards. Still, better than Habitat, and she might give me a job. She's a single parent, too – seems quite nice, what you can see of her under old cupboards.

Hey. Did you notice I said a single parent *too*? That's a giveaway and no wonder, with Josh disappearing at 8 am and reappearing at 9 pm or thereabouts. If I shuffled the baby in with four other babies, I doubt he could pick out his own with any confidence. Would he even notice if I gave it away? He might ask after it a few times – doing all right, is it, coming along nicely, is it? He'd probably only catch on a decade from now, because of the baby not being there to go to his Old School.

I am still shattered about Josh giving Tom the money to write *The Flasher's Guide to Feminism*. I didn't deign to ask how much but it rankles. I mean, what sort of vicious circle am I in? My ex being kept by my present spouse so that my ex can tell the world how ghastly it was to live with libby me and women like me. Josh says I must regard it as an investment and that he's merely trying to ensure me and the children of our rightful dues. He's actually drawn up some sort of contract about repayment of capital sum and royalties on the first so many thousand and rights on the paperback and heaven knows what else. What attitude should I take with Josh? Gratitude that he's protecting my interests, however misguidedly? Cynicism that he only wants to recoup what he's spent, supporting me and Tom's kids? Or silent contempt – I do a nice line in silent contempt.

Yours with worried blue eyes,

Martha

Cannibalism

Dear Mary

I thought we all agreed with Kate Millett that our Middle Eastern sisters needed our support in their battle to emerge from the veil and now you're saying Mo is back from Arabistan and you're both 'into chadors'. Mary, what can you and Mo *look* like, scuttling up and down Sebastopol Terrace covered from head to foot in black bags? What is appropriate in far-flung desert parts is hardly *comme il faut* up the Co-op. People will talk. People will come along in white jackets and take you away. And what on earth does poor Bobby-Joe make of it all? Just as he's getting to know you, you vanish behind folds of cloth, leaving him bereft of a single erogenous zone.

In some ways, of course, there is something rather appealing about the idea. Many's the time I've wanted to rush out of the house for a packet of fags and had to choose between getting all tarted up or going as I am and frightening the horses. Whereas if I could drop a black shroud all over myself, no one would know it was me. I'd just be a large black bundle padding through the streets, the ultimate asexual object. Instant privacy.

You know, the more I think about it, Mary, the more I think you and Mo may be on to something. Who's going to want to molest a shapeless mass? What man will whistle at an animated shroud? Talk about Reclaiming the Night – if we were wrapped up like that, they'd hand it back to us on a platter. We could get men to join in, too. That'd make rapists and muggers and other male disturbers of women's peace think twice. Imagine one of them pouncing on a black-draped siren from the mysterious East and finding, underneath, the heavyweight champion of Liverpool North? A couple of straight lefts and the beast would be put off sex and handbags for a good many moons.

And, apart from anything else, black figures flitting about in the night would put the fear of the Prophet into any man not about his rightful business. I've got an old black evening dress up in the attic and even I should be able to run up a chador. If it catches on, they might issue them on the National Health. Send me a snap of you in yours, so I can see what you don't look like.

I've had a great idea too, if a teeny bit macabre. You know my friend Lorna, the one who got a job as an autopsy technician and was rabbiting on about corpses fitting in so well with women's hours? I was pondering on this, thinking about a job for myself, when the bulb lit up. What is one of the very last bastions of male supremacy in the Western world, sans even a token woman? The Marines? The girls are in there. Miners? The girls are down there. Yes, you've got it. Undertaking. Have you ever seen or heard of a female undertaker? Ever caught a glimpse of a lady in a hearse, alive and well and looking mournful? And if not, why not? Women must have laid out corpses for hundreds of years and where are we now? Pushed back into the kitchen is where, cooking the funeral meats for the wake, muscled out of our rightful heritage by men.

So you know what I'm going to do? I'm going to find out what you have to do to be an undertaker (Apprenticeships? Day-release schemes? Evening classes?) and then I'm going to set up my own all-female business. Martha's Mortuary. Shiftwork only, ho ho. I think people would flock. I know I'd much rather put my body in the hands of women instead of some boring old fatty in a wing-collar and a top hat whom I wouldn't trust dead or alive. I'd be a sort of midwife, only the other way round; it's good steady work, ideally suited to family life and my clients could hardly object if I shut up shop now and then, in an emergency, could they? When you think about it, men being undertakers is positively unnatural. It's the same story as doctors, really. For generations, women attended at births and then, all of a sudden, a whole lot of men arrived, stethescopes flapping, and gave us the heave-ho. Why shouldn't I be the first to reverse that takeover? I could combine it with wearing a chador, for that matter. What could look more decorously mournful than that?

I just told Josh my idea. That man has no imagination. First he said what would the Department think, him having a wife in Undertaking. Then he said if I was going to start a fashion in black sacks, it might seriously affect the sales of The Flasher's Guide to Feminism because what man would want to flash at a black sack? Josh, I said, that is the whole point. Pshaw, he said, or something like it, and disappeared into a black sulk.

I have to stop writing now. Ben has just decided it is time

The Grim Flasher

he showed me how independent he is by going camping this weekend alone, with Flanagan. So will I buy him a rucksack, get batteries for his torch, sew up the split in his groundsheet, wash his sleeping bag, find a camping site, look up the trains, pack oxtail soup, sausages, baked beans, drinking chocolate, long-life milk, Mars Bars, Coke, toilet paper, apples, soap, tin-opener, saucepans, fork, knife, spoon, plate, Brillo pads and drive him to the station. Please.

Two seconds later, Flanagan's Mum is on the phone. As I know, she says, she – Flanagan's Mum – is a working woman and hasn't the time to get Flanagan equipped for the weekend. So will I, very kindly, get him oxtail soup, sausages, baked beans, torch batteries, drinking chocolate te tum te tum te tum. The nerve of these working women. What does she think I do all day long? Sit around in a face pack? Martha's Mortuary, here I come.

Yours, banging on death's door,

Martha

Dear Mary

Thanks for the snap you sent me in your last letter of you and Mo in chadors outside Sebastopol Terrace. You're quite right, I can't tell which is you and which is Mo, but why is my bewilderment merely 'a predictable bourgeois individualist reaction'? Even a duck-billed platypus might become a trifle disorientated if it couldn't pick out its pal in the next burrow from any duck-billed platypus that happened to wander by. I know, I wrote that chadors could have their advantages but this is ridiculous.

Do you suppose Iranian soldiers fighting in Iraq carry photos of their womenfolk back home that they can't tell from their enemy's women, never mind their friends? If so, it must be pretty boring for them back at the barracks. Here, have a look at my Fatimah, mate, says one, passing over a pic of black washing. Cor, smashing, says the mate, have a shufti at my old lady then, and down the line goes another Polaroid pin-up of laundry in vaguely human form. Anonymity in the streets is one thing but this kind of dressing could mean a man gets his meals cooked for a fortnight before he realizes his wife's moved out and his mother-in-law's moved in.

I dare say that proves a vital point about the interchangeability of women's servicing roles but it's not one I can contemplate without feeling a bad identity crisis coming on. Besides, I showed your photo to Josh and you wouldn't have liked his reaction one bit. He thought it was quite sexy. All cats are grey in the chador, he said wittily. They're obviously his version of throwing the car keys in the pool and gambling on who'd be in his bed that night. How do you know Bobby-Joe isn't fantasizing that he's got Mo under the blankets? Well, not Mo, perhaps. Raquel Welch?

I'm sorry I didn't write back immediately, but the life of a housewife is not conducive to outside interaction. What is it conducive to, I often ask myself? Sometimes I think I might as well reside permanently in a pot-hole for all the contact I have with the great panorama of twentieth-century events, including women's liberation. The microscopic happenings in

Home Sweet Home so distort all perspective that I frequently feel I'd happily swop the Sex Discrimination Act for any suggestion of what to cook for dinner that doesn't include spaghetti and meat balls.

Being a 100 per cent wife and mother feels a bit like living on Mars and trying to take an intellectual interest in world affairs on a planet 80 light years away. An interesting mental exercise, perhaps, like playing Scrabble in Latin, but equally irrelevant. You and Mo can easily live on a diet of abstract theory because nothing in your actual life looms up to confound you. But if I put the smallest liberating idea into action the backlash knocks me sideways before I can get the words out. Like I told Josh I was going to bed early and he'd have to give the baby his last feed. Which he did but forgot to change nappies so the poor little thing has nappy rash again.

I know I could push on until Josh got it right but the baby doesn't have Third Party Indemnity and how many personal battles can I fight over an increasingly raw but innocent bum? Again, I perfectly realize that I was not put on this earth in order to keep the fruit of my loins unendingly supplied with toilet paper but I fear I am already as conditioned as Pavlov's canines. One cry of despair from the smallest room and I'm rushing about shouting *mea culpa* and shredding up newspapers for the incarcerated loved one. Well, not shouting *mea culpa*, perhaps, but feeling it.

I'll admit it does them no good but how to break out of the vicious circle? I send Ben out to buy two pounds of leeks and he comes back, five minutes later, saying, 'What do leeks look like?' Ben, I say, how can you exist in the twentieth century and not know what leeks look like? Being conversant, if indeed you are, with Newton's Theory of Gravity, the Pythagoras Theorem, and the cycle of DNA, will simply not suffice. Leeks have their place in the History of Human Achievement, even if you can't get A-levels in them. It may be a humble place, unsung, unrewarded, not in the running for a Nobel Prize, but place it is.

A male who can pick out a goodly leek and process it into a Lancashire Hot Pot may possibly contribute more to the struggle for sexual equality than any amount of ideological jargon. You tell me, Mary, that your Bobby-Joe is a truly feminist man because he always says he *and* she, his *and* hers, men *and* women. Hurrah for Bobby-Joe. But can he pick out a decent leek at ten paces and make of it something fit to be ladled into mankind's (humankind's) mouth? If so, full marks. If not, hot air. And answer me this one. Who cleans

the lavatory at Sebastopol Terrace – No, don't fudge it with ifs and buts. Who, Mary?

In case you think I'm putting you down, I shall nobly admit that my money is not yet where my mouth is, not by a long chalk. You remember my telling you about the ludicrous Studs, that B-movie twit my friends were all swooning about? The one that calls them 'chick' and tweaks their bottoms? He came round unexpectedly the other evening when Josh was working late. Well, Josh is always working late. Anyway, he sat at my kitchen table, swilled my beer, called me 'beauty' and said nothing turned him on like a woman in the full bloom of maturity with her hands dug into a bowl of flour.

Actually, I had just decanted a Betty Crocker Cake Mix (add one egg and stir) but did I let on? I did not. You'd have thought I was making a week's wholemeal granary loaves, the way I got kneading. The man's a fool, of course, wearing that silly hat pulled down over one eye, talking in a fake American accent, either drunk or pretending to be. But I have the feeling, Mary, that under all that tough-guy stuff, Studs is just shy. Just a big, shy boy. He put his arm round my waist at one point and I gave a girlish giggle. I suppose I should have smacked him. Please send one chador knitting pattern, by return of post.

Yours, with needles poised,

Martha

Dear Mary

I've had this man Kev in all week repainting the stairwell because Josh said it looked like a stretch of the H-Block, what with the scuffs and gouges made by Ben and his elfin friends flitting upstairs. Between brush strokes, Kev has been giving me the benefit of his thoughts on the rich tapestry of life and my blood, Mary, is only just uncongealing.

The way I see it, Marf, says Kev, any man could kill *one* woman in an off moment, know what I mean? No, Kev, I say. Like if she's getting on his wick like. Nagging and that, says Kev. But this Ripper, topping 13 women, that's a bit much, know what I mean, Marf? No, Kev, I say. Well, there's a lot of Rippers about, Marf. Take this man goes to my pub. He's got a very funny attitude to women. I reckon he could be a Ripper soon as look at you. At *me* you mean, Kev, I say. Right, Marf, says Kev.

Well, this man, he bought this python. Ten pound a foot, he paid, so he's got about sixty quids' worth of python there and he brings it in the pub and he sits there with it, drinking his usual Pernod, Guinness and bitter. First thing, it wraps itself round this dog and the dog's yipping away and this woman starts shouting. Shut your mouth, you old cow, he says, and the publican says don't you talk like that to my mother, and there's a bit of a barney, but it settles down because nobody wants to call the police, due to this and that, you know. Anyway, then all the gels start coming in and shrieking when they see the python and throwing up their hands and spilling their drinks and this man is smiling away. He likes that, see? Giving all the gels a good scare.

But then, Marf, these other two gels come in and they're different. Oh, they say, look at that snake, Rosie. Oh, isn't it beautiful. And off they go, billing and cooing away at the thing and this bloke starts frowning. Then, all of a sudden, he bends down, picks up the python by its neck, drags it over to the bar, and thumps its head against the side until it's dead. It was like the python was only good for scaring the gels and when a couple of them weren't scared, that was the end of the python. Funny, eh? Takes all sorts, doesn't it, Marf? Yes, Kev, I say.

And that's not all, Mary. Kev says he reckons there are more nutters in front of bars than behind them and I reckon he's right and I reckon Kev's one of them. Two days later, he starts coming down from his ladder and telling me he can see Prince Philip's face on the ceiling. Next thing, he sees the whole Royal Family, up to and including Lady Di. Not surprisingly, the experience seemed to unhinge him. He didn't turn up this morning, so I've now got a stairwell blocked with ladders and pots and old sheets and Mother's arriving some time today, which is one of the reasons we started repainting in the first place.

I dread it. She'll be on the warpath within seconds, wanting to know what I've done to Josh to drive him away evenings, picking up the baby and saying 'poor little thing' as if it were Third World and asking Jane what's wrong with her legs that she can't wear skirts. Already she's pushed me several notches below depression level by suggesting, on the phone, that I have a face lift. Mother, I said (shocked out of saying Mummy for a change), I don't need a face lift. I'm 38, you know, not 101. That's as may be, she said, but if you leave it, the price will go up. Mother, I said, I can't lift a face that's got no lift yet, just because it'll cost me twice the money in 10 years, can I? It's Josh I'm thinking of, she said enigmatically and put the phone down. Two whole tears dripped down my nose. A week of her and it'll take a 10-ton crane to lift my face. Then Jane comes in and moans about Granny visiting. Don't talk like that about your grandmother, Jane, I hear myself say, I won't have it. Mary, sometimes I can *feel* my personality splitting.

Of course, I've done quite the wrong thing, mother-wise, getting the house looking reasonably nice. Your mother, Mary, is never going to come and stay at Sebastopol Terrace, is she? I can't see her coping with bare floorboards and that rat you say keeps popping up round the dustbins, no matter how cute you think he is. Has it occurred to you that what you think is one rat is actually twenty rats all looking alike? If I were you, I'd send for the rodent exterminator now, before one of them nips a hole in your waterbed and drowns you in your sleep.

Yesterday, I started on a round of phone calls to try to get Ben a place in some college if he does decide to leave school this summer with anything more academic than one CSE grade five. The first place I called, they put me through to the Department of Vocational Something-or-other and someone picked up the phone, said, 'I wouldn't do that course, if I were you, it's worse than useless,' and banged it down. Great confidence, that's inspired. Who was it? A disaffected student? An Illich de-schooler? A Tory mole? You've never had to plough through these college brochures, Mary, and you can thank your lucky stars. You need a degree, these days, just to work out how to get one. A degree, I mean. Oh God, there goes the doorbell. Hang on.

That was Mother, complete with twenty-four shopping bags, no change for the taxi and a foot already firmly stuck in one of Kev's paint pots.

Yours, wishing I had house room for a python,

Martha

Poor little thing

Dear Mary

I'm alone at last, in the stilly night. The babe has crashed out after the hard graft of jigging his cot 68 times across the room, Mother after the hard graft of seeing Harrods, and Josh after the hard graft of seeing Mother. I have just committed the mortal sin of switching on the central heating again so that I can take off two cardies and write to you. Josh did his usual Switching-off Ceremony at the end of March, leaving me and the baby the only two Eskimos in the old home igloo – the rest of them bundle off mornings to their various snuggeries and arrive home after work fanning themselves and saying phew, bit stuffy in here isn't it?

Josh's Department, Thatcherites to a man, has responded to the Leader's call for cuts by awarding him a secretary all his very own – until now he's had to make do with the dryads of the typing pool. Not that he mentioned this little perk to me. I called him last Thursday to say should I pay the electricity bill, since it was now an apoplectic purple and, instead of him, got this deep frozen Benenden voice that managed to fight congenital lock jaw long enough to inform me that himself was tied up at the moment. On the verge of saying we must all snatch our pleasures where we can, I lost my nerve and couldn't even bring myself to say I was his wife. Simply couldn't face playing that golden oldie role, the Trouble and Strife, interrupting His Godliness with some boring domestic plaint like it was his turn to peel the potatoes tonight. So I said ay am Lord Dewberry's seketery, ay hev His Lordship on the laine, and was put through pronto.

Josh was noticeably unamused but too canny to give the game away. When I asked could he pick up ravioli round the Italian on his way home, he said three bags full Lord Dewberry, dinner tonight it *is*, and rang off. What's more, he didn't have a chance to harangue me when he did get home because, just as he was opening his mouth, in sailed Mother to engulf him in her bosom, murmuring *dear* Joshua in that hushed voice she always uses on him, as if he were suffering terminal martyrdom. Marthadom?

She really has it in for me at the moment, that auld Mother o'Mine – something about the spring and the flowering sukebind always turns her against me. Yesterday, staggering back from a full day's shopperama wearing a new hat in the likeness of a squashed mushroom, she demanded, out of the blue, to be told how many pairs of socks Joshua had. Mother, I said, search me. Upon which she delivered herself of a moving speech about the fearful fragility of marriages when wives did not even know how many pairs of socks their husbands had. Loyally, I forebore to say that her precious Josh was one of those persons who wore his shirts tucked into his underpants, which fact, in any properly run country with a reasonable representation of females at the pinnacles of power, would constitute grounds for instant divorce. That and wearing shirt collars folded back over jackets and socks with sandals – matrimonial killers, every one.

Some minutes later, she took a shufti up our stairwell and said she didn't know how dear Joshua could possibly *work* with paint pots and ladders all over the landing. Josh, I said, goes to an office to work, Mother. A warm, tastefully furnished, close-carpeted bijou technological miracle called an office. It's *me*, Mother, that works in a hell of paint pots and ladders. Me.

Undeterred, she went on to say that she had tried telephoning me to tell me what time her train arrived but I had been *out*. Pause for implications to sink in. Daughter is Scarlet Woman, spends daylight hours togged out in Y-front frocks chatting up lounge lizards in sleazy Mayfair drinking clubs when should be suckling innocent babe and meeting clean-living Away-Day Mother at Liverpool Street. *However*. She had then phoned dear Joshua and got this charming girl who'd said Josh couldn't meet her due to dining with Lord Dewberry that night. Wasn't it nice, said Mother, that Joshua had such contacts and nicer still that he'd foresworn them in order to welcome his Mother-in-Law and she only hoped I appreciated him as much as she did.

You're always saying, Mary, that feminists should make friends with their mothers, but where do I begin? What possible way can I introduce mine to the Women's Movement? Say to her, Mother, do you realize you are a member of an oppressed class? Mother, who's squashed Father so flat all his life that he looks like a piece of lasagna with a moustache on one end? Mother, who wouldn't recognize oppression if it leapt up and garotted her? I read

Nancy Friday's book *My Mother, My Self*, and all I could think was how lucky she was, having such an amenable mother.

Anyway, the baby likes Mother. He's done nothing ever since she arrived but gurgle at her like something out of the Wonderful World of Disney. Good as gold, says Mother, I don't know *what* you complain about, oo's a luvvy babby den, coochy, coochy coo. Personally, I wouldn't be surprised if, somehow, the baby's dummy ends up half-way down her throat quite soon.

Yours matricidally,

Martha

grounds
for
divorce

Dear Mary

I have to hand your anthropological dissertation on The Role of Shopping in the Establishment of Female Bonding Mechanisms, for which no thanks. Men, you assure me, hunt, drink, tell dirty jokes, and observe footballs being moved about in order to cement masculine bonds. Ergo, I must be prepared to hump myself through Horrid's Jewellery Dept to achieve the same end with women, viz my Mother. Great. Help yourself to a PhD in putting down Marthas.

You've overlooked one tiny detail, though. Said men, in the pursuance of said bonding, take it for granted that the necessary rites are carried out together. Like they *all* shoot rabbits and Germans, they *all* swig beer, tell the one about the landlady's daughter, and yell themselves silly at Wembley. Whereas I am unable fully to participate in the Shopping Rite because (a) I haven't got the money and (b) I haven't got the money. A fact that makes one more unbridgeable gap between Mother and me.

My lack of the readies merely proves to her that I have led my disgustingly promiscuous (twice-married) life in vain since the only justification, in her view, for promiscuity or marriage or men in general is that the women who go in for them come out clutching enough lolly to buy up Horrid's Jewellery Dept. In the name of the Father, the Son, and the HG, of course. As Mother is fond of pointing out, she is a *Christian* woman.

Anyway, how come you're suddenly in favour of conspicuous female consumption? Whatever happened to Betty Freidan and her Feminine Mystique? Betty F's whole point was that all the Mr Bigs of industry and advertising were in a conspiracy to keep women in the home so that they could be sold things and now you're saying I should let them have their way with me. True, there is only one thing more boring than being a woman at home being sold things and that is being a woman at home *not* being sold things but it's the principle that counts. Isn't it?

The fact is, Mary, that you haven't got your finger on the

nation's economic pulse and no wonder. You squat rent-free in Sebastopol Terrace. Your electricity reaches you gratis, due to some nifty intervention by Bobby-Joe between the mains and your bulbs. Your food is lifted by nimble-fingered Mo (I know *property* is theft but where does a leg of lamb fit in, wafted out of the Co-op under Mo's chador?) and you fulfil the rest of your needs (ciggies, dope, sound) courtesy the dole. Which is not what I call grasping the harsh realities of Thatcher's Britain. I, on the other hand, live cheek by jowl with them, sustained only by hand-outs from Josh, courtesy the Department. And believe me, once you've joined the system, press-ganged by marriage and parenthood, the Good Ship Lolly soon Pops.

Take mortgages, for example. Our annual statement dropped on the mat this week to the cackles of the robber barons who lurk, these days, under the thoroughly respectable label 'Building Society'. Huge monthly sums go out in payment, the figures in the Balance column dwindle nicely and just as the mortgaged heart begins to soar – whoomp – it gets shot down by 'Interest' at the bottom, which pushes the Balance up again to almost exactly where it was before you started – out of sight. In the last twelve months we've paid out over three thousand pounds and managed to increase our actual ownership of this pile of bricks by exactly £394.98. At this rate, I'll be a heap of whitened bones before we own half the front door. Josh, it would appear, is working for nothing and if *he* is working for nothing, matie, what about me? What's ten times nothing? I've got a device for re-using bits of old soap now. You stick them all in a plastic thingie, dunk the thingie in hot water and press down, whereupon one brand-new piece of soap is supposed to emerge. In fact, you get a ghastly gollop of goo that looks like something the cat brought up – you see the lengths I'm forced to go?

The only ray of light this week was Studs calling round again, which should tell you something about the general state of gloom. In he rolls, fingers extended like a mad crayfish, ready for tweaking. Hel*l*o, Gorgeous, he hoots. How's my honey chile, honey baby, honey honey? Shriek, I go. Bridle, giggle. Things look distinctly up. Then I fetch him a beer from the kitchen and when I get back, he's started on Jane. Not that Jane is in any danger. Cut it out, *creep*, she's shouting in her usual forthright way. How I admire my daughter. How my heart sank. But the bitter end came when Mother appeared in her squashed mushroom hat. You're

Martha's *Mother*? says Studs, pretending to fall off his chair. Come on, baby, pull the other one. Sister, I'll believe, but *Mother* – who are you kidding? And Mother titters. She pats her hair and titters, while I stand there feeling like the pensioned-off wife in the harem.

Still, I'll say one thing for Studs. He doesn't give a toss if a woman looks like a piece of pumice stone, outweighs an elephant and is all of ninety-four. As long as she's a living, breathing female, he's in business. Is that the worst sort of sexism or should he be awarded some kind of medal for the world's most undiscriminatory behaviour?

Yours, only asking,

Martha

Dear Mary

Mother departed yesterday and in the resulting burst of euphoria I snuggled up to Josh and said would he love me just as much if I were cross-eyed, knock-kneed and had sticky-out ears and he said no. And I said you promised to love me till death did us part and now you're saying cross-eyes knock-knees and sticky-out ears would us part and he said he wasn't saying any such thing and I said he was and he said he wasn't and why was I being so illogical and I said I wasn't illogical and he said *women* and I said *men*. Then the neighbour's little girl came in to return some sugar and said what was the cat's name and I said Bimby and she said no, but what is its *real* name and I said to Josh isn't that marvellous, she knows the cat isn't *really* called Bimby and he said he called it Bimby and I said she means who is the cat *really*, to other cats, and he said oh God! and went upstairs. I think I'll have to join the Bhagwan and go orange, there's no understanding around here of the mysteries of life.

Then I had words with the children about fruit. I do not know the solution to fruit. I come home with two pounds of apples, a pound of satsumas and a bunch of bananas. I arrange them beautifully on a white platter in the middle of the table. Then Ben and Jane come in and reach for them and I say no, leave them, I've just bought them and they say I'm always saying leave them and then, when everything's gone all shrivelled, I say *eat* them for goodness sake, so what do I want? What none of them realizes is that fruit and food and things in the fridge and tins in the cupboard don't get there by magic. There isn't a good fairy about, waving her wand and, hey presto, baked beans and bunches of bananas. There's just me, Martha, making lists, slogging down to the shops and slogging back again. All they know is, they go out, come back and the cupboard's full. Magic.

Probably that's why I came home today from the supermarket with a hot toothbrush. I don't believe in your 'property is theft' stuff, I just have this very deep feeling that the world owes me something, even if it's only one yellow toothbrush, medium bristle. The thing is, buying provisions for five people week after week after week is an indeterminate sentence to hard labour. First, I have to check everything that's running out. Then the baby has to be parked with my neighbour because, otherwise, he'd get so squashed under tins they'd have to sell him off as battered goods, half-price. So all the time I'm shopping, I've got this little picture in my mind of him, mouth open, chest heaving, face purple, neighbour's hands closing round his throat, like a silent horror movie. Then I have to drag my bag-on-wheels down to the supermarket, get lumbered with the trolley with the stuck wheels that keeps forcing me round in a circle, fight through the aisles, load up with stuff I wouldn't be seen dead eating (Sugar Puffs, prune purée, sickly orange drinks), hang about in an endless queue, unload everything at the check-out, load everything again on the other side, pay out ridiculous sums for the privilege and then collapse with a silent but painful stroke.

So what I feel is the supermarket ought to reward me for working so hard on their behalf and, since they don't, I am forced to reward myself. Hence the toothbrush. They pretend they're doing us a favour, having everything self-service, and all the time it's us doing *them* a favour, trekking round their noisy, overcrowded food hangars so we can stick our week's housekeeping in their tills *and* pay for their plastic bags covered with their advertising. There was this old lady in there today, doing it her way. Not sticking toothbrushes up her jumper but quietly awarding herself consoling swigs of whisky while struggling to buy Whiskas for her moggy. By the time she arrived at the check-out, that old lady was feeling no pain and the bottle was tucked neatly back on the drinks shelf, a little bit empty. I gave her an admiring grin as I passed her. Bottoms up, she said, bless her OAP heart. What supermarkets ought to do, if they had any imagination beyond fleecing you, is give each worn-out trolley-pusher a prezzie at check-out. A pair of tights, a bag of sweeties, a toothbrush, *free*. It'd cost them less than shoplifting and cut down on that, too.

Glad to hear you've graduated from your Sub-Orgasmic Therapy Group. I'd have sent you a card, except they don't make cards to mark such earth-moving occasions, even in these permissive days. Something tasteful and discreet, like roses are red, violets are blue, Spring has come and so have you. Personally – and I'm not underestimating your triumph – I find the Big O soon sinks to the level of yet another household chore. Part of a list that goes 'buy green thread, spray apple tree, iron shirts, have orgasm'. Sort of a duty, really, that you owe your beloved, like buying polyunsaturated marge for his cholesterol level and sticking Vic up his nose for a cold. Still, at least your union with Bobby-Joe is not yet sacred, like mine with Josh, so you've got a little room for manoeuvre left, if you see what I mean.

Nevertheless, rising from the sub-orgasmic depths into the bright white light of fulfilled womanhood doesn't necessarily give you the go-ahead to include my private habits in your Exploring Politics Through the Sexual Act project. But more of that in my next.

Yours, in wifely modesty,

Martha

Dear Mary

I've been brooding about those fairy tales where Snow White, Sleeping Beauty, the Ice Queen, the Little Mermaid and other happily resting ladies get woken from their snoozes by a peck from Prince Right on the old liperoos. Male fantasies about arousing female virgins, what? But did anyone inform the ladies in question that once they're presented with the result of their awakened passions – ie a permanently insomniac infant – all they will desire in life is to return from whence they came?

The Princes I've kissed, hoping they'll turn into frogs on account of frogs don't disturb your kip like Princes do. In fact, my idea of a happy ending is a Prince whose kiss works the other way round and puts me to sleep for a hundred years, by Royal Decree. And if any wicked fairy is presently hanging about, aching to stick me with a spindle and several thousand years of shut-eye, she's only got to say and my Welcome mat is out.

OK, so I'm fatigued, whacked, bushed, zonked and clapped-out. As my friend Dorrie Carrie Bogvak often says since becoming a Mother in the US of A, Sleep? I'd kill for it. She had twins, poor dear, which guarantees her an unravell'd sleeve of care for life. My darling issue has taken to waking just as my eyelids close, with many a glad cry of whoop de do, bring on the girls, who's for tennis and such. I, needless to say, am his one wan guest, sole subject for his experiments in sleep deprivation.

Josh, woken just one time by my ninety-eighth nocturnal excursion, reared up long enough to ask how he was expected to support us all if he was *continually* disturbed and fell back unconscious again, leaving me petrified. Was this masculine blackmail or was it true? Admittedly, he's cross with me at the moment because he came back from the dentist with a frozen face and I didn't notice the difference but what *would* we do if he was laid off for incipient drowsiness? There's a lot of laying off about, these days.

Only yesterday he complained about his boss, Irene, the

one who looks like a Thirties film star. Not a great Thirties film star, you understand, just a B-grade Accompanying Feature. Anyway, Ms Bossy-boots has presented him with this form to fill in, assessing his own worth to the Department. It's got questions like 'List, in order of importance, the personal characteristics you possess that offer most value to your Unit' and 'What, in your opinion, is the optimum staffing level for your Unit?' I mean, why doesn't she just hand him a pearl-inlay pistol and tell him she's sure he'll do the honourable thing, like they did in the good old days? Then he could shoot her in the back and plead womanslaughter on the grounds of diminished responsibility (his) and ameliorated nagging (hers), excuses all judges find perfectly acceptable when men murder women.

The thing is, Mary, I thought she fancied him. I said as much to Josh and he muttered on a bit about how Irene is jealous of his new secretary, Cassandra by name and, I dare say, by nature. What evidence has Irene got for that idea, I asked in my professionally objective voice (a banshee shriek) and, with that, we were into a goodly bit of overtime bickering until Josh flaked out and the baby, bright-eyed and bushy-tailed, flaked in. From then on, in between poker games, chorus girls, the popping of champagne corks and all the other debaucheries of nursery night-life, I kept eyeing Josh's prone and snoring form. Could this protuberance under the blankets that I call Husband possibly arouse, in female office bosoms, the pitter-patter of passion?

Speaking of which, you asked me about my sex life, re your Exploring Politics Through the Sexual Act project. Fascinated to hear how you and Bobby-Joe practise Marxist dialectics in bed – him being Thesis, you being Antithesis and, whoopee, here comes Synthesis. Also you being the Shadow Cabinet and him being Benn and you being the EEC and Bobby-Joe implementing Conference decisions. What do Social Democrats do? Say American Express, that'll do nicely? Anyway, just put Josh and me down as having no politics to speak of at the moment, unless you count border skirmishes with him being Israel and me being the Lebanon. Personally, I reckon I'm No-Man's-Land till the baby's grown and then I'll be in a wheelchair, though I dare say there are things you can do in wheelchairs we wot not of.

To add to my burdens, Jane has taken to her bed with what she calls the glandulars and I call skiving off. She lies there in the bombsite of her bedroom looking like the wreck of the *Hesperus* and stuffing herself with Curiously Strong

The Fisherman's Friend.

Mints, the Fisherman's Friend. Some devoted and clearly certifiable young man appeared at the door on the second day of her withdrawal from the world, holding a bunch of flowers. As he entered her room, I heard Jane say 'Oh God, it's you. Oh do piff off.' The poor wretch starts backing out, his crest all fallen and, blow me down if she doesn't then shout after him 'Leave the flowers, you nerd.'

And he *does*. Slinks back again, dumps the bouquet and scuttles out, saying sorry to the wallpaper all the way down the stairs. Jane, I said after he'd gone, equality is one thing but this is ridiculous. A man takes the trouble to visit you in your bed of pain and you tell him to piff off and leave the flowers. More fool him, she says, swallowing ten more Fisherman's Friends. What, I wonder, would Barbara, Queen of Cartland, make of Jane?

Yours, not wishing to hear the answer,

Martha

Dear Mary

If we lived in the Middle Ages, I'd have the Black Death. As we don't, my red eyes, grey gums and black tongue must be due to the bout of sorrow-drowning I had last night. Not that any got drowned. On the contrary, several new ones rose to the surface like three-day corpses. The occasion was a dinner party given at the house of one Nigel, colleague of Josh, to exhibit his collection of Top People and put up with the odd Bottom Person like me, admitted on inspection of my marriage lines.

My sorrows started back at mill, as I'm putting on my sexy black number. Josh stops in front of me, eyes my cleavage and says that shows too much bust. *Bust*. My blood ran cold. Josh, I said, ladies in corset departments have busts. Mother has a bust. But when I, Martha, mate of your choice and sharer of your duvet, have a bust, all is over between us. Taking no notice, Josh adds that he thinks it's time the baby was weaned. You ought to stop, Martha, he says. Stop what? I said. Bustfeeding? Martha, *please*, he says, let's try not to be late again.

So I conceal the offending bust and the broken heart under a fringed paisley shawl and silently we drive off, to be met at a wee £200,000 Hampstead cottage by Caroline, mine hostess. Caroline leans foward when she talks and opens her eyes very wide, as if to convince you she's terribly awake. Nigel leans back and closes his eyes very tight, as if to convince you he's not. So nice, says Caroline, bug-eyed. Lovely, says Nigel, lids vacuuming in. Upon which, the fringe of my shawl snakes out, hooks itself to the front door latch and resists two minutes' tugging before it gives in. Ricocheting free, I burst in upon the party but not before the fringe has grabbed an umbrella from a stand and draped it tastefully at my left hip.

Next, I am clasped to the chest of a passing military man as the fringe entwines itself in his jacket button. He is forced to divest himself, I say we've got to stop meeting like this, Josh frowns. Undeterred, the fringe leaps at the watch strap of a young man dispensing drinks. I say I didn't know you cared, Josh frowns a lot more. Then I bend maternally over a small pyjama'd girl (Martha's so good with children), the fringe molests her, she breaks into sobs and several adults have to tear her away. I say how's that for a little fringe theatre, Josh pulls off my shawl with quite unnecessary violence and my bust is released for the evening.

From these squalid scenes, we progress to the dining table and I am seated next to a gent in a blazer and an extremely hostile moustache. During the next thirty minutes, through gazpacho, poached salmon, petit pois and duchesse potatoes, he tells me about sparking plugs. By the time the strawberries arrive, I know more about sparking plugs than whoever invented sparking plugs and, at the advent of the cheese board, the worm turns. I start telling him about the baby. I tell him all I know about the baby, what the baby eats and what the baby refuses to eat. I hold forth at length upon the baby's little ways. I am very animated about the baby, he is strangely still. As the brandy is poured, he heaves himself round to the woman on his left and leaves me alone, at last, with my Remy Martin.

And, believe it or not, Josh has noticed and Josh minds. What came over me, he asks when we get home. Do I not realize that men at parties are not interested in hearing about babies? Have I not learned that babies are hardly the ideal coin of conversational currency? That I have, Josh, I say. I am deeply cognizant of that fact. When a man's eyeballs glaze, when he stares at the edge of my right earlobe, when he fidgets like a soul with itching powder up his Y-fronts, Martha gets the message. Man is bored, says the message. And what do I care, says Martha. Does man recognize when woman is bored? He does not. He refuses even to contemplate that sparking plugs are not everyone's favourite thing. Fair do's I said to that man, do you have children? Yes, he said. Well, I don't have sparking plugs so Heads I win.

Why, oh husband, is it shameful of me to bore a man rigid at a party by talking babies and not shameful at all for him to bore me rigid talking of sparking plugs? Martha, said Josh, you've had too much to drink. Possibly, Josh, I said. That is, I grant you, a remote possibility and then I fell down.

I expect no sympathy from you, Mary, in recounting this sombre tale. I dare say, given such a splendid choice, you might plump for sparking plugs over babies. Nevertheless, there's a moral in there somewhere, if only my head would stop hitting me long enough to let me see it.

It's a mad mad world. One day, my newspaper informs me that a handwriting expert, in possession of a scrap of Lady Diana's correspondence, has proclaimed the astonishing fact that her loops and stems show Lady Di is 'not career-minded'. She has no career in mind, you hear me, Mary? Being Queen of England, with your head all over stamps and five-pound notes (albeit several feet below your Master) is not a career. At heart, Lady Di is a homebody who wishes no more than to stay at home for the rest of her life cooking toad-in-the-hole for hubby and ironing his socks.

That settled, I read this review of a biography of Edgar Allen Poe. Poe, said the reviewer, 'was cursed with a streak of self-destruction which prevented him ever succeeding at anything'. Aahh, I said to Josh. Shame, isn't it? I can't hardly bear it, thinking about E. A. Poe and how unsuccessful he was. Makes me realize just how fortunate I am, being this uncareer-minded housewife, peas in a pod with the highest Lady in the Land *and* being so much more successful than E. A. Poe. My goodness me, Mary, some people have all the luck.

Yours, counting her blessings,

Martha

forward thrust   anti-matter

Nigel and Caroline drifting in Space.

Dear Mary

Just because Mr Begin dropped a few bombs on Iraq's nuclear piles doesn't mean he's about to dedicate his life to CND, you know. The idea of you and Mo shedding your chadors, discovering your Jewish grannies, and vowing to shop-lift only Israeli avocados from now on makes me think the two of you have finally gone critical yourselves.

Menachim is only breaking the other boys' toys before they can break his, anyway, and he's not going to be interested in your plan for an Israeli task force that zooms about the planet demolishing nuclear bases. Though, mind you, it'd be nice if *someone* would. I get quite frantic, sometimes, dosing the baby with vitamins and orange juice and knowing, all the while, that his future is really dependent on some male killer-ape ensconced in a barbed-wire desert with his hairy great finger an inch away from The Button.

I told Josh I wanted to take the baby and go on a CND march this summer and he said no I couldn't, it wasn't Department policy. What *is* Department policy then? I said. Letting babies frizzle in their cots like Kentucky Fried Chickens? Having women and children running through the streets like so many living torches?

Do you realize, I said, that the only people likely to survive a nuclear holocaust are those that started it in the first place? Out they'll all burrow from their underground sewers, twitching their horrid little tatty whiskers while the last rays of the nuclear sun twinkle on their military brass and medals and you know what they'll do? If any unfortunate corpse shows signs of life, they'll bend over it, shout 'Stand to attention you nasty little person' and the whole awful process will start all over again.

Honestly, that's about the only consolation I can think of for not surviving. Getting an invitation card saying the Ronald Reagans, the Leonid Brezhnevs, a few dozen boring old Generals and their ghastly yes-men request the pleasure of your company on a burnt-out planet. RSVP. Enough to make anyone pray for a quick end.

Besides, I said, I'll bet the Department has got its shelter planned. I'll bet its shelves are stocked with Heinz Baked Beans, Kellogg's Cornflakes, and ten billion Sainsbury's pink toilet rolls. What, Josh? Hey, Josh. *Speak* to me, Josh.

But you know what, Mary? Answer came there none. What Josh actually replied was did I know we'd run out of bread? Oh dearie me, I said. Now that is a tragedy. Why, the tears are prickling behind my eyeballs just to hear you say that. How can I possibly contemplate anything more hideous than us running out of bread, unless it's you and Irene and your lady secretary cuddling together in the Department's nuclear shelter while your family fry outside.

I expect you'll feel it incumbent upon you to take Irene as a mate, afterwards, on the grounds that it's your citizen's duty to repopulate the earth with the clones of the kind of citizens that booked seats in nuclear shelters to begin with. Going on a CND March, I said, may not be that much of a jolly for the baby, jogging up and down on my back for a hundred miles, but what's the point staying home, measuring his feet to make sure his shoes fit, when, one day soon, he won't have any feet to fit shoes to?

I went over the top a bit, there, I'll admit. To make matters worse, two minutes later there was Irene, knocking her knuckles on the front door. Irene — Josh's boss and token woman by appointment to HM. In she comes, sits herself down, has a little man-talk with her employee about things too esoteric for my ears, and then puts all her papers ostentatiously away, smiling brilliantly at me the while as if to say the Big People have finished, now, let Children's Hour commence.

I flop down, green with exhaustion after cleaning up the baby, swabbing down the house, and cook, cook, cooking a three-course meal. Upon which, Josh swings his arm slowly out towards a bottle of wine, asks me if I'd like a glass, I say ta, and you know what Ms Bossieboots contributes at that moment in time? Aren't you lucky, Martha, she says, having a husband who spoils you so?

I sit staring at her, jaw at half-mast, while the real me picks up a machine gun, shouts Banzai and riddles her with bullets. Josh gives a cute and deprecating wiggle of his shoulders, meaning you *see*, Martha? Some people appreciate me. And the witch stays on for dinner because she says oh my how she miss family life. I imagine her family drove her out with rakes and hoes and pickaxe handles some time ago.

That night my innards tore free of their moorings and cantered about like wild things. Josh, on the other hand, being of a forgiving nature, felt like a bit of how's your father. Have you ever tried to make love with a mouthful of Rennies, Mary? Don't.

There's Josh being the Sheik of Araby and there's me going chomp chomp and trying to give him a CSE Grade I kiss without losing my lozenges. Finally, Josh stops what he's doing and says Martha, could you give me an appointment when you're through with those tablets? Josh, I say, it says on the package do not chew, do not crunch, let dissolve slowly in mouth. And then I add, in case of fire, break glass.

I do not know why I said that, I do not know why I say most things.

Yours, half-way to the nut house,

Martha

my hair!

the real me

1 July

Dear Mary

When you first wrote that Bobby-Joe was going, I thought you meant back to the Lone Star State, there to do what a man must do, whatever that is, but now you say not at all, he's out on his earhole on the grey paving stones of Sebastopol Terrace, never to darken the door of Number 2 again because you and Mo took a democratic vote, two to one against, and gave him the shove. And all because the poor Texan lad didn't do his share of the housework.

What house? What work? I don't wish to be gratuitously rude but I'd never have guessed that you and Mo were squat-proud. Last time I visited, there was this cucumber lying under the kitchen table so covered in mould it looked like a woolly cactus and I said to Mo why is there a mouldy cucumber lying under your kitchen table and she said because if she picked it up she'd be making a commitment to domesticity. And this is the lady who minds about Bobby-Joe not taking turns doing the washing-up? Has it occurred to her that he might not be able to locate the sink? It took me half an hour to twig that all those interesting fungi in the corner had dishes underneath and the new variety of Venus Fly Trap was actually your communal clettering stick.

I mean, let's face it, your place looks like a giant rat had run amok and gnawed its way through everything in sight. Unless I'd seen it with my own eyes, I'd never have believed that chairs and tables so chewed up could actually remain standing on all three legs. And you may think you've got some sort of order in there but, take it from me, not everyone searching for a toilet roll would necessarily look in the oven and not everyone could guess that the logical niche for sprouting beans is in the cistern.

So why should you both suddenly decide the wretched B-J isn't pulling his weight and dump him? You said yourself he was ace on the guitar and surely he played a bit role in the success of your Orgasmic Therapy course? Can't you find it in your heart to put up with *anything* in the name of love? When I think of what I endure day after day, year after year, screech screech of soap opera strings, all I can say is you're a hard woman, Mary. And if so, why am I sitting here in my cosy nest with my cosy man, cukes neatly stacked in the veggie rack, going green at the edges with envy? I cannot imagine.

Never mind, holsville is nearly here. Actually, I hadn't realized it was nearly here until yesterday evening, when I heard Josh say on the phone to his sec, the doomy Cassandra, that, yes, we were off in August to our little place in France. Then I knew it was the tent again, up the Dordogne. I wonder if Josh is aware he's had a baby since last year? Probably not.

Jane, interrogated as to her holiday plans, said wild horses wouldn't drag her to a canvas tip in Frogland; Ben threw himself about at the thought and produced a series of revolting noises but can I be sure they won't come? I doubt it. Plans, nevertheless, are afoot. Josh, for instance, is deep in the Michelin. Head stuck in the little red book, he reads out things like *"Cheval Blanc, Specialité; brochettes de coquilles d'estragon, turbot beurre blanc, sole braisée au Noilly, vins Muscadet"* and says, 'What about that Martha? Eh, Martha? What's for dinner, Martha?' — and I have to say bangers and mash.

It's so *unfair*, Mary. What is all that fuss about these *chef minceurs*, anyway? I've been cooking *minceur* forever, and who comes along and awards me four stars for my amazing innovations in ze kitchen? No one. Discrimination again.

All the real cooking goes on in homes, done by women — men just come in at the top of the pyramid wearing silly hats and call themselves *maitres de cuisine* because they've managed to make something edible out of two gallons of double cream, a haunch of venison and three bottles of brandy. Big deal. Whereas we women can produce a meal for eight out of six decaying veggies, a cube of Oxo and a pound of stale biscuits, which is what I call cooking. Besides, chefs don't have to put up with husbands pigging it and then moaning about their weight.

Last time Josh complained about his, I told him I knew a sure-fire way he could lose 20lb overnight and he said how and I said I could cut his legs off. Then he'd be the teeny toast of the town, like Toulouse Lautrec. I was feeling sore at the time, as it happened. You know that long boring saga I told you two weeks ago about how my shawl got its fringe caught in everything at that party?

Believe it or not, at the supermarket Saturday I bent down to gather up some tins on a low shelf and got my earring entangled in the hair of a small Chinese boy. I had to stay bent over him for ages in the most humiliating way, thinking I'd never heard of anyone who had to be medically severed from a Chinese child except, perhaps, a Chinese mother. What have I done to deserve such punishment?

Coming home, flushed from slaving over a hot Chinese child, I blew off to Josh about how I *must* get a job and save myself from all this. A job? he said. Did I realize, he said, that there were now 2.6 million unemployed and you, Martha, wish to add to that number? *Five* million, I said, sharpish. Five million and one counting me. I'm one of M. Thatcher's fudged statistics, remember? I *want* a job, there aren't any jobs, so I'm forced to wear a hat saying Housewife.

Perhaps, said Josh, you could take a course in Advanced Knitting.

Yours, with the needles out,

Martha

Tai chi chuan

Dear Mary

Are you at all cognizant of what the likes of you and Mo have done, with your Women's Liberationism? Are you aware that you've taken as nice a bunch of modest, sensibly brogued ladies as ever lay back and thought of England and turned them into a monstrous regiment of dirty old women? Transformed them into leering harridans in grubby macs who hang around street corners whistling at anything in trousers that innocently skips by? I've a good mind to shop you to Mrs W so she can stick you in the dock with the Romans, where you belong.

OK. Scratch that. Cancel it, wipe the machine, file it in the wpb. The fact is, I'm in a very distressed state about Ben. You haven't seen him since he was normal. He is now a Brobdingnagian giant. What with jack-knifing down to say googly-goo to one son no higher than my knee-caps and then arching in an S-bend to have a quick word with the other before his head vanishes for ever into deep space, I've got a permanent slippery disc. And if I say so myself, Ben looks terrible. His feet alone take several minutes to enter a room and that a human back-bone can support so many dangling appendages without collapsing like a pack of vertebrae is one of the minor miracles of ergonomics.

Besides that, he's got so many spots it takes a magnifying glass to see the boy in between. Ben flatly denies this. What spots? he says. You're always going on about my spots when I haven't had any for years. Then he asks for a pound to buy Oxy-5, for his spots. What spots? I say. You haven't had any spots for years, right? A cheap victory, I grant you, but I'm not one to look a gift horse in the mouth, can't afford to.

Anyway, yesterday the great lump says he's going out. Where? I say. Out, he says. I cherish these intimate conversations. Then it leaks out he's got a girlfriend. I am genuinely pleased. Fancy that, then, our Ben with a rosy-cheeked damsel, all braces and bunches, sweet sixteens both and never been kissed.

Upon which, Ben announces that said damsel is thirty-five. Thirty-*five*? *Thirty-five*? Mum, says Ben, your record's stuck. But Ben, I say, you're *sixteen*. *So*? says Ben. You an ageist, Mum or something? But Ben, I say, what on earth does a thirty-five-year-old woman want with *you*? And do you know, Mary, the twit gives a sickening smirk, adjusts his shoulder bones in the hall mirror, clicks his fingers at his reflection, and erupts out the front door squawking like a rooster. Leaving me, his mother, 38, alone and palely loitering. Is there such a thing as senile nymphomentia? How does she treat him, what does she say? Ben, you wash your hands before you come to bed, hear me? And just look at those nails. Will you for Pete's sake stand still while I talk to you, stop fidgeting, and *please* turn that music down before my eardrums puncture. Is that any sort of prelude to life's tenderest moments? The woman must be round the twist.

There I was, with the birds-and-bees all planned, ready for Ben's first whisper of romance. A motherly man-to-man chat about responsibilities and courtesy to the opposite sex and always using the necessaries. And now I'm locked in combat with a female pederast. It's too much. How am I supposed to mother an innocent babe and a sex-crazed teenage clown, all at the same time? Mornings spent sticking Heinz Chicken Dinner in a small mouth, one for Mummy, down the little red lane, evenings spent embroiled in a May to September saga of mismatched lust. No one woman can bridge such gulfs.

Josh is no use. He coarsened before my eyes when told and clapped Ben on the back for the first time since he learned his five times tables. I'm going to write to Ben's father and make him *do* something. At least it'll tear him away from his rotten *Flasher's Guide to Feminism*. Did I tell you he's sent the first chapter to Josh? Haw haw, says Josh, laughing immoderately, you must have a read, Martha. Thanks, but no thanks, I said. As it happens, I did catch a glimpse. The first page: How to Seduce a Feminist. Tell her, 'Oh, Ms Croggs, if you'd only put your hair in a bun and wear glasses, you'd be beautiful.' Vulgar trash and typical of my ex.

In the midst of these upsets my friend Lorna, the autopsy technician, appeared and said why didn't I come with her that evening and have my feet massaged by this marvellous man who could solve all my problems by rummaging round my insteps. So I went and he stuck his fingers quite painfully into my big toe and when I said ouch he told me that showed I was a deeply sensitive and misunderstood person, which is

so true, Mary. He also said I was pitifully exposed to other people's feelings and must wear a black cummerbund round my middle to protect myself from emotional vibrations that make martyrs of generous and vulnerable souls like myself. He guessed my star sign, too, or the one I would have had if I hadn't been in such a hurry to get away from Mother. The man is clearly psychic and the first for a long time to see into the real me. Such an aesthetic demeanour. Such compelling eyes. Such strong yet gentle hands.

Yours, strangely moved,

Martha

Dear Mary

Got about five minutes to write this before Josh, me and the baby depart for our place in France, ie *le tente*. Does tente mean tent? Probably not. In my experience, the more the French word is like the English the more it's different and usually rude. Have we got an *entente cordiale* at the moment? I can't remember if we've just stopped fighting about lamb or just started fighting about fish. I shall scrape the GB off the car on the other side, just in case. Do not wish to be pursued by enraged froggies down the N1.

Over the weekend Josh (generous to a fault? Oiling up the ladder?) announced he'd swopped Department hols with this VIP called Tinkerton-Smith because T-S and wife have marital problems and can't get away. I've met the Tinkerton-Smiths. They look like two rubber balls with specs on, it's a miracle they manage to have sex without bouncing. Anyway, I was furious. *We're* the ones who'll have marital problems, I said, if you think I'm going to pack for three and organize two others plus cats, goldfish and white mice, all in two days. Oh I told him, Mary. Out of the question, I said. Quite impossible. *Pas de chance, oubliez-le* and so on. I was adamant.

So we're off. Ben's gone already, on this morning's train to Mousehole and his Dad. He protested like mad about leaving his fish, his mice and his girlfriend, in that order, but there's a silver lining to every cloud – surely he'll meet a nice Cornish girl nearer his age, like thirty, instead of that predatory crone he's taken up with? Tom was none too pleased when I phoned but I didn't give him a chance to talk. I said Tom, your son arrives 1.45 pm, Penzance, today. His name's Ben, he's wearing an orange rucksack, you can't miss him. And I slammed the phone down on the rising rumbles from the other end. That was the bit I enjoyed. Ben can be guaranteed to sabotage *The Flasher's Guide*, at least for a while.

Jane was more of a problem. She mooned about complaining of being exploited, having to stay in the rotten house to feed rotten rodents. I'd told her she could have a girl friend in or go to her Grandmother's and Mrs Next-Door would come in to feed the beasts but Jane said she didn't have girl friends and mooned some more. Then, yesterday evening, she comes in with this stunning young man. I mean *stunning*, Mary. Well over six foot, marigold hair, cornelian eyes and medallions all over amazing pectorals. As I got up off the floor, Jane said this is Rover, Ma, a mate of mine. He'll stay for the month. So will I, I said. No, of *course* I didn't. I said Jane, look Jane, hullo Rover, look Rover, you must understand. I can't leave you both in the house, alone together. Why ever not? said Jane staring. Well, Jane, you're a girl and Rover is a man. You . . . I . . . it wouldn't do.

I dare say I came over a mite coy then, blinking and twittering and fluttering, while they both stood there and gazed at me, their eyes four blank discs of incomprehension. What? said Jane. Pardon? said Rover. It dawned on me then that neither Jane nor Rover would recognize sex if it fell on top of them in the dark. Between the two of them, they've obviously finished off the permissive society and buried it in a pauper's grave so they might just as well fill up the resulting free time scattering goldfish food on goldfish and mice food on mice. So I said, oh very well. Besides, in my sad experience, men who look like Rover look only at their mothers.

My mother, of course, popped up by popular demand to do her evergreen music-hall turn, the one with the refrain that goes 'what if.' What if, says Mother, Jane falls over the cat, breaks every limb and starves to death because Rover isn't there because Rover's mother's died and he's had to go to Buenos Aires for her funeral? What if ten thousand unemployed youths, brains bleached by the peroxide they put on their hair, riot in our back garden? What if a mad axeman escapes from Broadmoor, thumbs a lift to our street corner, breaks in and rapes Jane who jumps out of the front window? Not to mention the one about what if Rover or the longer one about Ben (falls out of train, fractures skull, gets amnesia and is never seen again). What would you do then, Martha? You'd never forgive yourself, Martha. Oh how we all clapped. This one will run and run.

One good thing, though – I'll miss the Wedding. What a happy deliverance from the Royal Charade! I've no wish at all to sit and watch while one poor little girl, the same age as our Jane, is sentenced to a life-time of flatties. And I know I can rely on you and Mo to give me no details whatsoever of the Wedding Dress. You haven't got a telly, anyway, have you? Mind you, I may be forced to watch in France, somewhere. You know how besotted the Continentals are about our Royals and I wouldn't want to be boorish, if anyone insisted. When in Rome, I always say.

And as Mrs Next-Door always says, you don't go on holiday to do what you *want*, do you, dear?

Yours, with the seat-belts clunked and clicked,

Martha

Dear Mary

Driven 1000 kms through deepest France, baby pogo-ing on lap, shrieking in earhole, whacking in face. Arrive camp shaking wreck, bruised neck to knees, sporting black eye, to be greeted by Hooray Henry in next tent who takes butcher's at me, says ho ho ho ho, who's on her honeymoon then, eh what? Did *not* drive 1000 kms to squat cheek by jowl with dread GB hearty sniggering about sex. *Sex* imposs. anyway. Baby's nose just reaches top of canvas cot, from whence he regards us all night long with unblinking stare.

Just glimpsed Josh's card to sec. Says 'Wish you were her'. Is this sloppy spelling or end of marriage?

Votre, sans un trace de ooh la la,

Martha

Dear Mary

Due to hitherto undetected EEC apricot mountain, baby has runs – ie baby sits, I run. Result: this postcard written under low cloud formed by fall-out from nappies incinerating in some foreign field that is forever England. Elsewhere, Old Sol works overtime. Yesterday, braving Josh's mutters, I appear topless on river beach. One glance at forgotten globes & baby goes into thirst-maddened-desert-castaway-crawling-towards-mirage-of-drinking-fountain number. V. embarrassing. Have to peel him forcibly off intimate anatomy to chorus of *dommages* from French mamans on brink of shopping me to Dordogne branch of NSPCC.

Votre, la belle dame sans merci,

Martha

Dear Mary

These past 24 hours have brought our little family remarkably close. Mainly because if we so much as touch the outside canvas, rain pours in. Il pleut, Mary, comme chats et chiens. Gigantic Citroen parked opposite to view (I thought) les foreign misérables, turns out to be Josh's dear old college chum Yves de Tiswas, come to convey us to his maison de campagne, complete with brocantes and meubles traditionelles anglaises (expensive bum-numbing wooden benches). Yves has a maid, too, an honest-to-goodness becapped, befrilled, be-black-stockinged maid. Josh now in deep sulk. He's worked his guts out, voted EEC since Heath was young, so how come Yves, a fool if ever there was one and lazy to boot, not to say un pouffe from way back, is rolling in francs? But Josh, I said, I thought he was your *friend*. What's that got to do with it? says Josh, enragé. Les hommes, quelle mystère ils sont.

Votre, wishing I was there,

Martha

Josh thinking about Yves....

Dear Mary

Am exstatically happy – Ekstatically happy? Something not quite right there but no Concise Oxford handy so who cares. Sun hot, wine cold, only blot on horizon pack-up time rapidly approaching. Baby brown as chip off Old Potato. Said to Old Potato, why can't we always live in tent, just you and me? OP replied 'And Ben *and* Jane *and* the baby AND your mother and let's not forget Studs.' Heart sank. Didn't know he knew about Studs, not that anything to know. Had flashback about day Josh came home early, found Studs carving leftover roast. Realize now any woman caught in flagrante with man carving husband's roast, worse than adulteress.

Yours attrappée bang to rights,

Martha

Dear Mary

Sorry no letter last week, just arrived home zonked out. Missed road, missed boat, nearly missed England. Bad trip. Hey, wait a minute, I'm not writing postcards any more. I can expand out of the glottal stops, stick in the odd pronoun, dust off an adjective or two, get into expressing myself full frontally again. Not that there's a whole lot to express. My tan has faded to what we housewives call dirty and the first faint spots of autumn have broken out across the baby's bum. Oh to be in la Dordogne, now that London's here. Well, all good things must come to an end.

Anyway, I got your card and I'm glad you're home, too. No lolling about in the ultra-violet for you, I see. No sooner do I turn my back than you scamper off to yet another Summer School. What was it, this time? The Experiential Ethos of the Feminine Principle, Logic or Myth? Something like that.

Honestly, sometimes I wonder about Wales. It was Wales you were in, wasn't it? Like California, when they tipped Britain on its side all the nuts rolled into Wales. Our nuts, not theirs. First they got hordes of hippies cantering across the Severn Bridge in the Sixties, kneedeep in cowbells, stiff with joss and Acapulco Gold, hellbent on filling in the Welsh valley with rotting plastic mattresses and throttling the natives with their awful macrame. And the moment they'd gone, in came the next wave, religious nuts this time, complete with woodsy altars to replace the nice, dull Welsh chapels. Daughters of the Moon. Kiddywinks of God. Church of Christ, Dentist. All that. What must God have felt, peering through the clouds (the Welsh do a nice line in clouds) and seeing all those loony little faces raised to Him, chanting mantras and arranging their limbs in inscrutable Eastern positions? A bit like the last of the Raj, I shouldn't wonder.

And now they're shuddering under the latest wave – batty Self-Improvers who rush over with their rucksacks and unspeakable sleeping bags to register for weekends in Ego Expansion and Ancient Kurdish Skipping Rhymes. Whenever you hear of a new group that's into anything light years away from useful, where are they doing it? Wales is where. Not surprisingly, they make bonfires of our cottages. I could find it in my heart to light a match or two myself. Yes, I know all that sounds the teeniest bit Fascistic and I know you'll think I'm being hostile but it's not meant that way. I am trying to talk about you first, like it says in those books about how to win friends. Do not push yourself, it warns in Chapter One. Listen to others' problems, ask them about themselves, learn to be a listener. Well, you've had your innings. It's all me from now on.

I won't say the place was a mess when we got home because it wasn't too bad. Jane had fought back the encroaching jungle in at least the kitchen, the bathroom, and our bedroom but she'd given up on the sitting room. Breaking in, I knew suddenly how Howard Carter must have felt, discovering King Tut's tomb. The very atmosphere was heavy with times past. Two vases of roses were almost perfectly preserved though, alas, as the door creaked open and fresh air rushed in, they crumbled into dust before my eyes. And, believe it or not. I found intricately emblazoned beer cans containing the actual fag-ends, left exactly as they were by the long-gone folk of yore. There were even the yellowed shards of Sunday papers lying open on the floor, where the last inhabitants had dropped them before the vault slammed shut. It was so moving, Mary, it brought tears to my eyes.

Ben had returned a week earlier, jaded by the highlife of Mousehole. He seems to have spent the time in what he calls his bed, actually a cage he's constructed of bookshelves cunningly interwoven with white mice, a few goldfish and two pots of ivy expanded into a trellis of greenery between him and the outside world. Within, he can be dimly perceived, a shy gorilla amongst forest leaves, munching through comics like *National Lampoon*, that disgusting American mag Tom saw fit to give him last birthday. How's Dad? I said. OK, he said. What did you do? I said. Nothing, he said. Sometimes I wonder will I ever stem the flood?

Josh, having put in an appearance at the office, stormed home very put out. Someone had moved his desk. They *had*. Stuck it under the window instead of sideways to the door and pinched his swivel chair. Poor lamb. Really, Mary, I don't know how some men bear their lot, do you? Just imagine coming home and finding you have to face due South instead of North, as was. Enough to snap the stoutest nerve. I said to Josh, I don't see you have any option but to resign. Otherwise, what shred of dignity have they left you? I mean, if people think they can push you around like that, next time you're away you might find you'd made a whole 180 degree turn, without a word of authorization or a single signed slip. And after that, anything might happen – you could end up press-ganged into the SDP. Do you know, the way my husband looks at me sometimes, I don't think he even *likes* me.

Yours, home and wet,

Martha

Testify! —

The church of Christ, Dentist.

2 September

Dear Mary

I don't know what to do about Rover. Here it is, September, and he shows no signs of leaving, nor does a ripple of anxiety disturb the delightful harmony of his brow. Jane says we can't come home from foreign parts whenever it suits us and chuck him out on the street and Rover stands like a block of polished steel and says uh-huh. When it *suits* us? I said. The way I feel now, Rover's welcome to move in with Josh and I'll chuck *myself* out on the street, if not the window. I believe this is what's called the post-hols blues.

I suppose, Mary, you couldn't put him up at Sebastopol Terrace, could you? Haven't you an odd cupboard free, now that Bobby-Joe has gone? Rover doesn't seem to have any direct connection with London, like work or friends or the theatre – have you noticed how ex-Londoners always say, of course, I *do* miss the theatre when they've never even seen *The Mousetrap*? It's true Rover doesn't do very much except look in the mirror and twitch his muscles but you can't blame him for that, seeing as how he's so ornamental. You could pretend he was a large and exotic parrot you'd bought to brighten up the home, albeit a bird daft as two planks who can only say uh-huh.

I wouldn't mind having him all that much but Josh would and he's under the illusion that Rover's already gone, anyway. He thinks he comes in the evening to see Jane but he doesn't know he sneaks upstairs after banging the front door hard like I told him to. All he's faintly concerned with is Jane's purity – is she saving herself for a husband? Whereas I know Rover's no threat – he's saving himself for himself. Do write and tell me if you can house him because I can't go on much longer concealing him in the attic like Mr Rochester's mad wife. Yesterday, him and Josh nearly collided on the way to the bathroom and I got so nervous I ate a whole treacle tart.

Ben went out yesterday and came back with the woman he calls his old lady and no wonder. You remember his aged amour, the 35-year-old cradlesnatcher? It was her and, much as I hate to admit it, she's really rather nice, even if she is only two years younger than me. She's called Wendy. Not, I grant you, a name that reverberates in the soul. No one is going to sing Wendy, Wendy, the most wonderful name in the world, but it suits her and she's very maternal. She picked up the baby right away and dandled him the whole time we were chatting. Ben got bored and went off to watch the Muppets and we got on with our girl-talk. Mind you, I kept an eye peeled as she left in case she showed signs of trans- ferring her affection from Ben to the baby and tried to smuggle him out. Come to think of it, she'd make a handy baby-sitter.

It's so odd, the way things work. For hundreds of years, fathers have been giving away daughters to men their own age, as if they were passing them on to another father and, in most ways, they were. But it should be the other way round, shouldn't it? Boys are so much more childish than girls. Jane could cope with practically everything when she was 12 but it still takes Ben about half-an-hour to tie his shoe laces. Perhaps, between me and Wendy we can start a whole new matriarchal trend. I can quite see myself walking up the aisle, Ben's hand gripped firmly in mine (stop it now or Mummy will smack), and depositing it in Wendy's capable grasp at the altar, knowing I can trust her to see that he brushes his teeth properly, up and down, eats plenty of green veggies, and has a bath at least once a week including back of neck.

She's a good thrifty housewife, too. Told me how she makes her own sheets and you know the price of sheets. Well, you should know. The only trouble is, talking about sheets makes me think of her and Ben lying under them. Yuk. I feel, now, I ought to get in touch with Wendy's mother, to warn her about my son. She lives in Bournemouth. I happen to know that interesting fact because Wendy said she had to visit her and Ben said oh why and Wendy said she is 70, you know, and Ben said well, you'd better run, then. He goes back to school next week. Thank heaven.

I got your letter explaining about your summer course in the Ethos of the Feminine Principle, Logic or Myth, and I say unto you it's Myth. Look, it sounds fine, arguing that if men cooked and women engineered, the battle of the sexes would grind to a halt but that's not my experience. When – when – Josh cooks, the merest turn of a wooden spoon becomes the essence of masculinity. His bechamel stirs him to the very peaks of machoism and if he produces even the tiredest-looking cake he reckons he's John Wayne, jingling spurs, funny walk, drawl, the lot. If ah'd known you was comin', ah'd of baked a cake, baby. Whereas Josh comes upon me repairing the boiler with a spanner I happen to have painted a face on, for no reason whatsoever, and he laughs tenderly like men do when they're thinking how deeply, lovably, and transparently inferior women actually are. And I titter back.

Yours, stuck in a gender trap,

Martha

Dear Mary

I wrote to ask if you could put Rover up at Sebastopol Terrace and you write back and say you can't 'on account of the CND'. What does that mean? Josh, who's taken a quite unaccountable dislike to poor Rove, says you've discovered what he's known all along, Rove's a human neutron bomb – he destroys people, not property. Which is very mean of Josh and also inaccurate, as he would know if I'd ever let him see the gouged-out floorboards in Ben's room where Rover drops his dumb-bells from on high.

The only connection I can imagine is that you've got CNDers staying while they're on some march but, in that case, they'd be classified as itinerants or nomads or something and Rove could come when they've passed on. Unless you're on some permanent CND shuttle service between Land's End and Chancellor Schmidt?

Yes I know. I sound irritable and I am. Ben is having the longest school holidays in the history of education. Every day he makes noises like he's going off, he disappears, I breathe a sigh of relief and abracadabra, he's back again. Just registering, he says, waving various bits of · blank paper. Really, I could almost suspect the school didn't want him, which is weird. Well, weirdish.

Yesterday, he came in, cleared his throat and said Mum, I've made a decision. My heart leapt up. He's taking French, I thought. He's really going to work hard. He's decided he's going to be a doctor. Wrong again. Mum, says Ben, I've decided what I want for Christmas. Christmas. Oh good, Ben I said. What a relief to us all. Wait till I tell Father Christmas, he *will* be pleased.

Besides Ben, there is the baby, once so sweet and lovable, now a home-breaker. Could the Martians have whipped the real infant away and left us with a wind-up intergalactic spy? When I put him down on the floor, he crawls off at top speed like one of those horrid mechanical toys that used to frighten me so when I was a kid. Mary, I swear he *whirrs*.

Jane stands there yelling do something, Mum, it's coming at me, don't let it get in my room. Also, he's taken to emitting unearthly shrieks. All of a sudden the mechanics fail, the limbs come to a grinding halt, a hole appears in the centre of the face and out of it comes a series of eardrum-perforating screams, as if he were permanently attached to a maddened wasp.

What really unnerves me is, he watches me while he's shrieking and his face is perfectly blank and sort of inwardly absorbed, as if he were passing on some message to an invisible walkie-talkie. Agent PZ254 calling Mars. OK, Mars. Mission accomplished. Multiparous Terran Female cracking up. What's more, there's Josh complaining all the time that he's aware food prices have gone up and he knows there's inflation but my food bills are ridiculous. Josh, I want to say, they're not ridiculous, they're Rover, but I daren't. Josh, hit in the pocket, is not a pretty sight.

Worse, I fear Jane may be falling in love with Rover. She kicks him a lot, jumps out on him from corners bellowing like that Japanese in the Pink Panther films and rolls her eyes heavenwards whenever he speaks, grunting Jeez.

I wish I could be philosophical about it all and think 'this, too, will pass' but that only reminds me so will I, and soon, if this goes on. You, Mary, who communicate only with adults, can have little idea what it's like to be locked for life in the monkeys' cage at the zoo. Ever so entertaining if you're on the outside, pushing snacks through the bars and looking forward to a nice cup of tea in a peaceful kitchen. Another thing altogether to find, when the visitors go and the keepers switch the lights off, that you're banged up in the chimps' tea party.

My only relief this week has been Lorna, my friend across the road. I'm not surprised she's a mortician technician, suits her down to the ground, ho ho. Last week they buried the grumpy old boy who ran the basket shop in the high street. Oh dear, I mumbled hypocritically, his poor family. Yeah, said Lorna, grief-stricken as newts they were.

Then she goes on about a girl she was on holiday with, the one with the wavy copper hair and emerald eyes and ugly. Apparently the kiddies on the beach had flocked around her. She's obviously got a magnetism for kiddies, I said. They're drawn to her. No they're not, said Lorna, they just wanted an eyeful of the holes in her cossie. As for Lorna's friend's husband, all she'd say about him was he had breasts the same shape as his wife's. Honestly, Lorna's inner life must look a bit like Ben's goldfish bowl, all green and murky and full of dark shapes.

Josh is no help. When I try and discuss Ben with him, he raises his face towards me and his eyes close, just like a sleepy-doll. I mean, I know Ben isn't his son but you'd think he'd take an interest for my sake. Last week I was moaning on about the lad and this time Josh didn't even raise his face. Look, I said, do you realize that sometimes teenage boys are really worried about some things, really disturbed, and their parents never bother and then, out of the blue, they kill themselves? He'll grow out of it, said Josh vaguely, it's only a phase. You can't grow out of death, I said. Hanging may do wonders for venison, but it is no maturing process for human beings. He wasn't listening.

About the only thing that gets through to him at the moment is the baby's shrieks. Is that why the baby shrieks? Clever thing.

Yours, deaf-aid off,

Martha

Lorna at work.

COLD STORE

DEAD AGAINST THE BOMB

Dear Mary

Josh entered the house at seven pip emma yesterday, bounced off Rover's pectorals in the hall, fell over Ben's bike in the kitchen, took the full blast of the baby in mid-aria, poured himself the sludge at the bottom of the holiday Pernod, said here's to the ladies bless 'em and *smiled* at me – I know he's smiling when the front of his hair moves. Ye gods and fishes, I thought, Maggie's made him Sir Josh. But no. Martha, he said, making toasting gestures at me, good news for you. The Boss has decided to stand for Parliament and I'm behind her one hundred percent so don't ever say again that I'm against your women's lib.

Well. For a moment there I thought the floor and I were about to come together. A frightful pain shot through my heart and buried itself in the region of my spleen. Ms Boss, MP? Just twenty-four hours ago I'd expressed a desire to attend my very small women's group for a very short time and Josh had come on like I planned to desert him for a career in Hollywood. He had, he protested, *papers* to go through and how could a man go through *papers* with a baby at his feet making noises like it was about to take off for Saturn? So I didn't go. And now we have Irene, already at the pinnacle of one male edifice, plotting to scale yet another with the one hundred percent support of my spouse. Furthermore, a spouse who's acting as if she's some sort of Joan of Arc for her pains. And the two of them couldn't blow their own noses without help from ancillary staff.

So there I am in an upright swoon, pinned to my chair by a ton-weight of envy and resentment and a headache coming on fast, when who should appear but the Maid of Orleans herself, clad in shining white Vanderbilt coveralls (I myself am modishly got up in Sixties bell-bottoms and some parts of a sweater Jane got tired of knitting). And Mary, the woman is iridescent. Nostrils aflare with the scent of power, face flushed across to the ears with naked ambition. She's fresh from some boat trip of women egging each other on to Westminster and she looks like the Bride of Dracula after a boozy weekend. Even the baby feels upstaged and cuts out suddenly on a high note.

And what does Josh, Knight-at-Arms, do? Goes across to the cupboard, takes out the bottle of champagne he's set aside for some intimate marital occasion like the day Mother kicks the bucket, pops the cork and pours froth all over the place while our foetal MP smiles and smiles. One of these days, that woman will smile me to death. Then, downing her champers, Irene sails over to me, puts one exquisitely manicured hand on my dish-pan appendages, looks moistly into my eyes and says Martha dear, I hope we can all rise to the challenge, look beyond mere Party prejudice and vote for me. We girls must stick together, mustn't we?

If I'd had the breadknife handy, I'd have drawn it across both our throats. And I trust, Mary, you're not thinking good for Irene, we need more women in Parliament because, if you are, don't bother to put a 14p stamp on it. Irene MP would do women like me about as much good as the rhythm method. Not only will she forget the ordinary woman's lot – she never knew it. She'll waltz about the corridors of power in her £300 Jean Muir number with a bodyguard of masseurs and coiffeurs plucking at her and appear night and day on telly to lecture such as me on the sanctity of marriage and the marvels of motherhood.

I tell you, that woman is the Marie Antoinette of our time, she even has a weeny thatched cotty in the Cotswolds where she goes and pats sheep. Any minute now, she'll be saying let them eat Textured Vegetable Protein. You're thinking she resembles Mrs T? Matey, she makes that lady look like Marx in drag. At least Maggie has momentarily experienced childbirth even if it was two for the labour of one and into boarding school before they could call her Mother, whereas Ms Boss has done nothing more female than stick her feet in stacked heels. Why in heaven's name should I support a person just because it wears skirts? So does King Khalid and he's in line for no feminist prizes.

Don't you *want* women in Parliament to defend your interests? said Josh, in bed that night. Yah boo sucks, I sobbed. And then, you know what? He puts his arm around me, gives me a little squeeze and says listen, Martha, let me spell it out. If Irene gets to Parliament, who gets to be Boss? D'you see, little Martha? D'you see why I'm behind her?

There's men for you, Mary, deceivers all. Vipers in the grass, snakes in the woodpile, leaders up the garden path and leavers at the altar. Poor Irene, poor silly dear, how's she going to manage in politics if she can't tell the difference between a pat on the back and a knife between the ribs? We girls must stick together.

Yours in sisterly solidarity,

Martha

23 September

Dear Mary

Amazed to hear that you and Mo were on that Women-for-Parliament cruise, too, and actually met Irene face to face. Or would have, as you say, if the ten tons of make-up she was wearing hadn't prevented her lifting said face above the Plimsoll line. Mean remarks like that, Mary, make me realize you are not so much a Sister, more a bosom friend. I hate to be brutally frank in return but I must tell you I'm not truly convinced, even so, that you and Mo are likely to lead me, your humble womb-defined female voter, much further along the path to paradise than Irene.

Does life as it is lived up Sebastopol Terrace say a whole lot more to me than Ms Boss's division-bell penthouse and Cotswold cotty? Answer, not a syllable. I won't go on about Motherhood again because I promise you I don't really count giving birth as among the outstanding qualifications for women MPs but is my choice of a life-enhancing economic policy stuck between Irene's Brylcreemed commodity-brokers overcharging on hoarded Third World coffee and your strategy of nicking Sainsbury's Instant whenever the whim strikes? I dare say you both succeed in redistributing some wealth but not, I'd like to point out, in my direction.

This analysis may be lacking in depth. We housewives find it practically impossible to obtain four minutes' quiet in which to formulate abstract thought. During the past half-hour, for instance, Ben has been padding up and down behind my left ear muttering tiddley pom tiddley pom tiddley pom, over and over. Ben, I finally said to him, other boys of your age do not spend their days saying tiddley pom over and over in this ridiculous fashion. Furthermore, Lorna's son, who is exactly your age, told me yesterday a great many interesting facts about the chemical that makes oak apples into oak apples and I must say (I added, meanly) I rather wished *he* was my son. Mary, all that boy did was look vaguely in my direction and say and was he? Was he? I said. Ben, what d'you mean, *was* he? Of course he wasn't, you idiot. He's *Lorna's* son. I mean, Alice in Wonderland, Mary.

Do you wonder I can't concentrate under these circumstances?

That sort of thing happens all the time with Ben. The other day we went and picnicked by the Thames, under a tree with a boat tied to it. Ben sat in the boat and said Mum, why have they tied that tree to this boat? They haven't, I said. They've tied the boat to the tree. How do you know? he said. Perhaps they think the tree might get stolen. You see? Is there such a thing as dyslexia of the entire personality and, if so, what's the cure? In my more optimistic moments (last one, June 5, 1978) I put Ben's behaviour down to what that nice Mr de Bono calls lateral thinking and only crude and ignorant people call barmy.

Be that as it may, such goings-on make abstract political ideas hard to come by and forces me to realize the appeal of the SDP who will do it all for us, and nicely, because they are nice people and kindly ignore the silly things folk like me say, such as get rid of nuclear missiles and so on, because they know we don't know what we're saying. Which, remembering the CND chums you've got snoozing on your floorboards, brings me back to the pressing problem of how to kick out Rover. He, along with Jane, is now manifesting all the natural gaiety of a vulture. When I make noises like he's got to go, Jane says he's a squatter and has squatters' rights and I say, quick as a flash, no he hasn't because we all share the same loo. That is legally correct, isn't it? So Jane says that one won't work because Rover doesn't use our loo because he's the sort of person that can't use other people's loos. What on earth does he do then? I said crossly. Goes at his auntie's down the road, she said. Well, can't he take a bit more than his kidneys to his auntie's? I said. No, said Jane, she's only got a bed-sit.

Really, it's too stupid. Can you imagine me fighting this one out in a court of law? Me: M'lud, the accused is squatting. Rover: M'lud, I'm not squatting, I pee at my auntie's. How did I get into this? Tell you what, Mary, this is the sort of complicated trivia that make up real MPs' lives. If you and Mo come up with a solution to Rover's floating kidneys, you'll have my vote. I'll put it to Irene, too, and may the best woman win.

Yours, ballot paper poised,

Martha

Jane
defending
the sort of
person who
can't use
other people's
loos

Dear Mary

Last week (reason why I didn't write) I got these agonizing pains, at least seven of them. My gums swelled up all along the molars, the glands under my chin felt like loose ball-bearings, my stomach took off for foreign parts, with only the occasional letter home, and the parts of me left behind got fed into a concrete mixer. Josh, I said. Do you ever get a pain so painful that if it went on longer than a quarter of a second, your nails would fall out? The flickery sort of pain, Josh, the kind that flashes up the soles of your feet, tunnels through your ribcage, streaks across your neck and explodes out of your left ear? The kind that makes you think God is skewering you for a celestial shish kebab? No, said Josh. But *Josh*, I said. Don't you ever get a very *small* pain? Even the teeniest twinge in, say, the third metatarsal from the right or just under your nosebone? No, he said. Sometimes I think I am married to someone not of flesh and blood at all. Sometimes I think they ran up Josh in some laboratory, wodged him together out of a strange, thick substance, like pressed-felt carpet tiles.

I couldn't even call the doctor, due to the fact that Kev is back and stripping the wallpaper from the bedroom wall. You remember Kev, who kept seeing the Royal Family on our ceiling? Marf, he said when he arrived at the door. They give me ESP in that place and I'm cured. Now he only sees Princess Anne's baby and that only occasionally, in the odd bit of wallpaper. Which, considering he saw the Queen, the Duke, Princesses M and A and Princes C, A and E before, is pretty well a cure by any standards. So Kev's large as life again, showering plaster down on the two of us, making me look like a long-dead corpse. If the doctor did come, he'd only diagnose lead poisoning or some other variation on what might be called a Decorational Disease.

Poor Jane had to cope with the baby because she's still on holiday till next week. I say 'poor Jane' but, actually, she'd got herself perfectly organized. She'd dump a bowl of shredded wheat on my tummy at 9 am and then take off, baby and Rover and all, to her friends in this squat. The baby arrived back every evening looking like he'd been forked out of an allotment, like a new potato. He was just one staggering smut. Jane, he's *filthy*, I'd say in shock horror. Yeah, she'd say he is, isn't he? She didn't seem to care at all, she seemed to think that it didn't matter, babies being filthy, because of them being washable and pre-shrunk and permanently-pleated. I got this nasty redundant feeling, especially since the only thing I could see through the grime were the baby's teeth, exposed in a blissful grin.

Why did Doctor Spock never reveal that all babies want in life is squats and filth? I reckon it's a capitalist conspiracy to keep mothers in the home buying 20 different varieties of baby-cleaning products. The advertisers hire troops of evil little gnomes to impersonate kiddies who *like* being washed and eating wholewheat muesli and Marmite, when all the time what really makes them happy is grovelling about in dirt munching old potato peelings.

It's a conspiracy that has put a stone on me. I dare say if I wasn't so fat, I'd feel less pain – obviously, the more there is of you, the more lebensraum germs have to work in. My trouble is, I don't think I'm a teapot, I think I'm a dustbin. I have this overwhelming urge to fill myself with left-overs. Down the little red lane, I say to the baby and the baby says ugh and down my little red lane go the stewed prunes, the pureed spinach, the chicken-and-carrot dinner, the soggy rusks, the chewed banana. *Pour encouragez les autres.* What's more, if anyone ever said to me, Martha, how do you fancy a fry-up of a dried-out pork chop, three cold roast spuds, six limp celery tops and a wedge of mouldy cheese? I'd say not a lot, thanks awfully. But that's what I eat, myself, every time I defrost the fridge. Oh look, world, I say. See what a good, thrifty housewife I am. There's not one left-over in *my* pantry. It's all neatly packed away on my hips.

Josh pronounced my illness psychosomatic, brought on by refusing to face the fact that I can't get into anything but my bell-bottomed jeans. It's true that nighties are the only garments that flatter me and I suppose you can't be an entirely well person while walking about in nighties. Perhaps I'll marry Kev. His monarchical interests might divert him from marital flab, unless he started seeing Lady Di in the folds of my spare tyre.

Oh, Mary, I've gone on about myself and there's you sunk in gloom because of Mr Benn, and threatening to defect to the SDP so you can ruin *their* vote for a deputy leader. Look at it this way. Isn't it nicer just to dream about a new decor for the Labour Party? When the old wallpaper is actually peeled off, you get horribly choked up with dust and debris and bits of asbestos fluff that set off a terminal respiratory ailment, quite possibly. Sorry. The metaphor is drearily domestic but d'you see what I mean?

Yours, coughing up old flock,

Martha

Kev spotting Princess Anne's baby.

14 October

Dear Mary

That was some bonfire you set off up here, Thursday. Three am, all's quiet and then brr, brr there's Mo shouting down the phone about Old Bill having got you for breaking into a sex shop. I tell Josh and, half asleep, he explodes. Good grief, he howls, who the hell is this Bill, getting his paramours to steal sex aids in the middle of the night? Can't he effing well resign himself to being effing well impotent like any decent man? Christ's sake, Martha, I know your friends are round the bend but do they have to be raving nymphos to boot? The poor man was all confused, you see, and to add to it, he'd accidentally switched on the bedside radio and some young mother was blethering on about the problems of raising kids in high-rise flats. Problems? bellows Josh. Is it any bloody wonder you women have problems, with half of you yakking all night on the radio and the other half raiding sex shops? If it were up to me, I'd have the whole lot of you put down.

I'm trying to explain to him what Old Bill means and about there being such things, in the twentieth century, as recorded broadcasts when in comes Jane saying it's very nice, she's sure, old people like us having a sex life, but do we have to wake the whole house and in comes Ben yelling is it a fire and we can all climb out the window on his trained ivy and then, to cap it all the baby lets fly and Mrs Next-Door starts hammering on the wall fit to bust her garters. By the time Friday morning dawns, Josh has served me with six parking tickets and my divorce papers and I'm into my fourth nervous breakdown.

We've picked up the pieces now but, Mary, are sex shops really worth all that hassle? I mean, I take your point about the principle of it all and women not being sex objects and porn fodder and that but it's a funny world that pops you, Mo and Mrs Whitehouse in the same bag. I'm sure Lenin was right, as you say, using any group to further his own aims but, personally, I'd happily sell a gross of tickling sticks rather than go through what I went through that night. What price a sex shop at the end of Sebastopol Terrace when I may never have a sex life again, because of it?

Seriously, though, I am on your side. We keep the Guinness Book of Records in the bathroom and it fell open the other day and inside it was some frightful magazine full of frightful women on some insane gynaecological rampage. Oh Lord, I thought. Not only is Josh short-tempered but he's a hypocrite as well. He wants his respectably wedded spouse to do what these women do for a wage packet I won't see in a month of Sundays. Why doesn't he put his money where his mouth is? Sorry, I'd like to have put that another way. And it turned out not to be Josh at all but something Rover left behind when he took off for his auntie's and all I can say is, I hope his auntie's OK.

But, Mary, I do understand what you meant to do by breaking into that shop. It's true, if the honest citizens of Sebastopol Terrace had seen all those sexy appliances spread over the street when they woke up, they might have joined your cause. Too bad the police managed to tidy it all up before morning and charge you. Of course I'll be a character witness even though, obviously, it'll cost me my marriage and Josh will get custody of the kids and two of them aren't even his and probably their *real* father is a mail-order subscriber to that very sex shop. What a mess.

Mother came over the day after your fiasco and when I told her about it, she approved, which ought to bring you out in a cold sweat. My Mother thinks bananas are pornographic. Goodness knows how I was ever conceived – I'd say my Dad must have swum over her, except he can't swim. When I mentioned the pains I had last week, she said I must have had an episcopal pregnancy. That, Mother, I said, is what the bishop said to the actress but she didn't understand. Most of the time, when I talk, she just stands there shaking her head and saying she's glad my grandmother isn't alive. So am I. She'd be over a hundred now and she wasn't a barrel of fun at sixty. All she ever said to me, when I was five, was I'd pass with a push in a crowd with the light behind me.

Apart from the aforementioned alarums and excursions, I've spent most of the week in the garden, cutting things back. You'd be better occupied, said Josh, cutting Ben back. That boy needs pruning a lot more than apple trees. You know, Mary, I sometimes think second marriages aren't a solution, especially when there are children. Josh and Ben have never been close, but, then, Ben and his real father aren't what you'd call intimate either. Ben said when he went down to Mousehole in the summer he only recognized Tom because who else but his father would be too busy chatting up Britain's only female porter to recognize his son? If that man is my father, said Ben, I think I should be told. I'm such a failure as a woman, Mary, that even biology isn't my destiny.

Yours, getting me to a nunnery,

Martha

Martha's mother as instrument of Lenin

Dear Mary

Oh boy, a whole lot of chickens came home to roost here last week. Wait till I tell you, you'll *die*. First, Daffy Murdoch calls – Daffy Jackson as was. You remember Daffy at school? The one who could hold her breath and make her nostrils click? The one who married the cricketer who must have been kinky about clicking nostrils? We've kept vaguely in touch since her son Godwin – *Godwin* – went to primary school with Ben. Anyhow, Daff says she's got a surprise for me and can she come over for tea? Tea I can't promise, I said, but there's plenty of mashed prunes around here, if you're into scraping them off the ceiling. She wasn't put off. Daffy was always a pushy girl.

So an hour later, there's Daff at the door and just guess who's with her? Old Friz-Chops. Yes, that slice of pressed ham with superfluous hair who sat beside you in the Upper Fourth. And, Mary, Friz-Chops looked *gorgeous*. I mean, as gorgeous as any female can look when she's got a dozen dead seals dripping down her back and a dead lamb perched on her head, which is, I'm sorry to report, pretty gorgeous. Hi hi hi, says Friz-Chops, smiling all over her pearlized lipstick and blowing kisses at me like I'm infectious. Fancy seeing dear Martha Muddle-Brain again! Honestly, isn't it *sad* how some people never grow out of using these infantile labels? Oh, but there was worse to come. Daffy announces that Friz-Chops has just flown over from New York and, Mary, sit down, you're not going to like this, she's just sold her first novel for one million dollars. Bucks, greenbacks, mazumas, lolly.

Now you remember Friz-Chops in English Comp? She couldn't write three words on A Day In The Life Of A Penny without boring us all down the drain. And this PhD in Anaesthetising Plumworth High has written a best-seller? Mary, there is no justice. Oh Martha, she coos, giving phoney little gasps of admiration at the sight of my blitzed kitchen. How cute, how mellow, how laid-back. Look, Friz-Chops, I wanted to say, don't you come in here, oozing your West Coast oil, and think you can get round *me*. Because with me, baby, mere money and fame and names in lights cut no ice at all, baby, not even half a cube. I mean, I wouldn't swop a single buck for my wondrous baby and my lovely Jane and my dear-heart Ben.

Just as well I didn't say all that out aloud because it turns out some benighted Wall Street type has hacked his way through the superfluous hair – which is momentarily waxed off – and fathered upon Friz-Chops four little Friz-Chops. Four. Mary, how can people be so irresponsible, in this day and age, as to indulge themselves in four infant carbon copies of Wonderful Them, when half the world is starving? No, it's beyond me, too.

The very cruellest blow of all soon follows. Jane comes in. My heart sinks a bit more because, well, I love Jane but certain women covered in dead animals might be so purblind as to find her a trifle graceless, a mite hoydenish, you know. And what happens? Introduced to Friz-Chops, whom Daffy reveals is known nowadays as Auriol August, Jane goes red all over, says not the Auriol August and asks for her autograph while Friz-Chops simpers. At which, Mary, I wished to be no more. Apparently, Friz-Chops is some sort of feminist heroine to graceless, hoydenish girls like Jane, on account of some non-fiction tract she wrote two years ago about how women put each other down. Have you ever heard of it? The Old School Tithe, I'm told it's called. When Jane's gone, Friz-Chops gushes horribly about what a sweet daughter I've got and aren't they heartening, the young women of today? Heartening? I can feel the first of many angina attacks coming on, if that's what heartening means. OK, Mary, you can get up now and dust yourself off. Isn't it all weird? I mean we were the ones with straight As for Composition at school, you and me. I even got a prize for that essay I wrote which ended 'and the traffic lights turned from red to green and to red again' which was, for a fifteen-year-old, a pretty good way of marking time's passage but where has time's passage actually got me? Josh and a sinkful of dishes is where. I could cry, Mary. I did cry, quite a lot. When Josh came home that night he said Martha, I don't care for that pink eye make-up you're wearing, it doesn't become you. Josh, I said, I don't care for that nose you're wearing. I don't go a bunch on those eyes and that chin and those ears you're wearing, either. Pack 'em in, Josh, or I might just leave for the Big Apple on tonight's Laker standby and sod dinner in the oven.

At the weekend I went to my Women's Centre and, do

Jane meets Auriol August

you know, they are all fans of Auriol August? Auriol? I said. Oh, she's an old mate of mine, we were just like that at school. And she still relies on me for advice and things, does Auriol. She *does*, Mary. People who've made a lot of money badly need someone like me to keep their feet on the ground. There, said Bess, you see, Martha? You're always saying you're just a housewife but here you are contributing your life experience to someone like Auriol August. Sisterhood is strong, said Bess.

That's so true, Mary. We must stand by each other, who else will? Auriol said, before she left, that any time I wanted to borrow her New York apartment, I'd be welcome. She's obviously trying to say sort of 'thank-you' for, sort of, times gone by, and I appreciate that.

Yours, nostalgically,

Martha

Dear Mary

My back is still aching but wasn't that a great party? About half-way through the day, I felt exactly as if I, personally, had thrown it. Martha, At Home, October 24, Hyde Park or Thereabouts, 11 to 6 pm, CND Banners Will Be Worn. I kept spotting people I hadn't seen for yonks. At Charing Cross, those three lovely Danish women who were at Manchester one year. In Trafalgar Square, Hans-Helmut hanging from a lamppost, that nice German punk I once got stranded with in a train strike. Along Piccadilly, Marie, Lorna's French au pair and then all those women from Birmingham where we stayed on that Women's Conference and guess who, Miss McDonald, our old maths teacher, wheeled down from Edinburgh and still going strong at eighty and the two Liverpudlians who gave us a hitch that time in Brighton and Jenny Cartwright up from Derby and Mrs Next-Door, still laughing herself silly, and Ron from the hairdressers and about thirty people from our street and, oh, about a hundred others. I'm hoarse from catching up with the news, shouting across streets, bellowing over tankards. Marie's had a baby, Kirstie's got married, Manuella from Rome has moved to Paris, Jenny's divorced, it just went on and on.

Going for a sausage roll, I bumped into my own ex-spouse, of all things. Up from Mousehole with a girl called Olly, aged about five and dressed like a Red Indian. I gave her a big hug. Well, she'll need all the hugs she can get, being with Tom. I'm only here for the beer, said Tom, and I believe it. He was more or less legless already and we were only on the Embankment. Look, I said, you come round and see your children before you scuttle back to Cornwall or else. I don't know if he got the message – we were parted just then by some street theatre – but, judging by her expression, Olly did. She probably didn't know about her new man's past. I'm the only person Tom is tight-lipped about.

And then, best of all, meeting you! There I was slogging past the Haymarket behind these two huge papier mache figures, Thatcher and Reagan groping each other in the most disgusting way, when out from under them for a breath of fresh air pop you and Mo! We must have held up the hordes for at least six minutes, jumping around. That bloke you were with, the one with the green hair and the gasmask, he was a dish. We met up later, you know. Jammed against the journalists' barricade, under the speakers' platform and from what little he said, he really fancies you. Then he took his gasmask off and Mary, if you don't fancy him right back, pass him on. What eyes!

He nearly started the only fight of the day though. There were these two journalists in front of us and one said, "Here comes the King," and the other said "You mean, the Prince of Darkness" and we looked up and saw they meant T. Benn. Well, before you could say CND, your bloke was tightening up their ties for nooses. I see why journalists have special barricades – it's to keep them safe from the public.

But it was a downer, coming home. The baby, on my back the whole day without uttering a squeak – obviously he'd only ever needed a quarter of a million other people around to keep him entertained – took one look at home sweet home and began his first bit of serious protest. Josh, who hadn't come on account of he thought Irene might be up in a helicopter and finger him for a fellow-traveller, was sitting there grumbling about how Thatcher was caving in by rescuing the BBC World Service.

What's the point, he complained, financing a lot of frogs, or worse, Englishmen *pretending* to be Frogs? Joke, he said hastily, seeing my face, but I know enough about that man to know his elaborate jokes merely conceal elaborate truths.

It's like that woman said from the CND platform, Mary. The world is run by old men. Old Reagan, Old Brezhnev and behind them shuffling the papers, Old Josh. Each one sunk in a fantasy of being Gary Cooper in *High Noon* when what they actually are is Count Dracula, back from a good night's necking to keep his cheeks rosy. Josh says I'm paranoic about Cruise etcetera but I say if I'm paranoic, Josh, so is half Europe and how are you going to find a bin big enough to take us all?

Next day, mother phoned and said had I seen all those Communists in London and wasn't it sad. Then an aunt phoned and said had I seen all those Lunatics in London and wasn't it amusing and then Tom appeared, accompanied by Olly. Poor man. I think he's actually afraid of his own children – he looks at them as if they were fireworks gone off at the wrong time. No wonder. Daughter Jane doesn't look

Mrs. Next-Door against the Bomb.

much older than girlfriend Olly, which must be a trifle unsettling for them all. No good really, using Grecian 2000 and sucking in your beer belly when Jane's around to blow the gaff.

I wish there was a gardening programme that advised you about husbands instead of plants. Dear Percy Thrower, My husbands aren't doing too well. One is curling up at the edges and losing its leaves and the other has blight. What should I do? And dear Percy Thrower could tell me to spray them with derris and all would be well.

Yours, preparing to dig them both over,

Martha

Dear Mary

What is it they say? A son's yours till he marries, but a daughter's a daughter the whole of your life? That makes my future look pretty bleak, I'll tell you, specially as I can't see anyone ever marrying Jane. I mean Jane ever marrying anyone. When I think of all the sleepless nights I've spent soothing her fevered brow, all the days I've slaved over a hot stove cooking her vitamin intake, all the years I've nipped in the bud so she could bloom, sob sob, and here she is turning on me. Holding me up as an object of scorn, looking down at me in my own kitchen, weighing me in the balance and finding me wanting – only Jane could believe *that*, with me going on eleven stone in my stockinged feet. Why do they always say stockinged feet as if women were born with webbed toes, like ducks?

Anyway, Martha, I hear you ask, what could a Saint like you have done to deserve such cruel ingratitude? What I did was buy a copy of *Vogue*. Yes, Mary, *Vogue*. It wasn't easy, either: I stood for ages in front of the rack, perspiring lightly. I read about A.J.P. Taylor's week and how much I'd get for a third-hand Citroen Dyane with body rust and how Saturn was in my Sun sign so I'd better mend my ways and getting goose pimples every time someone came near in case it was Bess or May or some other woman from my Group. In the end I snatched up *Spare Rib*, *Women's Voice*, *New Society*, *New Scientist* and *New Socialist*, stuck *Vogue* well down in the pile, paid and shuffled out with it under plain cover, flat broke. Then, when I'd made it home, I scuttled up to the bathroom, locked myself in and read it. And left it there, forgotten, on account of getting distracted by the ring Ben put around the bath two days ago.

Next thing I know, there's Jane sticking the wretched mag under my nose and saying what's *this*, Martha, in the doomsday voice of someone who's found a cockroach in their soup. Jane, I said, you're old enough now to know the sad truth. Your stepfather is a transvestite with social ambitions. We must be brave and try to help him up the ladder in his Princess of Wales hats.

But she just kept gawping at me, waving the silly mag, so I lost my temper. For heaven's sake I said, or possibly shouted. You caught me bang to rights with the loot. Guv, go easy on me and I'll tell all. No, but *why*, Martha, said Jane. Why schmy I said, or possibly shrieked. Because I'm hooked, that's why. Because I'm a pathetic *Vogue*-ridden wreck of the woman I might have been. You don't know the half of it, Jane. The lost years, trying to kick the habit. The endless weeks at Vogue Anonymous, baring my breast in front of them all, confessing to the Big V. Telling how, at first, I'd only buy one copy now and again, then how I found myself buying more and more, hiding them in my boots, in the cistern, in the freezer, spending the housekeeping, blowing the family allowance. Don't give me Oh Martha, Jane, that's how it was. But I battled. How I battled. I hadn't bought a *Vogue* for a whole year until today, the worst time of the year. Collection Time. Suddenly, the old urge came upon me. I had to know what the hemlines were doing. I *had* to. I staggered down the street to find a pusher, hands trembling, head whirling, and then I blacked out. When I came to, there was a *Vogue* in my handbag. Forgive me, my child, have mercy on your grey-haired mother. With you beside me, I can beat this evil thing. Cut it *out*, Martha, said Jane.

Good grief, what's so terrible? Have I sold my Sisters down the river for a mess of ready-to-wear? Are women's rights set back a hundred years by my fleeting interest in cinch belts? Will the Sex Discrimination Act fall in tatters because I doled out a quid for the stop-press on cardies. Am I a traitor to feminists everywhere because I want to know what length skirt to buy at Ron's Kooky Klothing, a far yell from Gay Paree.

Thank God for Ben. He came in then in his old black sweater, ancient jeans, and crumbling black boots. Tell you what, I said to him, I'll buy you a whole new outfit, anything you want, name it. Black sweater, jeans, black boots, he said; ta, Mum. Oh, go on, be a devil I said. Have dark grey for a change. You see, Jane? You want a slave to fashion? Meet your brother. Besides, I saw you coming out of Oxfam yesterday, don't think I didn't. We've all got our little habits, my girl, so it ill behoves us to point the finger at others.

Poor old Ben. He and Josh are at loggerheads most of the time these days, Must be something to do with the Primal Hordes – Josh the old stag and Ben getting up his antlers, I don't know. Josh is always nagging him. Don't say no in that negative way, he said to Ben yesterday in one of their set-to's.

How do you say no in a positive way? Or should Ben have said yes in a negative way? Josh obviously feels he's got to give out with the advice all the time too. You know the sort of thing. If you had more cold showers, Ben, your teeth wouldn't ache. If you stood up straight and put your shoulders back, we wouldn't have to leave the Common Market. If you ran round the block every morning, Sadat would be alive today. Helpful stuff like that.

Josh came in just now and said what's for dinner, Martha? Fried cholesterol, I said.

Yours, spoiling for a mixed grill,

Martha

Dear Mary

You didn't mention my *Vogue* true confessions in your reply –
does that mean you found them too abhorrent to dwell on or
has the Post Office had another of its hiccups? Perhaps
you've been side-tracked by true love at last? That bloke I got
crushed up against the CND platform with, is he – you know –
your bloke? From what I gather, you seem to talk about
nothing, together, but NATO Contingency Plans and the ethos
of Flexible Response but what your friends want to know is,
have you gone Critical yet? And, if so, do you have
Manouvreable Re-entry Vehicles (MARV) or are you still
using Terrain Comparison (TERCOM)? Only asking.

   We had our own limited strategic flare-up last night, it
being Guy Fawkes. Ben conned me out of a small fortune for
fireworks and we went over to Lorna's so he and Lorna's son
Zep could let them off in Lorna's back garden. Our garden
was out due to Josh going through his papers again and
accusing Ben of wishing to ignite a deeply important Fiscal
Green Paper with an indoor sparkler. Lorna and I spent most
of the time yelling through the windows at the boys – they
kept bending over their Catherine Wheels in a horribly
dangerous way. I ended up with a sore throat, shouting Ben,
if you go blind, don't think you're coming in here again (what
did I plan, to keep him stumbling about in the garden all his
life?) while Lorna shrieked incessantly watch out, you idiots,
or it'll be White Stick time for you.

   The fireworks were lovely, though. I said to Lorna that if
I were rich, I'd have them going all the time, like medieval
torches in my public rooms. Lorna said she thought it'd really
suit me if my hair caught fire. That sulphurous flare does a
lot for your skin, she said.

   Sometimes I think that woman lacks all human emotion.
After the fireworks, she and I were sampling her drinks
cupboard – full of holiday leftovers like Basque liqueur and
Occitane aperitifs and sticky Greek ouzo – when she tells me
her mother is dying and would I go and see her? Lorna, I said,
one thing a friend can't do for a friend is visit a friend's dying

mother. Dying mothers don't want to see perfect strangers, they want to see daughters. Mine doesn't, said Lorna. She's always said she doesn't want me at her deathbed because I'm the sort of person who would try to steal the limelight from anyone, even on their deathbeds.

Apparently, Lorna's mother was once a vaudeville artiste called Queenie King and led Lorna a difficult childhood. She gave a party, once, backstage, when Lorna was a baby, covered her all over with the guests' fur coats and forgot about her for the rest of the evening. Lorna was dug out at 3 am suffering from oxygen deprivation, which may account for her lack of a fully developed emotional life to this day. When Queenie first started on the downward spiral, Lorna would phone me and say could I give Zep his supper because her mum had take up her natural position again – flat on her back on the floor, surrounded by broken bottles. Lorna's spent the past three years committing her, and doctors have spent the past three years uncommitting her, because of the Cuts. That woman goes in and out of bins like plastic liners.

Have just heard the news about Princess Di's baby. Lorna says poor ducky, she'll have to have a Caesarean on account of the ears, which is typical of her unfeeling approach to the rich tapestry of human life. I think it's nice news. Heaven knows, I'll never have a grandchild, due to Jane refusing to be in the same room with any man apart from Rover, who refuses to be in the same room with Jane, and Ben being in love with carburettors and women too old to reproduce, like Wendy. I do envy pregnant women – it's the only time in your life you can do absolutely nothing and know you're doing something.

My heart sank yesterday. Delia Smith's put her Christmas Pudding recipe in the paper again, which means only six weeks' dithering time to the dreaded 25th again. Mother has already rung, like Christmas bells, to ask what my plans are, which is her way of saying she'll be catching the 4.45 pm on December 24 and will we please meet her at Victoria.

Martha

Dear Mary

I'm sitting here at the kitchen table, dead tired, in my dressing-gown, yawning my head off, all ready for beddy-byes and it's just gone 9 am. Ben's departed for school leaving note saying It Was Not Me Took the Creem Off of the Milk and Jane's departed for college leaving empty tins of oxtail soup behind her. Can oxtail soup be called a proper breakfast? What *is* an ox? Surely they don't grow in England? The poor creatures are probably shipped from India or somewhere, tails and all, in ghastly freighters, mooing. Or whatever oxes do. The baby is down on the floor with the cat eating Whiskas – he's particularly partial to the Lamb's Heart flavour – and Josh banged the door quite loudly as he went off to the office, saying all he ever wanted for breakfast was one bowl of Sultana Bran and why was there never any or was that too much to ask of a liberated wife?

Reading about the Russian submarine in Swedish waters had set his adrenalin seething. You see, Martha? He said. There's your peace-loving Soviets for you, floating missile bases skulking about under other people's seas, so much for your woolly CNDers. I must say I do *wish* the Russians would listen to my advice. The fact that they don't is I must admit, one of their least attractive features.

The news in general this week has packed some of the bags under my eyes. First, after that doctor gets cleared of murdering the baby, we're confronted with two hundred articles about how we're now only one step away from the gas chambers and me hardly able to cope with my perfectly healthy, presumably normal infant. Like that awful old prune Mugg who, I bet, has never so much as stuffed a teaspoonful of groats in a child's mouth, going on about legislation opening doors through which we'll soon be pushing those without whom we might appear to be better off. Such as that awful old prune Mugg, I say, and wish I hadn't.

Why is it that people who are against everything you believe in always make you react in exactly the way they're arguing? Why do I always want to kill everyone who wants to kill everyone? Then there's all that about spies, how they've given immunity to this spy and that spy so's they can track down some other spy. Perhaps these confessions will eventually lead to the uncovering of one really Enormous Spy, a sort of vast multi-national Spy's Spy, the Hundredth Man, entirely covered with micro-dots and poison-tipped umbrellas and so camp he can hardly walk.

And then there's the business about loyalty in the Labour Party. Funny, that. Josh is always on about loyalty, too. The thing is, people who want your loyalty inevitably mean 'in spite of' what you really believe. So being loyal always means going against your conscience or concealing your deepest beliefs or whatever. Otherwise, they wouldn't have to ask. Josh says I should be more loyal whenever I ask what he really *does* in the Department – ie shut up, do what you're told, them that ask no questions get told no lies. At his last office party, he put his arm round my shoulder said this is my loyal little wife, Martha, and I had an instant attack of the Anthony Blunts.

By the way, Josh has announced that we have to give a party before Christmas, we owe so many people. He may, I don't – I only know two people. I can't hardly recall the last real party I went to, while Josh is always having drinkies after work with his mates. I suggested we hire a hall or a pub or something but Josh said never, people expect to come to your house for hospitality. There's nothing hospitable about our house, I said, unless you think peeling wallpaper and sofas covered in cat's hair hospitable but he was adamant. So I'm going to throw a Come As You Aren't party. I shall appear as a female executive in T bar shoes and I'll dress Jane up as Miss World and Irene will arrive in curlers and a pinny and you can take everything off and come as a sex symbol and Mother can be a doormat.

Mind you, it might bring on Josh's incipient identity crisis. He's obviously none too sure who he is, always leafing through his Diner's Club catalogues, yearning for cuff-links and shirts and bathrobes with his initals on. Do you anticipate becoming an amnesiac shortly? I said to him. Losing your memory and waving initialled hankies at concerned coppers? He wasn't amused but, then, he rarely is, these days, poor man. Sometimes I feel so sorry for him. He wanted a wife and a baby and he even quite fancied the idea of ready-made kiddies like Jane and Ben but none of us, I'm afraid, have come up to expectation, especially not when compared to Diner's Club families. If he'd ordered us on spec, we'd all have been returned by now, without obligation.

I know he envisaged me in a hostess gown, waiting for him at the door with a mixed Martini and the baby, flushed and rosy and quiet in Nanny's arms and Jane, pretty as a picture in broderie anglaise, hanging on his every word, and Ben frightfully intelligent in pebble glasses, asking for advice, and our only real problem the shortage of schools for extremely gifted children. Instead of which . . . well, I won't go into that, it's too depressing. I had a different picture of him, too, but I mind much more that we disappoint him than that he disappoints us, I don't know why. I do try, now and again. I painted my nails on Monday but by Tuesday the bits were flaking into the fishcakes and Josh said it was unhygienic.

Yours, face down in the Kelloggs,

Martha

Josh's vision.

Dear Mary

Here is a wee snatch of seasonal verse for you:

Ortum leaves are tumbling down
To fertalize the sogy groun

I found it in Ben's pocket. With any luck, it isn't his. I can't tell his handwriting because it drifts in a different direction every day. Like ortum leaves. And Jane's been nagging me about Rover. He's got nowhere to spend Christmas, she says, so what am I going to do about it? I say that Christmas is a time for taking in frail old ladies, not huge Mr Universes who will eat the whole turkey and all the mince pies while trying to catch glimpses of their beautiful selves in the Christmas tree baubles. Besides, Rover's living with his auntie down the road, so what about her? She's Jewish, says Jane. In that case, I point out patiently, Rover's Jewish and won't want anything to do with Christmas, anyway. Rover, says Jane, is not Jewish because he. Then she goes very red. Because he *what*? I say, steely-voiced. Because he, she repeats and suddenly discovers she is extremely late for an extremely pressing appointment and shoots off. Leaving me with nothing but suspicions darkening my door.

Only a month ago I was forced to have a talk with Ben, after he and his geriatric girl-friend Wendy had spent about 15 hours sealed in his bedroom with a padlock on the door and a notice saying Keap Out This Meens You. Josh wouldn't have a talk with him. Josh said let Tom have a talk with him and I said what? The facts of life through a megaphone from Mousehole? Anyway, I've got Jane and Ben to prove that what their father knows about you-know-what could be put on the end of a you-know-what. So I said to Ben, if you're you-know-whating with Wendy I only hope you're you-know-what. What? said Ben. Well, I said, is Wendy on the thingummy, that's what. Yes, said Ben. Are you sure? I said. Sure, he said. I see her take it just before.

And now I've got Jane to worry about. She knows all about you-know-what and thingummies, of course, but what's she doing about it? I suppose I'll have to have a talk with her now, too. One thing about me, though, Mary. I'm absolutely out front with the kids about you-know-what and thingummies and so on. As a parent, I consider that essential, nowadays.

Because of this awful Christmas party Josh says I've got to give, I went out and bought myself an address book and all that's done is reveal on a hundred empty pages what I already knew. I don't know anybody. I've got you and Mo and Mother down and my American friend and Auriol August the Famous Feminist Author, to add tone, and that's it. I don't know the addresses of people I actually see, like Bess and May and Lorna and, anyway, that's only eight out of the population of the world, which is probably too minute a percentage for a computer to calculate. To compensate, I started to cut things out of the papers and magazines. In the end, I said to Josh, look, I've got a really efficient address book together now. If you ever need to know, there's everyone here from the Art Work Director of Gay Collective Digest to the Deputy Under Secretary at the UK Embassy in Qatar. Same man, I shouldn't wonder, said Josh.

By the way, why are you and Mo going on that March for Jobs? I mean, someone might give you one and then what would you do? I know it's the principle that matters and everything and I don't want to be rude but Mo with her purple hair doesn't come across as the world's most instantly employable person and the last time I saw her on a demo she was holding a banner saying I Won't Be A Wage Slave. I will. Or, at least, I'd rather be a Wage Slave than a No-Wage Slave, which is what I am now.

I know you keep saying I'm *earning* the money Josh gives me (I mean *pays* me) and I know I am, too, but does he? I wish the Department would send the housekeeping in a nice computer-printed brown envelope, so I wouldn't have to thank Josh. At the moment, I just sort of snatch the notes awkwardly but the words 'thank you' will keep leaking through my teeth. It isn't that I mind thanking him that much, only it gives Josh the wrong impression. Lorna goes to extremes. She gets her old man to push the money through the letterbox and she picks it up from the mat. That's silly, Lorna, I said when she told me. Silly heck she said. The Medium, Martha, is the Message. Perhaps she's right. The only wages I get for myself these days is when I post off the coupons that come in my ciggies. I get ever so excited when the money comes back but there must be easier ways of earning a living than tarring up your lungs smoking 200 fags for a pound.

Lastly but not leastly, yes, of course I'll be there as your character witness when you come up for pillaging that porn shop but for goodness sake, watch yourself. It'll be no good at all me going on about how your father was this deeply wonderful General who killed half a hundredweight of people in wars and other background info judges like to hear if you're effing away in the dock. And do remember, judges dress funny so you must, too. Borrow a modest black number from someone, put some Cherry Blossom pearlized lipstick on, and don't say Old Bill or anything *at all* about women's lib. Just come on like you're a respectable virgin lady who had a sudden turn as she passed the dreaded Spot because it sullied all you hold dear, including the sacred memory of your mother who died on active service with Mothers For The Bomb. One thing more, *don't* plead PMT or they'll prove you're on the Pill and haven't had a PM to be T about since two days cum Tuesday last Michaelmas.

Yours, packing twin-set and pearls,

Martha

GIVE

Lorna's system.

Dear Mary

The morning after I got back from you, I came down stairs, put All-Bran in my tea-cup, poured boiling water on it and nearly choked to death. Then I went upstairs and came down again, to have another go at starting the day. All your fault. Mercy may descend on young and single women as the gentle rain but on me, a middle-aged wife and mother, it falleth as a concrete brick from heaven. The magistrate lets you and Mo off with nothing but a warning, thanks to me perjuring myself silly in the witness box, but who's around to speak up for *me* when I get home and find Josh pronouncing the death sentence, suspended only so long as I do not stir from the broom cupboard for the rest of my wedded life?

Naturally, I hadn't told him of my starring role at Sebastopol Magistrates' Court. Apart from anything else, I'd reckoned on being home and dry before he'd got himself and his papers shovelled out the office door. As it was, I made it on the stroke of midnight, swaying very slightly from the effects of our celebratory substances, and oh wow, did this Cindrella hit rag-time. If there's one thing Josh cannot abide, it's me being out of the house when he comes home and, in case you think that's touching, the other thing he cannot abide is me being *in* the house when he comes home. He's always said Away-Day tickets proved British Rail is run by Reds to lure wives from their marital duties. Now, he knows.

Your Mother phoned while you were gone, he said, among other things. She was *very* worried. She said she had never permitted herself to leave *you* when you were young but that was, of course, before Women's Lib. I had to lie to her, Martha, for your sake. I had to say you'd gone to nurse a sick friend. I didn't leave my young, I said. Who d'you think *this* is? And I stuck the baby in his arms, to keep them still. Shove Mother anyway, I said. That woman got Power of Attorney from God to make her family as miserable as possible in His Name. My poor old Dad couldn't smoke or drink because Mother's friend God was a non-smoking teetotaller, not to mention a non-you-know-whatter, and what was good enough for Him was good enough for my Dad. How I got born at all is a secret to this day between Him and her. At any rate, Dad was never consulted.

But defending yourself only gives you a headache and you don't get legal aid. Next day, the polyunsaturated fat really hit the fire. Irene, she of the nuclear hairstyle, charges into Josh's office waving a copy of your local rag, the *Sebastopol Clarion*. Heaven knows how it got into *her* clammy hands; smuggled down a thin blue line from a Moral Majority cell at the bottom of your road, I suppose. And there, on the front page, was a blotchy likeness of you and me outside the Court, headlined 'Bra-Burners Warned in Porn Shop Plunder'.

This, of course, confirmed Irene in her worst fears of me. Now she thinks I'm the Mrs Big in some sleazy Copenhagen Connection, aided and abetted by a delinquent baby. Josh did me no good at all by saying oh god, this time Martha's gone too far. A most unsavoury business, Josh, said Irene. Not *at all* the sort of thing the Department expects of Department Wives. And she swept out, squashing underfoot, on her way, most of Josh's promotion prospects.

I did try to make Josh understand. Look, I said, when that old school friend of yours, Woolly Something, came up on a charge of doing beastly things in bushes, you did your bit for him in Court. That, said Josh, was entirely different and, besides, it was a ridiculous charge and, besides, the magistrate was old Bendy Baxter who knew as well as I did that old Woolly had *always* done beastly things in bushes, so what was the good of sending him to prison and setting a bad example to the criminal classes? Talk about male bonding.

Well, what can I do to make it better? I said. If I ring Irene to explain, I'll only get her under-secretary and have to leave a message so garbled she'll think she's had an obscene phone call and get above herself. Anyway, Josh, Mary and Mo weren't doing anything beastly like Woolly. They were trying to stop pornographers degrading women. And you know what my husband said? He said wake up, Martha, be realistic. Who do you *expect* pornographers to degrade? Budgies? Wake up? I haven't closed an eyelid since. Why is it that whenever the Women's Movement strikes, it's *my* foundations that wobble, not yours? Is that fair, Mary? Where's the Retirement Home for Distressed Ungentlewomen, not to mention their sex-war-shocked Issue?

Still, what can I do but soldier on and pretend I can't see the cracks? Our party, in case your recent legal triumph has wiped it from your mind, is next Thursday. On second thoughts, stay with the wiped mind. The thing's going to be a disaster, anyway. Ben did the invitations for me and wrote 'Drinks at Moon' on them all so the guests'll turn up at 12 midnight instead, or the barmy ones will. I'm too depressed to care.

Kev came in an hour ago with the bloke he'd said he'd find to repair the fridge. This is Merv, Marf, said Kev. Merv'll see you right. Merv didn't. Merv's just gone, leaving the fridge *and* me broken down. Remember old Paddy, Marf? says Merv. Sad about old Paddy. Took a clot on the brain, down the Star and Garter, not been the same since. Know young Joe, Marf? Bad about Joe. Come down with his lungs something rotten, wouldn't recognize him. Seen old Mrs Collop, Marf? No, you wouldn't. Took to her bed with the kidneys, August, she won't be up again. Remember Irish Ted, Marf . . .?

Yours, gone down with the mouth,

Marf

Irene points out item of interest to old and broken man.

Dear Mary

Not a squeak out of you since you stumbled into the night with Rover ranged round your shoulders like a giant stole. Range Rover. Did you get caught in his medallions and have to check into casualty to have him surgically removed? He wasn't supposed to *be* at the party – Jane smuggled him in. Now she's locked in her bedroom shouting 'just resting' to all inquiries, like an out-of-work actress.

Mary, you did *understand* about Rover? He has to be gay, and choosey with it, mostly choosing himself. Jane's still young enough to think she could be the light on his road to Damascus but you and I know different, don't we? Yet why no word? If Rover were a *normal* man, I'd have called in the police by now to drag the canal for your body.

It took me three days' work to prepare for that party. Just moving the sofas back revealed enough cats' hairs to knit another cat. The one I've got moped about for a while in the melee and then fainted. She always faints when she feels she's being ignored. I dropped her on Josh's lap (laps being things people have who aren't pulling their weight) and she spent the next hour licking his hair, under the impression that she'd found her long lost kitten. I wouldn't lick Josh's hair, and I'm married to him.

Bess popped in to give me a hand, along with some child she was minding. He's a bit *disturbed,* she whispered. I can tell that, I whispered back, he's done exactly what he's told since he came in. Unlike Ben, who is, of course, perfectly undisturbed. To prove it, he ate every second canape we made, walked round and round and *round* the kitchen table as if he thought, keep this up long enough and that table will play a tune and, later on, had to be put to bed by Studs after swigging the wine he was supposed to be passing around. Studs said Ben's last words, before flaking out, were 'when do we get to Calais?'

Mother came in to help, too. Mother's help consisted of standing at my elbow saying I wouldn't do *that,* dear, if I were you but, then, when did you ever listen to your Mother?

Also getting cups of tea for Josh, clucking. Which, interpreted, means how much better off you'd be, poor boy, if I were your wife instead of her. Well, there's only eight years and Mother's hats between them, so I wish them all the luck in the world.

Then Merv and Kev turned up, delivering our crates of wine which they kindly proceeded to unpack, mostly down their gullets. Cheers Marf, they'd say, each time I looked their way. Cheers Merv, I'd say. Cheers Kev. With hindsight, those cheers were my undoing. Josh kept shooting sidelong glances at me, the kind Chinese waiters give when you're eating late, like they could just restrain themselves by some Oriental isometrics from plunging a dagger in your heart. Keep stroking the cat, Josh, I said. Cheers.

At some point the door bell rang and the party was off. On. In bounced the Tinkerton-Smiths, fuelled by marital discord, their specs alight with mutual hatred. In leaned Nigel and Caroline, him backwards, her forwards. In swayed Irene carefully balancing her hair on her head like a seal with a ball. A Departmental Venus surrounded by waves of pinstripes all saying wonderful and very true and there you are, Josh, jolly good. In came Lorna with her mother Queenie, risen from her sickbed for the occasion. Queenie had to be unhooked from one of the pinstripes later – it's not that I think women are too old for sex at 75, but shouldn't they wait to be asked? Or is Queenie the earliest known specimen of Femina Liberata?

And there were you and Mo, along with those five unisex persons covered in badges saying 'I love Wimmin'. So do we, har har, chorused the pinstripes, and got sardines stuffed in their buttonholes for their pains. Mother said to me, Martha, Mo is charming. She may look a little eccentric but she's got her priorities right, not like some I could mention. So I asked Mo what she'd been on about to Mother. Just told your old lady how me and Mare gave that shop a good dusting over, said Mo. Halfway through, Auriol August mainfested herself, entirely covered with furry mammals, and Josh disappeared with her for some time, to show her his etchings. Being Josh, he actually has some. And I consoled myself with a dear little man called Carruthers. Well, he must have another name but I prefer Carruthers. Down, Carruthers, I said at one point. I am down, he said. So sweet. I think he's taken quite a shine to me or, at least, to the parts of me he's met.

About midnight, Irene came at me through the smokey

haze with her tongue out. This is it, I thought. Confrontation time. Then I saw the tongue was bleeding and, in a flash, remembered that jar of olives Jane had broken on the way home. I did think we'd got all the glass out with rinsing. What'll I do, I asked myself, if she falls down dead from powdered glass? Will I be arrested for murder, like a Victorian jealous wife? I covered up well, though, you would have been proud of me. Looks like scurvy to me, Irene, I said, are you getting enough vitamin C? Have an orange, do. Have two. But I needed a good few stiff ones after that, I can tell you. I don't recall much more of the party. Josh says I sang three verses of Knocked 'em in the Old Kent Road and collapsed, to the giggles of Mrs Next-Door which, added to her usual menopausal giggles, rendered her more or less uncontrollable.

The morning after, Josh announced that he'd come to the end of his tether. Tether? I said. What's a tether when it's at home? Put your tether in triplicate, Josh, and get Irene to sign it and I'll give it due consideration.

Yours, at the end of something or other,

Martha

More From Martha

Introduction

Once again, dear reader, Martha the Faint-Hearted Feminist takes pen in hand to pour out her heart and various other of her internal organs (spleen, bile etc.) to her enviably liberated friend Mary, her sister under the skin. To recap:

Martha (38), erstwhile wife of Tom, the oldest hippie in the world, and mother of two, Jane (18) and Ben (16), is presently married to Josh, a civil servant, with whom she has produced a relatively new Baby (going on 2). Tom has vanished into darkest Cornwall with a variety of adoring nymphets, where he is writing his projected best-seller *A Flasher's Guide to Feminism* and from whence he sends few words and fewer pennies to his one-time near and dear. Martha, slightly dented, soldiers on in London, coping as best she can with the vagaries of family life in the Eighties which can be pretty damn vague, no member thereof being entirely clear as to the role he or she is expected to play. Even the cat has lost full confidence in her cathood and faints now and again from the strain of wondering if she should try to be a dog. Only Josh, meticulously turned-out at all times, is perfectly at ease in his God-given position as Head of Family, Breadwinner and Man. Or would be, if only his mysteriously restless wife and her offspring would see it his way and grant him the proper respect due to his central importance in the scheme of things.

Mary, on the other hand, being younger than Martha, was free, white and twenty-one when the tidal wave of the Women's Movement surged across the Atlantic and hit these shores in the late Seventies (I'm Betty, Fly Me). She was therefore ideally placed to shape her ends to the new currents and meet liberation head on. Her consciousness held proudly on high, she vowed never to succumb to the blandishments of men and never to join the ranks of trammelled women bound by matrimony to unreconstructed husbands whose children they had borne and whose houses they wife'd. Instead, she devotes herself to the women's cause, unhampered even by the minor exigencies of the human race — the base from which she militates is a rent-free squat in a Northern city where she lives in ideological squalor with her comrade-in-arms, the mechanical genius Mo. Untouched by the fears and doubts and conditioned reflexes suffered by most of her sex, unburdened by their responsibilities, free even from the State's demands (Mo has by-passed the electricity meter and hooked straight into the mains) she battles gamely on her oppressed sisters' behalf in the purest possible way.

Sadly, Mary's principles do not always adapt easily to practice and the Marthas of this world, try as they may, cannot always rise to the heights expected of them by the Marys. Certain problems remain intractable, like the obstinate maleness of sons or the vexed question of who cleans the lavatory, and Martha is sometimes hurtfully ungrateful for Mary's efforts to put her on the straight and narrow.

The fact is that in many ways housewives were overlooked in the explosive beginnings of the Women's Movement. Hardly surprising. For thousands of years women had been confined to domesticity, forcibly roped off from that wider arena where men played their power games, so the first thrust of the struggle for equality was, naturally enough, outwards, away from hearth and home and all that the old order implied. No one fights for what *is*, only for what might be. Free contraception, abortion on demand and twenty-four-hour crèches were among the first demands issued by feminists but they all spelled out the same message — Sisters, get out of the house. For women like Martha, more or less hopelessly stuck in it, the message, however obviously right, seemed to come too late.

Nevertheless, it is Martha — imbedded in the home and the archetypical feminine role — who is at the grassroots and who must cope with the myriad complications inherent in these demands: contraception is vital but the decisions it imposes are agonising. Twenty-four-hour crèches sound fine if only babies would raise no objections. Abortion on demand is essential but does not, in itself, tidy up all the messy emotions common to human beings, men and women alike. Equal pay for equal work is only justice but what about the unwaged work that Martha does? What about the dear enemy, men? There is no such thing as a blessing unalloyed and no one is more aware than Martha that every silver lining has a cloud. From under that cloud, wet and often bowed, she writes her letters.

1983   Jill Tweedie

Dear Mary

The Great God Snow has decended from heaven and spread his glorious wings over the tip I call a back garden. Gone are the rusting Whiskas tins, the soggy Sainsburys cartons, the mouldy mop-heads, the bits of Ben's bike and in their stead we have white magic. A trifle spoiled, it's true, by me having been caught unawares by the weatherman with two of Josh's nightshirts still on the washing line. There, they have taken up attitudes of icy indignation, much like their owner.

The cat, whenever Nature calls, picks her way through the wintery fluff like a very old OAP, flicking her paws fastidiously. She has refused to catch my eye since the party. All is by no means forgiven. With a bit of luck, she'll soon decide to pack her food bowl and leave home.

As Rover has, I gather. You realise he's probably snowed-in at Sebastopol Terrace till Easter? I was quite taken aback when you wrote me about him. If you recall, I was the one who first drew your attention to his stunning outward trappings, but I must say I never glimpsed the inner qualities of a Zen master you seem to perceive. 'Rover,' you write, 'has discovered the art of just *being*. He is a true lily of the field.'

Well, I grant you he toils not, neither does he spin. Nor talks, nor thinks, nor moves that much, I'll bet though that Solomon in all his glory didn't wear sweat-shirts inscribed 'Throbbing Gristle'. But how is he so wonderfully free of sexism? Wonderfully free of sex, yes, but if that's going to be our goal, the human race hasn't long to go.

Do bear in mind that no matter how charming Rover looks, stuck like a Buddha in one of your alcoves, he is only ornamental. This is one Zen master who hasn't the energy to clap one hand, never mind wash one dish. And when I think that you threw Bobby-Joe and his guitar out on the streets because he didn't pull his weight. I'm here to tell you that Rover doesn't even play the guitar and he thinks elves come out at night to do the housework.

Josh and I have settled down into a white flag situation since the party. The one thing going for me — Irene has let it be known around the department that she quite enjoyed our do, in spite of her lacerated tongue. How Freudian that was, when you think about it. I don't like what she says so she gets her tongue cut. God moves in mysterious ways His wonders to perform. With a little encouragement He might get His mills going and grind Irene exceedingly small. 'We were amused,' Josh says she said, and went on to remark upon the interesting life Martha must lead, with all that free time.

'Do you?' said Josh, in a voice that meant and if you do, stop it this instant. At the time, I was up to my elbows in nappy soup. 'Does it *look* interesting?' I said. 'Ah, *ha*,' Josh said, shaking his head enigmatically. Perhaps he thinks the nappy soup, the baby, him, Ben, Jane, and Mother are mere covers for some Mata Hari activity I've undertaken. Like I'm some sort of KGB mole recruited in Moscow at an early age and instructed to camouflage my real purpose with wet nappies. If so, Josh, Brezhnev's forgotten all about me and, by the time the order comes through to activate me, I'll be the oldest spy in the world, not to mention the fattest and tiredest.

As it happens, I'm on my own this week for once. Mother sailed off with the baby for a few days 'to feed him up', she said, as if he were a famine victim. Ben and Jane are out all day. I should get on with things but what things? I'm as institutionalised as any long-term prisoner; I don't know what to do with my freedom. I wander about the house picking things up and putting them down again.

I could go shopping, but what with? I could partake of the cultural life of this great city. The British Musuem. Art galleries. Fringe theatre. Porn movies. I could, but I don't. I think I've got agoraphobia — two minutes in the garden and I feel an invisible elastic band tugging me back to the kitchen. Even the phone doesn't ring. I tried reading this really interesting book about women's psyches studied through primate behaviour but I kept breaking off for interruptions and when there weren't any I had a passing panic attack. At least, if Rover was here, I could stare at him.

It's like this woman Mother knows, the one person in her life who really turns her on. The poor old robot gets up at seven, sticks on her pinny, and goes into an eight-hour orgy of scrubbing and polishing and dusting and washing every day and twice on Mondays. She scrubs the shed door and the post that holds the clothes line, says Mother in the voice she uses for talking about God. Apparently she keeps that up until she drops into her bed at 9 pm and, Mary, you know what? Not a soul ever crosses her spotless doorstep to see all the things she's scrubbed and polished and dusted and washed. I get goose-pimples all up my arms, just thinking about her. Could I turn into her? A haggard old Sorcerer's Apprentice, forever beating back the forever advancing dust and not even a sorcerer to do it for?

Josh came home just now, sat down, and buried his head in the newspaper. '*Talk* to me, Josh,' I said. 'I'm too tired to talk,' he said. 'Well,' I said, 'Snap at me then. Give me a bit of a growl, try a snarl or two. I'll even settle for a yell.' So he yelled.

Yours, enjoying the sound of a human voice,

Martha

The Sorceror's Apprentice.

Dear Mary

They've just proved what I always knew in my bones. A survey published last week found that only five per cent of the men in the entire labour force have wives who don't work. After I'd read that, I stood in front of the mirror. And there she was, outlined in the twilight, a rare glimpse of a large female mammal on the verge of extinction. Too big in the body, too little in the head, Tyrannosaurus Regina. We shall not see her like again.

Mary, I'm an endangered species. Why aren't you and Mo out there, protesting at the gates of the Department of Environment? Save the Marthas. Any minute now, Aspinall, Durrell et al, will be making Josh an offer he can't refuse and whisking me off to a Safari Park, where they'll talk about releasing me, some day, for rehabilitation in the wild and invite zoologists to take their PhDs in me. All I ask, Mary, is, when you visit, ignore the signs saying Do Not Feed the Martha and throw me a cream bun, okay?

I told Josh about the survey. It's true what I've been saying all this time, Josh, you see? I'm a non-working wife, I'm in a tiny minority, what do you make of that? The majority, said Josh in a pompous voice, is always wrong. Can this be so? Or is that just a useful quote to prove he's always right?

Anyway, I made a New Year's Resolution on the spot. Whatever else I do in the coming twelve months, I'm determined to get some sort of a job and that's final. To this immediate end I flipped through the Sits Vac in the paper today and came across an ad for a Word Processor. It said applicants had to have In-depth Word-Processing-Implementation Experience and it added 'and be familiar with Wang equipment'. Wang equipment? And me a married woman? Cheeky devils.

What's In-Depth — Word Whatsit — Whatsit *mean*? I asked Josh. It means, he said, someone who's an expert in rabbiting on, should suit you down to the ground, yuk yuk. You see the sort of support I'm going to get from *that* quarter? Never mind. When I've become the first female In-Depth Word-Processing-Implementation tycoon, I'll implement Josh to process his in-depth words right down his throat, see if I don't.

Honestly, Mary, you can't imagine what people expect of you when you're Just a Housewife. Lorna — who's only got a part-time job — rang up yesterday and said she'd been too busy to get a wink of sleep so would I please give her a couple of my dreams to tell her Jungian shrink tomorrow? And if that doesn't take the candle, Flanagan's Mum (who reckons she's Mrs Thatcher's natural heir because she stocks shelves at Tesco's) called round to ask would I visit my doctor for her, Monday, seeing as how she was rushed off her feet.

I thought she meant she wanted a prescription picked up, which was nerve enough, but no. I've got, she says, this stabbing pain here, feel? And my mouth's all dry and my breath is shocking. Dear dear, I said, backing off. So could you, please Martha, tell the doctor where you hurt and I'll take the medicine. Look, I said, donating my body to science when I die is one thing but schlepping it round surgeries on other people's behalf is another. What do you think I am, a mobile Rent-A-Symptom? Oh go on, be a love, she said, I've got so much work with Christmas and all. Have you? I said. Funny, that. All I do is click my fingers and bearded gents flop in my grate, clutching acceptable gifts.

If it weren't for me and women like me, our families wouldn't have any Christmas. All week I've been queueing for stamps and sending off cards, signing them Love from Martha, Josh and the Children. All week I've been buying presents, wrapping them and writing on them To Ben Love Josh, To Jane Love Josh, To Diddums Love Daddy. Also To Josh Love Ben and Jane. Also To Jane and Ben Love Tom. Also To Mother Love Josh and Jane and Ben. Then Josh says, Martha, buy yourself something from me if you see what you want on your wanderings (wanderings?). Great. So I buy slippers, wrap them up and write To Martha Love Josh on them so that Mother can say, on Christmas Day, oh Martha, how thoughtful Josh is. I don't need a family at Christmas. I could just stand under the tree and play pass the parcel all by myself.

By the way, I think I've sent you the wrong packet. If you get one saying To Dad Love Ben and Jane, send it on to Tom in Cornwall, would you? He can be very tetchy if he thinks the kids have forgotten him. I'll get a letter in the New Year complaining that I've made them selfish.

Still, I've got Carruthers. Remember Carruthers, the wee mannikin at the party who kept making passes at my knees? He appeared the next afternoon, pretending he'd left his little woolly mittens behind (his Mummy should tie them round his neck) but I knew he'd come to try his luck again with me. He was ever so nice and polite and didn't take offence at all when I ran at him with a spoonful of mashed potatoes, mistaking him a moment for the baby. He said he thought I was a wonderful girl. Girl. He also said Josh was a lucky dog.

He asked if I'd like to have a bite with him some time and I said I couldn't, because of the baby, but he was welcome to a bite with me. What with dogs and bites and him woofing away, it was all a bit like a visit to the vet, but he ate up his scrambled eggs like a good boy and scampered off. Leaving behind him the only mysterious present I'm likely to get this year, labelled To Martha from Carruthers.

Martha

Giving Carruthers a bite.

Dear Mary

Christmas is over
The geese are all dead
Please to put a hole
In old Martha's head

No, it wasn't that bad, actually. Nor, I hope, for you. Did you take my advice and decorate Rover instead of a tree? I bet he looked a treat, all lit up, with baubles taped to his pectorals and a fairy on the top his bonce. Just be quite sure he's stripped and out before Twelfth Night or he'll bring you bad luck.

We hung our Christmas tree from the ceiling, because of the baby, and it looked like nothing so much as a missile about to be launched through the roof. Pray the Goddess that that is not an omen. Josh has been very preoccupied with Poland, though whether his preoccupation has to do with their noble struggle against oppression or their imminent bankruptcy is not crystal clear. Amazingly, he took himself off to Hyde Park Corner for the Solidarity march. He didn't join in or anything — if he had I'd have known our last hour was nigh — but he did stand and watch. I couldn't.

It sounds terrible to say so but, just between you and me, I'm dead scared of the Poles. If we were living in the Middle Ages I'd have to admire their particular Holy Roman brand of courageous patriotism but the way things are I'm terrified their death wish (fuelled by religion, which was always hot on death wishes) will drag us all into the final conflagration, willy nilly. Sad, but I've come to fear courage. Cowardice seems so much more mature, more natural, less likely to put a price on all our heads.

I know nothing is worth the human race being blown to kingdom come but do men? Can they envisage what it might be like or will they wake up to reality too late, hitting their thick heads and saying sorry, world, made a bit of a cock-up there, meant well, too bad nobody else will get a chance to mean well again. Do they realise there'll be no medals handed out in the Final War because there'll be no hands left to hand them, nor chests to pin them on? There won't even be consciences to be conscience-stricken with.

Still, we're only human aren't we, which means we can all manage to banish real fear on festive occasions and substitute irritation. Like the way I felt when the doorbell rang on Christmas morning and there was Tom. I didn't mind so much — after three glasses of Baron Alban Vin Mousseux (called Champagne in our house) I wouldn't have minded opening the door on Dracula — but I was a bit afraid of Josh's reaction. I needn't have worried. Tom's method of entryism was to dump a wadge of papers in Josh's arms, the finished manuscript of his *Flasher's Guide to Feminism*. Remember that? Josh cheered up no end. Never thought you'd pull it off, old boy, he kept saying, fingering through what he saw as his loan paid off and possible riches to come.

Mother, however, is not so easily seduced. The very sight of Tom in the same room as Josh and me made her sniff promiscuity in the air and, from then on, she behaved as I imagine a really professional madam behaved in a Victorian brothel, putting on a wonderful act of pretending the gentlemen had only come for a chat and preparing regally to overlook their occasional disappearances upstairs. Poor old Dad, on the other hand, already confused by unaccustomed snorts, obviously thought that Josh and Tom made up two halves of one Martha's Husband and was only startled that one man could get around that much.

I was glad Tom came, though. Jane was pleased and so was Ben and the baby took to him no end. Tom, you see, has a real talent for Father Christmas ho-hos, unlike Josh, which is what babies like. I soon saw that whatever confrontation might take place, it would be over the baby, not over me. I could see them duelling for the baby's favours where neither would raise a finger for mine, boo-hoo. However, all was solved after lunch. Everyone went fast asleep. Even the baby flaked out for an hour, his chocolatey face sunk in my best Serbian embroidered cushion.

Now they've all departed and tomorrow is New Year's Eve and we're not invited anywhere, the two of us. The thing is, we couldn't go anywhere anyway, because of the baby, but nobody's asked us so I can't even say Miss Otis regrets she's unable to dine today and so on. I feel sad, thinking of the rest of the world dancing about, popping balloons and hugging each other. Bess and May have asked *me* to a Women's Collective party and I'd like to go but it's no men and I can't bring myself to leave Josh alone, staring at his big toe. How about putting on a frock and coming. I said to him; but he didn't even reply. Once again the married woman hits the dust, lynched by conflicting loyalties. Will I find my heart's ease next year? No. —

Yours, watching telly in a twosome,

Martha

PS. — I opened Carruther's present in the loo. It was a tiny picture frame in the shape of a heart, with nothing inside. Is that significant? And, if so, in what way? Perhaps the New Year will reveal all.

Josh and Tom sucking up.

Dear Mary

I promise you I already *knew* that you and Mo were very close. I'm *sure* you're just like sisters. I *believe* she's a wonderful woman. I *understand* that you'll always respect and love each other because you're always straight and out front with each other and I *do* think it's great that nothing will ever come between you, least of all a man.

Okay, you can come clean now. It's El Rover, isn't it? I told you to get rid of him pronto, Mary. He's the eye of the hurricane, our Rover is. Never speaks, hardly ever moves, but above his golden curls the storm clouds gather. Jane has only just recovered from her bout, not that you realised at the time. I know she's recovered because she's given up eating again — back to the anthrax nervosas, says Josh.

Mary, you have to ask yourself, what do you see in him? We all know what you see *on* him but I'm talking about the inner man, if Rover has one. He's one-dimensional, you know, a cardboard cut-out. Walk round the back of him and check. Not easy, I grant you, with a person propped up at all times by a wall. But do remember, beauty is only skin deep. I said that to Lorna, and Lorna said well, how deep do you want it? Handsome kidneys? Good-looking lungs? Anyway, what a waste if you and Mo come to blows over a man who thinks a thing of beauty is a boy for ever. Well I bet you that's what he thinks.

To tell you the truth, Mary, I'm disappointed in you and Mo. When you recall all the generations of women who've only been loved for their looks and how we've all fought not be regarded as sex symbols, and now the two of you are falling in heaps over a male sex symbol (emphasis on *symbol*). You can't even say gee, Rover, you're pretty when you're angry because he's too lazy to be angry.

End of lecture. If you detect a hectoring note, it's brought on by the stress of my New Year diet. Grapes. Sour grapes, sweet grapes, green grapes, black grapes, an infinite variety so long as it's grapes. Well, I can't expect to break the jobs barrier clad only in nighties, can I? The house has already got a grape pip underlay. I once saw a man on television who'd built a model synagogue out of the pips of oranges. Could I build a home extension, d'you think? If I swallowed them, would they grow? Perhaps I could start an internal vineyard and produce Vin de Marthe — a lively little wine, if a trifle domestic. Chateau Moi.

Also, I'm fractious because I've been attacking Ben's room, or it's been attacking me. If I don't get it under control now, it could spread to the rest of the house and wipe us all out. Ben made a lot of noise with the vacuum cleaner but to little effect, mainly because he left it to its own devices in the middle of the floor while he stood swinging the tube round his head to make it hum.

Opening his cupboards, forty-two brand-new silver patisserie boxes fell out. I was unable to ascertain either their provenance or their destination. Asked, Ben explained that he dunno. Did they fall off the back of a lorry? I said. Can you inhale them, inject them, smoke them? Do you plan a new EEC patisserie box mountain? But answer came there none.

Ben seems, if anything, more distrait than ever. One evening, he ate two plates of meatballs, a small pumpernickel loaf, four slices of plum pud and three Granny Smiths, drifted out of the house and phoned in a half-hour later to say Mum, have I had dinner? Another evening, he asked for a tin of tomatoes and some spaghetti to take to Flanagan's house and cook for the two of them. So off he went. An hour later, the phone rings. It's Ben to say the meal is ready but he's forgotten Flanagan. The wretched lad is still upstairs in Ben's room, waiting.

I've given up worrying about him getting a job when he leaves school in the summer. Now, I only worry about how he'll manage to sign on. I mean, can he sign? On? Does he inhabit the same world as us? Last time he and Flanagan exchanged words (about three months ago), I overhead them. Ben said to Flanagan 'Policemen don't eat oysters,' and Flanagan said 'Oh.' Eleven years of education for this nugget of misinformation. What's more, he couldn't write it down — he can't spell oysters.

Lorna has her problems too, I'm glad to say. She charged in yesterday, saying she'd just beaten back a plague of social workers, all howling 'why woollies?' Why *what*? I said. Turned out Lorna'd been going on about her endless chores having to wash the woollies and so on and the social worker had said 'why woollies?' Lorna threw a tantrum. That's all I need, she kept shouting. Some boring woman interfering in my life, squeaking 'why woollies?'

Bess, who happened to be here at the time, said she saw

the social worker's point. People like you, Lorna, do sometimes seem to be making your own burdens, she said. You could buy synthetics and throw them in the washing machine, couldn't you? Oh could I? yelled Lorna. And what exactly am I freeing myself for, by not buying woollies? Running a literary salon? Learning to fly? Becoming England's Disco Queen?

Poor Lorna, she's tired. We both are. Some neighbour of ours is concealing a rooster about their back garden. Every morning this week we've been woken at dawn by a cock, crowing. I said to Mrs Next-Door — catching her in between giggles — are you woken in the morning by a cock? Leave off, she screeched and had to be dragged outside.

Yours, nodding off,

Martha

GIVE!

Lorna running a literary salon.

Dear Mary

Can you believe it? A girl hitches a lift, the driver rapes her and the judge talks about her 'contributory negligence'. I do wish I could have been there with you and Mo, picketing the court. All I've been able to do is stick Women Against Violence posters across every downstairs window, which leaves me stumbling about in Stygian gloom, tripping over the baby. Even Josh was tight-lipped about the verdict. It took Mother to throw her lot in with the Law, phoning to say there, Martha, didn't I tell you not to let Jane hitch-hike, let this be a warning to you, why don't you ever listen to your Mother? I banged the receiver down on her, I'm proud to say.

Mother gets *The Times* so I expect she collected her ammunition from their leader. Did you read it? Well, don't, it'll bring on an attack of the Red Brigades. The wretched thing was actually headlined Lock Up Your Daughters and my belief is it was written by the Judge himself, maundering on as it did about foolish girls and how careless it was to hitch a lift with a rapist. I swear, reading it, I could *hear* the dry knuckles of the ancient legal hand creaking as it scratched away with its little quill pen.

I tell you, Mary, if I got the writer in my car I'd pull off his wig, unhook his wing collar, peel off his Damart long johns, unwind his spats, rip the suspenders from his ghastly silk socks and drop him, mother nekkid, in a layby. Officer, I plead contributory negligence. The foolish beak sat in my front seat with the top button of his waistcoat undone, need I say more? Of course, what contributory negligence really means is being born female. It is perfectly obvious to the keen legal mind that if women didn't exist, men wouldn't have to rape them. Lock 'em all up for ever, and bingo, no more rape. One silver lining to the cloud, at least: the girl had the courage to report it. Without that, we wouldn't have had the ludicrous verdict and the exposure of these male attitudes in all their yukkiness. Still, good on Rover, standing outside the court with you both. Wonders will never cease.

Our rooster has fallen silent — I suspect Lorna crept out in the night and topped it. Not that the dawn's new quiet has done anything to quieten her. I went over the other evening to borrow an egg and she was having a right go at her old man. I know what *you* think, she was shouting. *You* think I'm bossy and dominating, don't you? Oh *yes* you do. Well, I'm not d'you hear? There isn't a bossy or dominating bone in my whole body, right? So just don't start or I won't be responsible. Bossy and dominating, *huh*. Lorna, I said, as hubby scuttled upstairs, I don't like to interfere but. Said Lorna, if you don't like it, don't do it, okay Martha?

What a mood she was in. Turned out she'd had a nasty session with the dentist — and him with her, I imagine. Bloody man went on and on, said Lorna, about how I got holes because I didn't brush my teeth properly. Three minutes night, morning, after every meal, up down, in, out, gargle, rinse, spit. I said to him look, it's a short life, what do you want me to do? Give up my job and devote myself to my teeth? Did anyone ever die of plaque? Next time he comes at me with that drill, Martha, I'll garotte him with his own dental floss. Trouble with you, I said to him, is you're into S and I'm not into M.

I took my egg and ran. In that state, Lorna could make even one of her corpses sit up and beg for mercy. Anyway, one good thing, I've lost three pounds this week on the grapes and already I can almost zip up my jeans. I'm hungry all the time, a sort of nagging ache, but I pretend it's a war wound and I've just got to endure it. I know you think, as you wrote last week, that dieting is an unfeminist activity and I should just let my body find its own level or something, but would it? I'm ashamed to admit it but I've never stopped eating because I'm full because I never *feel* full. I simply have to take an intellectual decision. Stop now or else.

I bought a package of delicious gooey biscuits yesterday for the kids and it had an expiry date on it. An expiry date. I mean, what kind of people keep delicious gooey biscuits around *too long*? Before I started dieting, I ate this whole cake and it said on the package, sufficient for six. Six what? Garden gnomes?

Ben went back to school again on Thursday, thank heavens, and Jane starts college next week. She told me at breakfast that I should have let her be there when the baby was born. I'd like him more, then, she said, we'd be bonded. Jane, I said, I wasn't that keen on being there myself, never mind asking you. So she says I'm old-fashioned and didn't I know that, these days, *everyone* gives birth with *everyone* around. Well, I said, I give you my word. Next time I'll send out the invitations well in advance. Martha requests the

pleasure of your company at her Birthing Day. Please bring your own forceps. Masks will be worn. Water will be boiled.
Next time? Am I mad?
Yours, with a wild surmise,

Martha

The Next Time

Dear Mary

Starting at college again has brought Jane out in a new rash of non-specific irritability. Coming home, she walked in as I was saying *poor* Mrs Thatcher to Josh. Immediately, her face went critical. Poor? she said, why poor? Jane, I said, Mrs T's only son Mark is lost in the desert, that's why poor, and she's been crying about it. I don't believe it, said Jane. What do you mean, you don't believe it? I said. It says so on the news. I could feel myself getting all hot under the collar, I don't know why. Jane, how can you *not* believe that a woman and a Mother gets upset and cries when her only son is lost in the desert? I just don't, said Jane.

So then we had a long boring wrangle, with me saying of *course* Mrs T. was crying, *naturally* she was crying and Jane saying huh and yeah and in a pig's eye. Really, I was confounded. And then Jane says she's only doing it to win the next election, like those Hollywood stars who are always getting lost and things and then they pop up with their pictures in the papers and everyone says aaah. Jane, I said, how can you *be* so cynical, how can you . . . but we had to stop there because Josh came out from under his papers and said would we mind taking our high-level political discussion elsewhere because he had papers to go through.

Two days later, Jane slaps a newspaper in front of me and says there, what did I tell you? I know, Jane, I said. He's been found and very nice too. But listen, says Jane and she reads out Mark saying 'We were not lost. We knew where we were, although we weren't where we were supposed to be.' Jane, I said, it's no good knowing where you are, in the Sahara, if nobody else knows where you are. You can't sit around in the sand saying I know where I am to the vultures, can you? Well, *he* did, said Jane and we were into another long boring wrangle. Mary, I'm all for young people having a healthy disrespect for politicians but to deny them all human feeling *and* accuse them of manipulating yours. Well. The trouble with Jane is, she simply doesn't know how to argue, either. She doesn't know the *rules*. Then, of course, I got your letter saying Mrs T. wasn't crying and it was all a plot to take our attention off the rail strike. Oh *Mary*.

To change the subject quickly, I had a little fling this week. V. embarrassing, really. My tiny swain Carruthers phoned and said would I like to have lunch with him and I'd said yes before I'd thought at all, it just popped out. I mean, I'm happy to have lunch with anyone from Carruthers up — and from Carruthers there's a long way up. So after I'd scrabbled in the cupboard trying to find a skirt and asked Mrs Next-Door to come in and laugh at the baby, there was Carruthers at the door, looking ever so dapper in an elfin suit and a weeny anorak. And, Mary, you won't like this, over the Steaks Diane in this quite posh restaurant, Carruthers said I love you.

It was terrible. I didn't think I'd heard him right and I said what? and he said I love you, again. At which, a piece of steak Diane got itself stuck in my throat and I coughed and spluttered and Carruthers punched me in the diaphragm because he'd read that colour supplement where it said that's what you do and my eyes streamed and this dreadful Mafia-figure in a dark suit came over and asked us to leave. Obviously thought we were having some ghastly marital hullaballoo. Like me saying, dear, there's something I've got to tell you, we're hopelessly incompatible because you only come up to my elbow.

I didn't tell Josh. I mean, I didn't *not* tell him, I just didn't tell him. You can't go around telling your husband that his wife has been told she is loved by half a male person, can you? I'm still quite amazed, myself. If there were only two of Carruthers, one on top of the other, I might be a bit thrilled. When I got home, Ben was there, sent home from games because of the snow and reading some magazine. Look, Mum, he said, there's this whole lot of men and women advertising here about wanting to meet and describing themselves and that but, Mum why do they say at the bottom 'object matrimony?' Like, if they object to matrimony, why do they advertise? So I explained that one and he said oh and then he said, Mum, why do they say 'looks unimportant?' Why do they want people who look unimportant? Honestly, Mary, that child makes my back flare up. Okay, so he can finally read, but what good's that if he can't make any sense of the words? Or was he having me on? I don't like to ask in case he wasn't.

And to add to my burdens, Josh said this morning that the papers he'd been going through were actually Tom's manuscript of *The Flasher's Guide to Feminism* and, Martha, it's good you know, really very droll, ha ha. Ho ho, I said to the baby, highly risible, I'm sure. But then he went off and left a large package on the kitchen table for me to post, with the address of a famous publisher on it. That's his way of making sure that I'm involved, an accessory after the fact. So I can't say, afterwards, nothing to do with me because he'll say but Martha, you posted it. So I didn't. I took it upstairs and stuck it under hundreds of pairs of laddered tights in my laddered-tights drawer. We'll see.

Mother has ushered herself into my life again, via the phone. She said Martha, I was deeply hurt when you put the receiver down on me and some people would find such behaviour impossible to forgive but I am a Christian woman and I am prepared to forgive and forget. Never mind forgiving me, just forget me, I nearly said. But didn't.

Yours, trapped in the family's bosom,

Martha

Carruthers in love.

Dear Mary

I'm not sure that being lamed for life by a rogue pram sufficiently justifies your latest broadside against Mothers and all their works. Aren't some of your best friends Mothers? Anyone would think we constituted mankind's worst peril since the Black Death, the way you carry on. Why mankind? There's nothing very kind about man, nor some women I could name, either.

We must get this straight between us or it'll end in tears, as my ma used to say when she hit us with the hairbrush. Of course you've got a perfect right to declare your private parts out of bounds to babies, though I do think calling the little dears 'squatters' is going it a bit, especially when you're a paid-up squatter yourself, in the council's womb, as it were. And, of course, some women have babies for all the wrong reasons and leave them littering the streets for you to trip over but every human being does occasional things for the wrong reasons, why pick on women?

When they asked that man why he climbed a mountain, he said because it's there and everyone said goodness, how profound. Well, there are women who have babies because it's there, 'it' being all that internal machinery going full blast from thirteen on, chugalug chuff chuff boopedyoop, like a high-tech factory and what's the point of a factory if the owner gives it nothing to fac?

A *real* empty factory might be a tax dodge or waiting for a subsidy or something, but no one cares about a woman's thirty-odd years of useless chugalugging, do they? Before I got pregnant, I often felt I was living over a coal mine, keeping my workforce unemployed for no good reason. Besides, someone's got to produce the odd baby, if only to give CND something to march for.

Okay, you can't abide the way Mothers barge about the place as if they were an occupying army, scattering the population into the gutters as they sweep past with their prams. But it's a bit much to write, as you did, 'the other day some walking Fertility Rite, armed with one of those multiple pushchairs that hold eight babies clamped in a straight line,

23

rammed into my shins and looked outraged when I protested. Obviously waiting for me to say what an honour it was to be permanently disabled by her ghastly progeny in their unguided missile.'

Some of us, Mary, are not so confident. I slink down the High Street with my push-chair, pulling my forelock and apologising all the way for both our existences. Sorry, excuse me, sorry, so sorry. As if the baby were a secret pervision I ought to practise behind closed doors, like wearing rubber undies.

There are parts of the world, my friend, where people actually worship infants and keep them around all the time so they can talk foreign baby talk to them. Fat chance, here. Now that they've got this campaign against dogs, can babies be far behind? Next thing, I'll be applying for a licence, filling in forms for permission to enter the inner cities, dodging black vans with baby-catcher nets.

My life feels increasingly rickety, these days, like an old cane chair you'd better not sit on too hard or you'll hit the floor. By the time I've got the baby up, scrubbed, changed, and stuck full of muesli, I'm gibbering. Can you OD on vitamins? I take six doses a day of yeast, calcium, B12, A, E, and C and all of them only just keep my eyelids from closing down. Josh says I must get out and about more. Out where and about more what, I asked him.

Do you have any conception, Josh, of exactly how dreary my life really is?

Do you realise that even Ben's goldfish had a change of aquarium at Christmas, not to mention the excitement of two whole new water plants to set their little hearts beating? I can see by their silly slack jaws that they're hardly over the turmoil yet. If I were a tribal mother in the African bush, I'd be participating in whatever tribes do but, being pale English grey, I'm only allowed occasional glimpses of my mate and older children and compulsory twenty-four-hour stares at my infant. I mean, this morning I caught myself looking forward to a phone call from Mother, explaining how unsatisfactory I am.

Never mind, says Josh, we'll be hearing from that publisher soon and *The Flasher's Guide* will sell for a fortune and we'll be rich and you can hire ten Norland Nannies and spend all your days in the Mirabelle, brushing crumbs off your mink. And all the time, the manuscript was tucked upstairs in my laddered-tights drawer. When he'd gone off, I retrieved it, wrapped it up and posted it.

Well, so what, Mary? You have to work the system. I've

unleashed Tom's male chauvinist piggery upon an unsuspecting world because it's my only hope and my only payment for being saddled with one man's two children and another man's one child. My Wages for Housework. I promise you, if it sells, I'll buy a Home for Slightly Battered Wives and enrol myself as its first resident. What larks, Mary, eh? What larks.

Yours, counting her free-range chickens,

Martha

Ten Nannies Dancing

Dear Mary

It is three of the clock on Monday the first of February in London, England, the British Isles, Europe, the World, the Universe, and I have just become a career-person. Stuff being Tom's ex, Josh's spouse, Mother's daughter, daughter's Mother, and the House's wife. Now I can call myself an Employee and soon, I dare say, a Partner. Oh glory be. I told you I'd do it in the New Year and I've done it. Today Annie's Attic, tomorrow the world.

Yes, Annie's Attic has opened sesame and I'm in. Remember I wrote you, this time last year, about that single-parent woman two roads away who ran a junk tip? Shop. I've been trudging by daily ever since then, having a friendly word with the owner as I passed. Like 'morning' and 'afternoon' and 'bet that old bed's seen a bit of ooh la la in its time', that sort of thing. And this morning, my mouth swung ajar all by itself and my voice said how would she like a part-time assistant and she said what sign are you and I said Libra with Saturn rising and she said done. And they think women aren't businesslike? None of your havering about and references desired and CVs in triplicate please for us.

Then she invited me into her office — well, we sat round her paraffin stove — and she wants me three mornings a week, nine to one, and she'll pay £2 an hour and I'm hired as of next week. Mary, that's £24 weekly, cash in hand, on the nail, in the bag, and up the Tax Inspector. Which makes £48 a fortnight, £96 every three weeks, and £192 a month. Fantastic, eh?

Best of all, of course, I can bring the baby with me because she's got a child, too, and she can't go buying with it so I'll be minding them both. It fits like a jig-saw. Annie turns out to Helen in fact, call me Hel, everyone does, I'm Gemini. Annie passed away two years ago, she was Virgo but we hope not intacta, seeing as how she was 83 when she went to the great junkyard in the sky.

Hel's daughter is four and she's called Troy, isn't that sweet? Hel's auntie has minded Troy till now but she can't any more, she has turns, says Hel. It has to be *meant*,

Mary. Children can't damage junk so they'll have the run of the place without me worrying about them breaking things what are broke already. And who knows, one day I could brush aside the cobwebs on an old painting and next thing it's up at Sotheby's, a long-lost Rembrandt, and I'm rich. Hel and I are rich.

How time fies, it's 10 pm now and all noisy. I told Josh about Annie's Attic and, surprise surprise, no cheers. First question, how much? OK, so it isn't £192 a month. Josh's lips moved and in no time flat he'd managed to whittle my salary down to £96. Typical. Not that I'm sniffing at £96, so why should he? Then he went into a long boring moan about how he'd have to check it out because it could affect *his* tax, mumble, mumble. I pointed out to him that the tax people were not about to get the big hullo from me but that just launched him into further pomposities about men like him in positions of trust and he had his reputation to think of and honesty being the best policy and we'd never get away with it, anyway, and so on. If I insisted on working, he said, nobody was to know what job I was doing, did I hear, *nobody*.

What do you think I'm going to do, I said, hold a Press Conference? Enter as Businesswoman of the Year? Besides, Josh, I said. If you persist in defaming my job like this, I'll sic my Union onto you. We Junk Handlers and Amalgamated Mattress Recyclers are a proud bunch and we'll take no stick from effete white collar workers like you. Oh tat off, he said nastily. Oh yeah? I said. Well, mate, when I tat off with my Rembrandt, don't ask for a share of the loot, right?

Not content, he starts on the baby. What sort of environment was it for His Son, spending his tenderest years in a jungle of rusty fridges and rotting sofas? Had it occurred to me that a large part of Annie's Attic might be highly infectious? Old cushions aswarm with Lassa Fever, carpets hopping with fleas, uncut moquette alive with dandruff, cupboards rife with wood-worm? I promise you, Josh, I said, first hint of holes in the baby's legs, first ear to crumble and I'll have him sprayed with Rentokil at my expense.

All Josh could do then was run through the gamut of painfully predictable Helen jokes. Hel's teeth, Hel on earth, Hel's Angels, Hel and high water, Hel's bells, he left no Hel untouched. Quite finished, have you? I said. Then the Hel with you, I'll do what the Hel I want. Jane came in at that point, looked at our faces and said what the hell is up with you two? Now Josh thinks he was the last to know.

And talking about men being the last to know, I happened to see Lorna last Saturday in Sainsburys, with a spare bloke attached to her trolley. Having coffee with her later, I asked who he was and her neck went all pink. Your neck's gone all pink, Lorna, I said, come clean with your friend Martha. So she did. D'you know, I could have sworn that Lorna was far too bad tempered for anyone but Mr Lorna to love, even if she is what we housewives call top-heavy. Size 38, C-cup, as I happen to know, having done her laundry once when her washing machine broke down.

Anyway, she's having an affair. Or rather, being Lorna, she's momentarily transferred her hatred of men to Another. I won't darken your ears with the details, suffice it to say that he was up her stairs yesterday. And, said Lorna, can you believe what that B said afterwards, Martha? Putting on his horrible socks, he said Lorna, you were good. Condescending rodent. I put him in his place sharpish. I said, Mister, you should see me with a man I *like* —

Yours, wincing for mankind,

Martha

In Annie's Attic

Dear Mary

This is the first free moment I've had to write and say thank you, dear woman, for sending me that lovely hippie-type bead-bag to hang round my neck — and fancy it being made with your own fair Rover's hands, daisy stitching and all. That lad's come on a treat under your wing. Josh says it looks like a dwarf Shetland's feed-bag but he's only jealous because no one sends him presents for his job.

Actually, I already feel I've been working so long I'm about due for a gold watch. I'd have made £32 by now, except for Helen being a bit strapped for the readies and not managing to cough up more than sixteen quid. But what do I care? I'm so used to working for nothing I can still hardly believe I've earned sixteen quid by the sweat of my brow.

It *is* sweat, though. Not so much the shop, more the children, as I might have guessed. Or child, rather. Helen's daughter Troy is a peachy angel-face, all feathery curls and pansy eyes and neon smiles. She sits on an old armchair in a pretty frock, looking like a bud that's fallen off a rose tree, good as gold and smiling away. But I turn my back for a second, turn round again and there she is in the same place, demure as pie, her skirts spread out like petals and she's done twelve whole terrible things.

On Monday, while I said wrong number on the phone, she squeezed a can of oil into the till, covered a wall with blue chalk squiggles, made confetti of three second-hand paperbacks, cracked a jug right across its Present From Broadstairs motif, permanently embedded six toffees in quite a nice sheepskin rug and emptied lemonade all over a pile of mattresses, leaving a very squalid stain. The Destruction of Troy.

The baby, on the other hand, thinks he's finally been let in through the Pearly Gates. He spent the first two mornings gazing around him in rapture and eating two moth sandwiches Troy fed him. He reckons Troy is the best thing to happen to babies since mother's milk and drools like a dirty old man whenever she whips past him on her way to sabotage pastures new. He is, of course, filthy all the time.

Friday, he spent four hours crawling through carpet rolls and nearly got sold to Mrs Next-Door who bought one to cheer herself up, though in my humble opinion if she gets any more cheered-up she'll go down with a double hernia.

But in spite of all the extra work, the job's lovely. Sometimes I feel like the Queen, sitting on my armless rocking chair and waving graciously to the passing crowds. If I say so myself, I'm doing Helen proud with my contacts. Bess and May lugged off an old filing cabinet for the Women's Centre, Lorna had a cup of tea and paid out for a blotchy reprint of Monarch of the Glen, a Valentine gift for hubby she said, looking shifty, and Rover's auntie hobbled up Wednesday to buy an ancient typewriter with the X missing. Who needs an X? I said. Here's a second-hand Roget for 20p. Any time an X comes up, a quick flip through Roget and you'll never need an X again, I guarantee. Oh, I'm getting to be a real hot-shot saleswoman. Only thing is, I've just remembered that Rover's auntie's name is Xanthe and even Roget won't come up with a substitute for that.

The one real drawback is the old boy who comes with Annie's Attic. On Monday, when I opened up, there he was stretched out on one of the beds. Smelly old devil, turf him out, tell him you'll call the cops if he comes back said Helen, but I didn't have the heart. Poor old nutter, he's so far gone on after-shave he thinks I'm the original Annie.

I must say, though, Helen isn't what you'd call scrupulous about my hours. She wears about sixteen hundred bangles so I can tell when she isn't coming, which is most of the time. The first two mornings, she didn't come back till 2 so, Friday, I brought the baby's lunch. There I was, on the pavement outside, sticking a spoonful of pureed apple into a roll of carpets and making encouraging eatie-up noises while a man passing by tripped over his boots, seeing me.

Meanwhile, back at the ranch, Josh's eyes have gone all beady with peering round to see what he can complain about that I've neglected for my job. I caught him standing on a chair in the middle of the sitting room the other evening. Why are you standing on a chair in the middle of the room, Josh? I said. Just checking these bulbs, he muttered, but I know he was feeling up the chandelier for dust.

As for Mother, I haven't dared tell her about the job yet or she'd start sending Josh food parcels and consolation cards. You're out an awful lot, Martha, she said on the phone yesterday, her voice creaking with suspicion. Well, Mother, I said, can't afford to let all this Spring sunshine go begging, can we? We're out all day in the park, the baby and me, and he's blooming. But Martha, she said, it's done nothing but rain all week. Never mind, I boomed, babies don't shrink, do they?

Yours, jolly hockey-sticks,

Martha

Dear Mary

One thing about being a woman, you do get to see life from all manner of angles. Compared to me, Josh spends his days in a fur-lined pouch, like a middle-aged Roo. A car to seal him off from the streets, mahogany and chandeliers at the Department, discreetly swish restaurants at lunch-time and upper-crust colleagues around him all saying I was at school with him, awful little toe-rag, whenever someone frightfully grand is mentioned. And if he's very good, he gets a visitation from the Minister, so he can fill his under-oxygenated lungs with a nice strong whiff of the corridors of power. Everything in his garden is lovely except for the home bits. Me and the children are Josh's slum area, his urban blight, the place where the riots happen. I wouldn't be surprised if he's got plans for demolishing us and putting up office blocks.

Nobody notices me much, either. If Princess Di really wanted to be private, there's no point zooming off to exotic islands entirely surrounded by telescopic lenses. All she's got to do is huddle herself into a shapeless quilted coat, pull a woolly hat down to her eyebrows, load up her arms with plastic bags, stick herself behind a crummy sort of push-chair with a crummy sort of baby in it and nobody would give her the time of day, even if she asked for it. She'd be Mrs Anon, like me.

Every now and then, though, I'm allowed to visit Josh-land. One moment I'm squatting on a broken stool in Annie's Attic, brewing up tea on the paraffin stove for me and old Charlie, who wouldn't care if I had two heads and pincers as long as I let him sleep off the after-shave behind a cupboard and the next moment I'm cheek by jowl with Top People in a high chair at Oxford. High something. That was last Thursday, when Josh's old school friend Jeremy (awful little toe-rag) asked him to dinner at his college and looked away long enough for me to slip in, too, in my best ethnic frock. Ethnic frocks haven't got waists and neither have I. I could have smuggled in a whole Indian family under mine and no one the wiser. Come to think of it, it would have been more fun if I had.

Things went wrong from the start. Having drinks in Jeremy's rooms first, in came this Methuselah figure, an old boy in much worse shape than Charlie and wheezing like a grampus. So I got up from the sofa to give him my place so that he could have his heart attack in a sitting position. Next thing, there's Josh's hand on my shoulder, pushing down fit to crack a clavicle. Don't move, he hisses into my hairspray, that's Jeremy's *scout*. Hullo, what have we here, I thought. Some sexual kink I've never heard of? A love that dares not speak its name in case its false teeth fall out? But I realised almost immediately, of course, that it's merely the Oxonian custom of having geriatrics as body-servants and calling them boyish names to camouflage senile decay. Still, I can't say I felt easy, slumped on my fanny while a palsied old person slopped vermouth all over my shoes.

Nor did I feel any easier, later, perched several feet above assorted young persons in a panelled hall, picking at my plate and wondering who, below me, could look up the holes in my knickers. It's a task in itself, making conversation with strange men in black shrouds who don't want to know one thing about any aspect of one's life. I fell back on asking questions about the history of the college and got told the answers, which wasn't a barrel of fun.

Then, suddenly, everyone stood up and trooped off the platform. Josh, who'd been talking animatedly with a basically very plain woman if you don't count long blonde hair and a cleavage like the San Andreas Fault, nudged me as he passed and hissed take your *napkin*. Apparently, a napkin covered with gravy and lipstick opens doors in Oxford. So I took it and followed the rest of them across and around and up and along till we came to another dining room with, in it, another dining table at which we all sat down. I mean, Mary, it was Alice in Wonderland. If I'd had a teapot, I'd have put my head in it.

At that point, Josh started hissing like he was about to go off. Psst, Martha, the port goes *clockwise*. Psst psst, Martha, the snuff box goes *anti-clockwise*. Psst psst *psst*, Martha, no smoking till the port's been round *twice*. Honestly, Mary, I didn't dare pick a grape for fear I'd have to stand on my head and sing 'Moon River'. The man on my left kept saying to me *silly, isn't it* with the soppiest grin on his face and goose pimples of ecstasy all up his neck. And they say men are the logical ones. Fiddling about with bits of silver? Weirderoony.

I tell you, I sighed with relief to be back in the real world of the kitchen before my grey cells finally snapped. On inquiry, Josh loftily informed me that such rituals had made England what She is. I'm afraid you're right, Josh, I said. An emerald asylum for the terminally deranged. But, Mary, he's serious. He really gets quite emotional about the idea of a long line of loonies stretching back into the dim and distant past, all sitting round tables telling each other which way to push bottles. But Josh, I said, what does it all mean? Where does it get us? Gives young men a sense of tradition, said Josh. But what *gain* is a sense of tradition, when the tradition is something as barmy as anti-clockwise bottle-pushing. It's like saying my ancestors were nutty as fruitcakes and what was nutty enough for my ancestors is nutty enough for me.

Mary, I think we ought not to continue fighting for more women at Oxford. One mad sex is quite enough. We can't afford two.

Yours, pushing the hoover backwards down the stairs,

Martha

The love that dares not speak its name.

Dear Mary

How on earth did you manage to get our Rover enrolled in the Sebastopol Terrace Men's Group? Don't you realise that men's groups go in for consciousness-raising, too, and Rover hasn't a consciousness to raise? I once, accidentally, stuck a large pin in him but he didn't notice and when he was staying here I never heard him say anything more discursive than uh huh, though he always said it quite nicely and without any obvious sexist bias. It's not that he's dead, exactly, more in very deep hibernation but I can't see him adding much to the topic of men's liberation. He's already either so unliberated as to be nearly catatonic or he's so liberated he's out of sight. Will we ever know which?

Jane's taken a distinct turn for the grumpier since you took him away, that I do know. She got sent a Valentine card in February and when I asked who it came from, she said some wimp. Jane, I said, a man has gone out, bought a card that says 'Knowing me the way you do, Of course you know that I like you! But even though I know you know. Today it's nice to tell you so!' and posted it to you with his own hands. Doesn't that make you think a bit kindly of him? Terminal wimp, said Jane.

The only person vaguely of the male sex my daughter seems to tolerate is old After-Shave Charlie down Annie's Attic. Every day, on her way back from college, she stops by and says 'how you doing, Charlie, all right, mate?' Yesterday I told her, Charlie's too far gone to know you from Queen Victoria, he can't even get his eyeballs focused on you. I like that in a man said Jane.

Annie's Attic, as it turns out, is a haven for human as well as wooden throw-outs. The latest inhabitants are Noreen and Baby Noreen. Noreen is eighteen years old and weighs as many stone, plus an additional eight pounds for Baby Noreen, whom she keeps tucked among her spare tyres and pulls out now and again to groom.

First time she dropped in, I made cooing sounds at the top of the baby's head and she tugged it out, held it up, smiled fondly and said that's my girl, she's a born killer just like her

Dad. All of two months old and a born killer. Whenever she cries, Noreen says she's off again, the bugger, after me nibbles and she rummages about in layers of bodice, preparatory to revealing several acres of mammary glands while I rush about for a screen between her and the public. What you doing that for? she said when I propped it around her. Only natural, init? Every woman's got nibbles. Not like Noreen, they haven't. Hers are bigger than most of the baby. When Charlie caught a glimpse, his rheumy old eyes focused for the first time in years. I don't know what Helen would say if she knew her place was turning into an itinerant doss-house and nursing parlour but she doesn't know — she's never there but Fridays, when she arrives in her van to unload yet more flotsam and jetsam on me. Yesterday we were so hemmed in by a consignment of forty-eight huge desks that we lost Charlie and Troy for almost an hour.

I live in terror of something falling on the baby (mine, not Noreen's). An old Dimplex radiator did fall on one of the little marmalade kittens that hang about here and when I heaved it up there was the kitty all flat underneath, like a squashed orange. Noreen picked it up and stuck it under her jumper, along with Baby Noreen, and an hour later it emerged with only two bent whiskers to show for its ordeal. Baby Noreen looked a bit the worse for wear, though. She had superfluous fur all over her face.

Josh is into whining, his way of protesting at having a working wife. This week's whine was about Ben and Flanagan and their set of old drums (purchased in secret by me from stock). Noise Against Racism, Josh calls them and says if they don't stop, he's going to set the British Movement on them. They practise up in Ben's room. You can't actually hear the drums as such, only a sort of dull zonk from the floorboards and bits of plaster in your soup. It's Ben's animals I worry about. When those drums really get going they set off a tidal wave in the goldfish bowl and the mice vibrate like they'd been wound up too tight. It can't be *good* for them, Ben, I said, it'll loosen their insides. Naah, said Ben, they like it. They *like* it?

It's already done us all good, though, me having this job. For the first week, Ben kept trekking over, saying Mum, there's no bread and Mum, there's no cornflakes and Mum, where's the kitchen scissors. Before, I'd have felt guilty, I'd have thought it was my business. Now I say Ben, I'm working, go get some bread and some cornflakes and *look* for the scissors.

I'm even getting quite brisk with Josh. When he asks where

something is, now, I say I don't know. First time, he couldn't believe his ears. You don't *know*? he said. That's it, I said, I don't know. He hasn't got an answer for that. He'd like to say don't know *ought* to know but even Josh is aware he can't get away with that these days.

Of course, he may divorce me shortly in the hope of finding a new and better doormat but, somehow, I doubt it. They don't make 'em like me any more, not young, they don't. And even *I* am not like me any more, quite. Who'd have thought Annie's Attic would be Josh's Waterloo?

Yours, flexing her muscles,

Martha

Charlie focuses on Noreen.

Dear Mary

Whatever happened to sisterhood? Your last letter gave me quite a shock, going on about how I must realise I'm being exploited by Helen. Mary, Helen is a woman, also a mother, also working-class and, thus, trebly exploited. Quadruply, really, if you count Wages for Housework. She is also a single-parent struggling alone in a male world doing a male job, lugging furniture around in a van, and she isn't strong, she told me so. Something about having a deranged kidney, knocked sideways-on, she said, by Troy's birth, oh dear. She's at the bottom of the heap, is Helen, so how can she be an exploiter? She'd need someone to exploit who was at the *bottom* of the bottom of the heap and that is not me, Mary. I've got a house and a husband and things and I'm middle-class, so that rules me out as one of your exploitees, doesn't it?

Of course, it's true she hasn't paid me for a while and she does tend not to turn up when she's supposed to, which means I end up working rather longer hours than we agreed and I do more or less run the shop as well as looking after Troy and After-Shave Charlie and Noreen and Baby Noreen and answering the telephone and writing the odd letter and keeping the books but I don't mind a bit. Not a bit. In fact, I'm enjoying myself for the first time in years so how can I be exploited? I mean, I'm not an idiot. I see that I'm very convenient for Helen but, then, she's very convenient for me and money isn't the only currency, is it?

There's no use my confronting Helen, like you say I should, because she's got financial worries and I haven't. Well I have, but I'm better off now than I was, even without getting all the money I'm owed and if I had some show-down on principle with her, I'd only be cutting off my own nose because I'd be back in the kitchen again with nothing, not even fun. Mary, I know you're right, really, but somehow, in my case, being right is wrong. Or irrelevant. Or potty. Or the view from Sebastopol Terrace is just very different from the view from Annie's Attic. Or the view Annie's Attic might have if the windows weren't so filthy. Must get round to cleaning them.

Besides, doesn't it shake you a little to know that you've got Josh on your side? He's temporarily given up his union-bashing hobby and appointed himself my shop steward. Yesterday he said look, Martha, unless you're paid every penny you're owed by this time next week, I shall have a few words to say to this Fanny's Attic myself. I'm not a man to stand by and watch while his wife is exploited. I'm your *husband*, Martha, and I won't have you treated like this. Like what? I said. Oh for heaven's sake, said Josh, what do you mean, *what*? Not getting paid for the work you're doing is what. I presume you're hardly in the business of giving your labour gratis to any Tom, Dick or Harry, are you? Certainly not Dick or Harry, I said, what sort of a girl do you think I am? Tom, now, yes. And some other man whose name escapes me at the moment. Like Josh.

After that, a number of interesting phrases were suddenly heated up and tossed about in the air, rather like Pancake Day. Phrases like what about love and doesn't marriage count for something and has it come to this and what do you want from me and I never thought when I met you and various other more pungent epithets. Even Willy Shakespeare got dragged in, with his unkind winds of ingratitude and so on. Who could have guessed that my pin-money job, which I do while I sweep while I beat while I clean, could possibly stir up so much how's your father?

Talking of which, why is it that every time I get my father on the telephone and say Hello, Father, he keeps bellowing Who's That? How many daughters does he think he's got, when I'm an only child? Oh, life is so complicated. All I know is that thanks to the deep concern shown by both you and Josh, I shall soon be done out of the only job I've ever had and ta very much. Lorna says I should practise a little data drop-out, which is computereeze for lies. What I say is this:

Oh what a tangled web, gee whiz,
When first we tell it like it is.

Never mind, I shall continue to make hay and hope the sun shines. At the weekend, some man sold Helen about three hundred second-hand badges, which we've now got stuck up all over the place. Noreen has bagged one with a picture of an eagle and RSPB written across, which she keeps telling everyone means Royal Society for the Prevention of Birds. Well, them eagles is wicked, see, she says. They go swoop on our babies and take em off up their nests and eat em. *Course* they got to be prevented. She's pinned Baby Noreen's nappies with a badge that says I May Have a PhD But I'm Not Stupid.

As for old Charlie, he's sitting there on the pavement all crumpled up, with his hair falling down his vest and his eyes spilling down his poor sunken cheeks, covered all over with badges saying Gay Vegetarian. If that doesn't put them off veggies and sex, nothing will.

Yours, with naught to lose but her brains,

Martha

Dear Mary

I got that copy of the *Sebastopol Clarion* you sent me and read every word, thinking there must be an item in it about you. My heavens, there's a lot of funny goings-on down your way. What did you make of that man a neighbour found, who'd been three days stuck up on his bathroom ceiling with bits of black leather? And what was that yobbo doing with that goat at midnight back of the Wimpey? I couldn't make it out. I hope.

Then I read your letter. You sent me the *Clarion* because there wasn't one solitary word in it about the Sebastopol Terrace International Women's Day Strike and what more proof did anyone need of the decadent and trivialising influence of the media? Mary, you're right, you're right, you're right. Who'd willingly read such filth? Well, what can you expect when most journalists are men?

The only tiny thing is, perhaps the ignorant MCP hacks didn't ignore it on purpose. Your strike, I mean. The trouble is, it's only single women who haven't got jobs and don't do any housework and haven't got children who squat in Sebastopol Terrace so it might be a bit difficult to tell when they're withdrawing their labour. I'm not blaming you or anything (I might possibly be envying you) but you and Mo don't actually get out of bed most days 'til gone 3 pm, so perhaps the roving reporter had roved on by then. If he'd had any wits, of course, he'd have checked the shop-lifting statistics that day. I bet they took a nose-dive.

No, forget I said that. I'm only a bit narked because you said I should have gone on strike, too. How, exactly? If I'd refused to feed the baby, Josh would have gone off to the office as per usual and what could I have done? Sat in bed counting the baby's screams for twelve hours? My only public recognition the old broom banging on Mrs Next-Door's side of the wall? Have a heart, Mary.

In fact, the only thing that went on strike around here was the cat. She marked Women's Day by being sick. She's a fastidious sort of cat so she isn't very sick somewhere, she's a tiny bit sick everywhere. And ends up depositing a neat little mound in Josh's shoe, which I firmly believe she did to show Sisterhood with me because she's the only female who's noticed how long I've been trying to stop Josh leaving his shoes around the kitchen. Unfortunately, a man doesn't look at his best when his heel's hitting foreign substances in unexpected places. The cat's feeling sole-sick I said with a snort, which wasn't a good idea. It doesn't get me anywhere, laughing at Josh. I'm just as aware as he is that he's got this cosy office bolt-hole to run to, where no one would dream of laughing at him, never mind being sick in his shoe. And, to be fair, who wouldn't prefer to be in a place where people took you seriously, if we had the choice?

Now Josh keeps saying in a low monotone, how many other men have to endure cats being sick on them and wives laughing? No good asking me, Josh, I said, how can I tell? That's the trouble with marriage, we're so isolated from each other we've no way of knowing what goes on behind other couples' four walls. Mr Next-Door says how many other men have to endure wives laughing, that I *do* know, but they haven't got a cat, is that better or worse? And my father used to say how many other men have to put up with wives who spring-clean on Christmas Day and Lorna's old man keeps asking how many other men have wives who are undertakers and smell of formaldehyde in bed and, in his case, my guess is not a lot. But you never know. No Gallup Poll is ever going to come up with even the vaguest average on married persons' peculiar habits. You remember what Tom was like about clocks, don't you Mary? Well, then.

What I wonder is, will there be any future for marriage once all wives find out what all husbands have always known — you can only rest at work? Annie's Attic, which isn't noticeably far from a loony bin, is a haven of calm compared to home. Perhaps because, however blotto Charlie is or fat Noreen is or amok Troy is or sick the kittens are, I don't feel guilty. In Annie's Attic, it can't be my fault.

Oh, Mary, before I forget. Can you believe these medics who say all women should have their babies in hospital and in the way they decree. That really got to me. Blimey, there are few enough things we can do in our own way in our own place in our own time and if having babies isn't one of them, what's left? When our cat's going to have kittens, she wanders around and we all creep after her, shoving cardboard boxes full of nice warm blankets under her nose, which she always ignores. It would be much more convenient for *us* if she gave birth in the boxes instead of slap in the middle of my double bed but, being a cat, nobody would dream of making her. But they want to make us.

What I say is, the medics should feel free to shove their hygienic swabbed-down disinfected labour boxes under our noses but if we choose to give birth in our own double beds, standing on our heads, that's our business and any interference is a diabolical liberty.

Yours, wishing I led a cat's life,

Martha

Dear Mary

Talk about guilt on the gingerbread. There I've been toiling away at Annie's Attic but enjoying myself no end, so of course I have to be punished. Storm clouds build up, back at the ranch. In theory, my part-time job should do wonders for the family, giving Josh a golden opportunity to blossom out emotionally, get close to the kiddywinks, express his long-stifled paternalism, excavate his buried talent for nurturing and reveal the warm, caring, parenting person under the pin-stripe. In practice, he's at home even less than before, terrified (I suspect) that one apocalyptic day he might get back before me and be forced to confront three dishes in the sink shrieking 'wash me'. The result is a residential vacuum in which Satan has taken up squatting rights.

For a start, Jane has taken to throwing off her garments in public. I was the last to know, of course. Lorna told me. She'd got it off a woman at a funeral who'd got it off another woman at the funeral who'd got it off the corpse. The word was, Jane had stripped at two parties, a disco and in the middle of the heath at mid-day. Rubbish, I said, Jane doesn't take her clothes off to go to bed, never mind cavorting about heaths. Coming home, I said to Jane, let's you and me have a cosy mother-daughter chat, shall we? At which infinitely tactful, supportive and restrained remark, my daughter reared up, whinnied like a frightened filly, wobbled the whites of her eyes and shouted God, Ma, you're not going back to Tom? Caught completely off guard, I said go back to your *father*? D'you think I'm quite off my rocker? Which damage I then sought to repair by saying Jane, you shouldn't say such things about your father, whereupon Jane said she wasn't saying any things about her father and, bingo, we were right in the middle of a cosy mother-daughter scrap.

Anyway, I finally managed to drag up the subject again and told her what I'd heard, squeezing her arm in a comforting way while Jane said ouch several times, peevishly. Not that I think it's true, not for a minute, I ended. Yes, it is, said Jane. No it *isn't*, I said, don't contradict. Oh, you may have taken off a cardy here and there but your mother knows a thing or two about men, believe me. They poured drinks down your throat, didn't they? They gave you exotic cheroots. They kept egging you on. You were very silly but you didn't know what you were doing, did you? Yes I did, said Jane. Well, there you are then, I said. What d'you *mean*, you did? Stupid blokes tried to stop me, said Jane. Pathetic nerds! I was pulling their clothes off too, till the twits galloped off.

The shame. Come back, B. Cartland, all is forgiven. And that's not all that's abnormal on the home front. Josh sidled over to me the other day, positioned his mouth an inch from my ear and said had I noticed anything odd about Ben? Everything's odd about Ben, I said, with quiet pride. I gave him a sandwich the other day and he said it had bones in it. Bones, in a marmalade sandwich. Martha, said Josh, looking round shiftily, Ben never leaves the lavatory seat up. He what? I said. And if, said Josh, it's never up, perhaps it's always down. Then he looked at me meaningfully. What are you on about? I said. Next thing, you'll be saying the baby's been spotted reeling about with a bottle, up Piccadilly, and a cache of arms have been found in his nappies. I warn you Josh. You cast any more nasturtiums at my children and I'll go back to Tom (has Jane got second-sight?).

Josh, of course, stalked off and I, of course, shouted after him the unforgivable. What about your son Billy, then? You haven't see him for five years, does that mean he's bound to go off his trolley and flip his lavatory lid? Josh, the image of injured dignity, turned round, said if you *remember*, Martha, Billy is in Australia and if you *remember*, Martha, I gave him up for you. Upon which I sobbed, but to an empty stage. It's not even true, Mary. Josh left Billy and his mother ages before he met me but it didn't half make a crushing exit line.

Only good news is, I've lost weight, or perhaps I just think I have, compared to my day-time companion, Big Noreen. She doesn't care. Spends the first hour of each morning feeling around herself, checking that eight hours of night starvation haven't robbed her of a precious ounce or two. Your Dad likes a bit of flesh, your Dad does, she mutters to Baby Noreen, hauling her out for a breath of air from between the maternal rolls. Can't abide a skinny woman, your Dad can't. Noreen, he says, you make them others look like bacon rind, you do, and that's the truth, straight up.

Lucky she's big, though, it has its uses. Monday, hauling stuff off the van, I glanced up and there was Irene, Ms Boss, smooth as pie in a pussy-cat bow, practically under my nose. So I ducked behind Noreen. Extraordinary . . . colleague . . .

wife, said Irene, peering in the shop with a friend. Dump . . .
never satisfied . . . women's lib . . . ridiculous. Then she
bumped into old Charlie in his pavement chair, drew her
skirts aside, flared her nostrils a bit and swished off. To
reveal, plastered across her tailored back, one of our
window stickers. JUNK, it said, There's more life in Charlie
than meets the eye.

Yours, laughing up Noreen's sleeve,

Martha

A motherly chat.

Dear Mary

If all this Argy-bargy over the Falkland Islands has done nothing else, it's acted on the males of this family like a sackful of Sanatogen Multivitamins with Added Cold Steel. Josh shed ten years the minute he heard they'd invaded and has frisked about ever since like a large pin-striped lamb, giving me loving little pats as if I were an Argentine Junta and personally responsible for the whole crisis. Ben, who has never noticed the faintest ripple of a current affair in the sixteen years of our acquaintance, is now au fait with every detail of the fiasco from the direction of the South Atlantic winds to the precise number of torpedoes on a Hunter-killer submarine (Tony Benn, please contact) and daily sings entire choruses of 'Rule Britannia' in the loo. Tom rang up from Mousehole to remind us all that he was born in Comodoro Rivadavia, which irrelevant news was greeted by Josh and Ben with many congratulatory sounds, as if Tom had won something. What about CND, Tom? I said. Sea and what? he said.

Also, Mother rang up to give me her recipe for mock corned beef, since I wouldn't be buying the real thing any more. I never did, Mother, I said. You always told me how horrible it was, eating it in the war. That's as may be, she said, but we don't want those Argies thinking they're depriving us of anything, do we? They're a fascist dictatorship, Martha, you know. I know, Mother, I said. Ten days ago, those would have been words of praise from my old Ma.

Only Jane and I remain consistent. Jane consistently calls everyone concerned, from M. Thatcher to the Falkland Island penguins, war-mongering wankers and I consistently say oh dear, I hope nobody gets hurt. I did try to tell Josh what Lorna's hubby'd heard from a passing oil man, that their slogan was Keep the Falkland Islands Rhodesian, on account of the people being rather to the right of . . . but Josh cut me off with the sort of glare that said I was Lord Haw-Haw and ought to be shot at dawn. It is all very bewildering. My solution is to settle all the Falklanders on the good ship *Canberra* for a permanent round-the-world cruise but who listens to me?

Nor has there been any respite at Annie's Attic. Big Noreen's bloke, the born killer, was had up last week for bonking some man on the bonce with a bottle. It's not right, says Noreen 'E thought the geezer was one of them Argies and 'e did 'is duty like a True Brit, 'is pride overcome 'im, know what I mean? As for After-Shave Charlie, he's almost sobered up for the first time in a decade, solely in order to communicate to us a blow-by-blow account of exactly what he did to them cunning bleeders in the war. The last, the first, the Boer, *which* war, Charlie? I said. *The* war, acourse, he said. Tell you something, Missus. The sun has never set nor never risen nor never will without Our Boys is fighting someone, somewhere in this world. Makes you proud, don't it? Charlie, I said, it certainly do. Does. The old boy would join up tomorrow if they'd have him and, I'll tell you, one blast of his methylated breath and Galtieri's goons would fall like ninepins, never to rise again.

The Attic closed for four days at Easter, just enough time for family hostilities to break out all over. Mother went to church on Sunday and returned blowing steam from all gussets, a result of being forced to pray for peace by a vicar she threatens to denounce as Red under the dog-collar. She looked like a hot, cross bun and said poor baby seven times in a minute to the baby, who looked like a chocolate-coated Easter Egg.

Then Ms Irene Bossiboots turned up for a Resurrection Riesling accompanied by the roughest toughest hunk of knotted biceps I've ever seen. Tattered denim jacket, faded jeans, seven-league cowboy boots, leather strap round eighteen-inch neck, greasy bandanna round greasy head, a real bone-freezer. This is Ron, said Ms Boss, he's my hairdresser and, my dear, what this man can do for my hair is unbelievable. She's right. Every time I see her hair, I don't believe it. Cheers, said Ron, downing the Riesling. Then he said did anyone here *begin* to understand why we were all supposed to go potty with rage because some itty-bitty island half across the globe had had its Union Jack taken off it? I could get all those islanders *and* their sheep into my salon and still have space for my Tint 'n Perm unit, he said. If he hadn't stepped on the baby at that juncture, raising the resulting Cain, I think Mother and Josh between them might have split every one of his ends.

Still, at least spring has sprung here, if only in patches. My friend Dorrie Carrie Bogvak writes from Boston that they've just had two feet of snow tipped over them and if she ever manages to tunnel out again she's going to emigrate with the twins to any old fascist dictatorship in any old banana republic that can guarantee her she'll never see another snowflake. She sounds very low, poor thing. She says time's running backwards in America, like a bad film, and she's hourly expecting to be put on trial in Salem and burned at the stake as a witch, due to campaigning for the Equal Rights Amendment and having a wart on her chest, which they'll think is a third nipple and proof of her witchery.

I wrote back and told her time wasn't exactly running forwards here and when it gets back to the *Mayflower*, she should nip on board and be reeled back to Southampton. I'd meet her on the quay in my wimple, shouting God Bless King James, and we could have a nice cup of tea before we went off to colonise the Falkland Islands.

Yours, packing the hard tack,

Martha

The pinstriped lamb.

Dear Mary

We had a sticky little scene here last night. Josh and his personal assistant Cassandra came back together from the Department so that she could put in some overtime personal assisting in what she calls the *dwawing room*. Cassandra, you may remember, is that Benenden reject who's so posh she can hardly talk and so skinny it's a wonder her knickers stay up. If they do. Care for a drink before we start, Casso? said Josh. Ah'll have a gin and toto, Josh, with just a smidgin of limono, said Miss Doom. Yukko, botho. Anyway, we all dived into the booze and the next thing I know, the Doom is saying oh Mawtha, must tell you this divine stowy. This man wants to be a woman so he has a sex-change opewation and aftewwards his chum says *do* tell, was it awfully painful and the chap says it was agony, actually. First they have to, you know, cut it awff, and then make a sowt of, you know, dent, and that was all utterly toothie-peg-clenching. Then they give you the silicone injections for the new bustiboos and that was sheer hell. So the chum says but what was absolutely the most screamingful? And the chap says oh, that was when they came to take my brain out. Then Miss Doom lets out this tinkley laugh. Tinkle, tinkle, she goes, tossing back the few lank strands, and Josh goes haw haw.

I inhaled two fingers of Vat 69 and nearly choked to death. Then I got up awff the floor and said in my Queen Mother voice, I shuggest to you, Miss C, that shince shome evidently conshider you a woman and, therefore, sans grey or any other matter, you have no recoursh but to hand in your notice pronto and take up your true poshition in life, as an under-inflated rubber dummy at your local shex shop. Upon which, I schwepp out.

Later, Josh had the unoriginality to tell me I had no sense of humour. Very true Josh I said. That went splosh in the kidney-shaped basin along with the brain. Unfortunately, those of us with hollow heads can't do a whole lot. Can't cook, can't wash, can't iron, can't earn and can in no way be trusted to clean precious little baby bottoms. Ever so sad, isn't it? God, Martha, said Josh, is it absolutely incumbent upon you to take everything so literally? Cumbie whatie? I said. No use using those long words on silly me. And I popped my eyes and swung my arms and sagged my jaw and dribbled all down his suit.

But on to more rousing affairs — your plans for the Pope's visit, already well advanced as I see from the snaps you sent. Now, Mary, you're getting into deep water here and you could find yourself splashing about in some very strange company, like Alice in the pool of tears, you and Pastor Jack Glass and the Reverend Paisley and other dodos. Remember, Popes have friends in high places and one of them has cornered the market in nasty come-uppances such as Flood, Fire and Famine. These are called Acts of God because no one's left to follow them. I thought the picture of you and Mo as the Pill, in a yellow dinghy, was very novel but Rover sheathed from head to foot in rubber I found a trifle tasteless. The Pope, said Josh the other day, is a fine man and he's certainly put Poland's troubles on the map. He certainly has, said Lorna, and whenever Poland's troubles are on the map, bingo, the rest of us all fall off. So then came the long, boring argument about what you must or mustn't do about aggressors, with Josh droning on about how he, unlike some others he could name, believed in fighting for democracy and self-determination and the right of every individual to speak his mind and for heaven's sake, Ben, will you shut up while I'm talking or I'll blip you.

Anyway you're right, the Pope has to be lobbied on behalf of women, though it'll do no good. You can't get at Infallibles, you see. They just turn round and say look, you horrid little person, I'm Infallible and I'm wearing my Infallible Hat, so shut up while I'm talking or I'll excommunicate you. Josh has a fit of the Infallibles about once a week, so I know the symptoms. Besides, if the Pope does catch a glimpse of you rolling about in your dinghy or Rover stomping about in his sheath, he'll only forgive you.

Did you hear about those scientists who discovered the fossils of six-foot penguins? How I wish they still existed, there's something so comforting about the idea of six-foot penguins, like waddling duvets. Weird, isn't it, how penguins have shrunk and shrunk over the eons and horses have grown and grown. What I say is, evolution's a funny thing. All that fauna and flora getting up to the oddest tricks for survival — insects disguised as flowers, flowers disguised as insects, snakes pretending to be desert, zebras pretending to be shadows and butterflies pretending to be leaves. Any minute now, some smart-alec creature will notice that we're on the planet too, with all our flotsam, and it'll start disguising itself as a beer can or a plastic mug or a bit of farm machinery. Or me.

Next time we meet, up the Pope's, make sure I don't bleed green. On second thoughts, life might be better as a creature. Most of them don't mate for long.

Yours, rapidly evolving,

Martha

what are you looking at

Carruthers meets a six-foot penguin.

28 April

Dear Mary

If Spring is here, can Arctic blizzards be far behind? Yesterday breakfast, while Josh was turning Shredded Wheat into bigger and better Josh and I was wresting a dripping bin liner out of the bin, he raised his head briefly, regarded my person, and said didn't I think it amazing that a woman like Irene always managed to look so feminine doing such a masculine job? Caught in mid-flight across the kitchen to the garden dustbin, I froze, causing an instant fall-out of festering veggies, mouldy chicken bones, and a tidal wave of tea leaves.

Once frozen amidst a piquant cloud of eau de rubbish, I spent the next two seconds blinking back an errant hot tear and trying desperately to back my voice out of its throat without crashing into anything. How to counter so many terrible implications whilst still keeping all the bits of me together? What to say first? Like, is emptying the rubbish a *feminine* job? And is lolling knee-deep in carpets telling people what to do, *men's* work? Is looking feminine while dining on expenses at posh restaurants some sort of triumph of gender over role, some womanly mountain scaled?

Eventually, clearing my throat of the mammoth frog that had taken up squatters rights there, I asked Josh in what way, exactly, did Irene's femininity manifest itself so wondrously. But by that time, the cunning B had picked up warning signals. Already half-way out of the door, briefcase like a shield across his chest, he said good God, he hadn't done a survey on it or anything, perhaps it was just that she always wore skirts. And then bang, the front door closed and I was left standing, mouth agape, heart readying itself for an attack. Mary, I couldn't put anything together. Masculine, feminine, job, no-job, skirts, trousers, what did it all *mean*?

One thing I realised right then, I hadn't a chance. I met the man, I fell in love, the sky turned blue, the birds sang, I said I do, and the next thing I know I'm in mucky jeans emptying out the rubbish. Whereas Irene met the man, trampled all over him, got to be his boss, the sky turned blue, the birds sang, and the next thing she knows, she's in a Jean Muir frock and

Arpège, stomping at the Savoy on the taxpayer's money.

I mean, how can I wear frocks, doing what I do? How can any woman scrub floors, clean loos, wash nappies and play mine hostess at Annie's filthy Attic, in prairie skirts edged with broderie anglaise? Or have I failed because I couldn't make time to get into a frock and earrings and whisper huskily into Josh's returning ear did you have a good day, oh King of my heart? Knowing perfectly well that if I did, he'd only assume I'd spent the intervening hours lying on a chaise longue reading French novels.

A no-win situation if ever I saw one. Josh is obviously so conditioned he can't see the wood for the stocking-tops. In his mind, being a housewife is a feminine role and so I ought to look like Marilyn Monroe doing it, while Irene, being his boss in the Department, has a masculine role and yet is just so damn *bustin'* with womanhood that against *all those odds* her sheer femininity triumphs.

I can't bear it, Mary, I can't cope with it at all. I've done everything a woman should; married, stayed home, had children, brought them up, and my husband thinks Irene, who isn't married, has no children, works in an office where she bosses him about and is arming herself for an onslaught on Parliament is more feminine than me because of the way she can afford to look. And do you realise, that goes on all over? *All* women in top jobs, up to and including Mrs T., always wear skirts and practically all women who are at home raising children wear trousers. And yet we're the ones at the butt end of jokes about who wears the trousers. It unhinges the mind.

I went upstairs an hour ago and dragged out the suitcase containing my summer wardrobe. Grand title for four short-sleeved T-shirts to top up jeans instead of four long-sleeved sweaters. Not a skirt in sight — I've even forgotten the mechanics of wearing them. What do you do with the two straight bits that reach down from the hem-line to the floor? You have to put them in stockings, don't you, at least until they've gone brown. And what happens at the end of the stockings, apart from holes? Flatties? At my age I'd look like mutton schlepping about as lamb. Heels? How can I heave the baby about, in heels? Despair, Mary.

Yes, I hear you. Josh has fallen for Irene. A woman who's done everything he thinks a woman shouldn't, everything he's stopped me doing and his four paws are in the air for her. He thinks she's more feminine than the mother of his child because she isn't the mother of his child and can wear pretty things without infants being sick down them. He sees her all the time because he isn't married to her and I hardly see him at all because I am. Mary, it's so unjust I could scream. I *am* screaming.

Yours, aaaah,

Martha

5 May

Dear Mary

Daffy Murdoch's just been regaling me down the phone about when she and her husband weren't speaking and he started coming home later and later from the office. On her own again for the umpteenth evening, something snapped. She broke six plates, pulled out every drawer, spread out all her worldly goods across the floor, turned their tiny hall into the St Valentine's Day Massacre with red paint, up to and including bloody handprints smeared down the walls, left a note cut out of newsprint saying: We Got Your Wife, and departed. Give him a fright, she thought. So straight away he rang her mother, her mother betrayed her and when she came back he wouldn't say a word to her for weeks. Just like old times it was, she said.

And then there was my American friend Dorrie Carrie Bogvak, when she first had the twins and things were tough all round. She got so desperate slaving over a hot two-ring stove that one afternoon she emptied meatballs in tomato sauce and all the mashed potatoes on the floor, unplugged the Baby Belling, stuck it on top of the mess, picked up the babies and did a flit, leaving a note for her old man saying Your Oven's In the Dinner. But, as she said, what man's going to take you on with three-month-old twins when even their rightful and legal father is none too keen, so she had to patch it up, poor dear. Or, rather, mop it up.

Would that I could afford such drama but I can't because of the children. They are my hostages to fortune but also to any chance of plain marital speaking. The luxury of an all-out bang-up shouting match can't be had when they're around. I tried launching into a mini-scene with Josh, the evening of the morning he broke my heart with his remarks about Irene being more feminine than me, but Ben came in just as my voice was hitting a thoroughly therapeutic High C and I had to pretend I was mid-way thorugh 'the hills are alive with the sound of music'.

That night, I tried a bit of hissing under the sheets but my hisses were drowned by Josh's snores. How can I make him realise the extent of my wounds? I lie beside him, sniffing, and all he does is occasionally brush my side of his face like I was a female mosquito. Obviously he thinks if he just keeps saying cheerful everyday things like *what* a nice day and Martha, this shredded wheat is *delicious*, I'll come round.

But I won't, this time. Now he's changed his tactics. Ignoring the fact that he's cut me to the quick with his gushings about Irene and is probably having an affair with her, he says why are you looking so glum, Martha? and I say *because* and he says oh God, you're not still on about *that*, are you? You wouldn't believe, Mary, how hard it is to make your loved one realise that your life's blood is sploshing at their feet. In view of this, I have no alternative but to take up your kind offer and absent myself until such time as Josh understands the near-fatal blow he has delivered. Telling him over the top of the *Telegraph* only makes me feel a nag as well as everything else. Josh. What? You've broken my heart, Josh. You what, Martha? I'll tell you one thing, Martha, that Tony Benn ought to be shot at dawn, Martha.

You said in your letter I should come to you if the going got rough and it couldn't get rougher. I won't stay long, I promise, how can I, with Ben still a child in all but feet? The baby will have to come along, of course, but he's in a quiet phase at the moment and even his shrieks are quite thoughtful and don't last that long. I've told Helen I've got to leave Annie's Attic. She said oh dear and sighed a lot and talked about how they always told her she shouldn't rely on married women. No man could have said better.

Big Noreen is going to take over while I'm gone. Just remember, take the baby out of the chest of drawers before you sell it, I said, and she shook all over. She told me when her Born Killer gets on her wick, she hits him over the head with a bottle and that rearranges his brains nicely, know what I mean. As for old Charlie After-Shave, when I shouted in his ear that I was off, he gripped my hand and said give them Argies hell. Well, at least he's got his wars straightened out now.

Jane and Ben took the news calmly. Just popping up to see Mary, I said, only for a few days. Jane said who's going to cook the meals for me and Ben said I need a new pair of Levi's, Mum, and could Flanagan stay while you're gone. Martha, sadly missed by one and all, tra la.

I haven't let Mother know my plans, she'd only be confirmed in her lifelong view that I was born a runaway wife. Why can she always be relied upon to take my husband's side against me? If anyone ever dared to take Father's side against her, she'd swat them into fly paste. I did ring her yesterday in a weak moment but I only got Father shouting who *is* this when I said hullo Father, so I gave up. Lorna wasn't exactly supportive, either. When I dropped round to her Funeral Home to say cheers, be seeing you, she put on a cadaverous voice, said today happened to be her fifteenth wedding anniversary and what a good thing some women took their vows seriously and stuck by their husbands, in spite of marital infidelities on a scale that I, Martha, wotted not of.

But Lorna, I said, *you're* the one having an affair. I *beg* your pardon, she said, rigor mortis setting in. Lorna, you told me about it yourself. Ah, she said, *that* one. You don't want to take any notice of *that* one, Martha. My old man doesn't and he never had it so good.

Whatever that means. Anyway, Mary, I'm leaving my Dear Josh letter on the mantlepiece, which I expect the cat will eat, and I'll be with you all in Sebastopol Terrace this time Thursday as ever was.

Yours, darkening the door,

Martha

Dear Mary

I shall be forever grateful that you let me and the baby stay so long in Sebastopol Terrace. But it *is* nice to be home. I have this lodger in the attic now. I did it out as part of my new life-rearranging Master Plan and if I say so myself because no one else will say it, when I'd finished it looked a dear little dell, a veritable glade of soft *eau de nil* punctuated tastefully here and there with a sort of squashed liver colour that is quite unique, due to the beetroot juice that the baby squirted in a workman-like way at the walls. There are cute paper lanterns dotted about and the bed is a bower of teeny cushions. Utterly sweet.

Unfortunately, the lodger turned out to be a wispy and none too clean mole in his late twenties named Judas. Not a name calculated to arouse any natural warmth in a landperson's bosom — who gets the thirty pieces of silver, him or me? When he told me what he was called I said 'are you sure?' which may not have been polite but was deeply spontaneous and he said, in a very meaningful way, oh yes, he was only too sure. Unsettling, wouldn't you say? Perhaps his name is really Fred or Clive, like anyone else's but he's coming to terms with some inner trauma situation. Not on my premises you don't, I wanted to shout but didn't.

You may be asking yourself why I let a thin, dirty and gloomy male rent my pretty room instead of a plump, clean and cheerful female. I do not know the answer to that. All I know is that Judas was on the doorstep at 6.30 am on the morning the ad came out and lying on the bed with his shoes off saying 'I'll take it' while I was still trying to slam the front door in his face.

He is a writer. 'What do you write?' I asked by way of gaining time before I told him he wasn't going to write it here and he said I'm having a stab at thrillers and I said how's it going and he said it's killing me. Well, he's got the hang of the terminology, anyway. We'll just have to see how it goes and at least it's bringing me in a bit of loot while I brood.

Being a landperson is going to be my job for the time being. Even Annie's Attic is too frail a place to let the baby have his head in any more so I've resigned myself to not climbing the executive ladder and storming the corridors of power until he's in school. I have to watch him every minute at the moment, otherwise he simply charges at the nearest object and knocks it down. The rooms downstairs look very odd. Nothing but bare surfaces, everything else is stuck several feet above ground as if we were waiting for the Thames to flood. I am determined to save at least half my dishes and a few favourite bric-a-brac from the storm.

Jane has moved round the corner into a squat very nearly as laid-back as yours at Sebastopol Terrace (goodness, how useful American words are). She shares it with an amazing bunch of girl punks whose hair stands up in tufts of glorious technicolour. I mentioned the word 'punk' to Jane and if looks could kill, my ashes would have been scattered on the spot. Not punks, Ma, she sneered, punks went out yonks ago. Well, I said nastily, what is it that looks like a punk, talks like a punk and smells like a punk but isn't a punk when it's at home? A human being, said Jane grandly and swept off. Swept in again sharpish, though, when she got a whiff of food.

Of course, I'm supposed to be this Single Parent Family now, with Josh grumpily renting a neighbour's flat 'while you come to your senses' as he graciously puts it to me and only Ben still with me, if Ben can be said to be *with* anyone or anything. But there's nothing very single about my life yet. Yesterday evening I cooked for six, including all of us (Josh too) and Judas, who happened to be passing by as I served the stew and was invited to participate before he fell in.

Josh looked him over as a potential co-respondent (he does this to every male passer-by) and the light died out of his eyes almost immediately. He then asked Judas what kind of books he wrote and Judas said I'm having a bash at a thriller and Josh said how's it going and Judas said it's murder. How long can he keep up this literary chat?

My own dear Mother is still puzzling as to how my new lifestyle has managed to hit depths unplumbed by my old lifestyle. If she weren't so loyal ('friends tell me my worst fault is loyalty, Martha') she'd write to Mrs Thatcher about me or shop me to the *Sun* as a Moscow agent hired to undermine All We Hold Dear.

On her first visit after I got back from your place she went on so much about the Loneliness of the Long-Distance Josh that she brought tears to her eyes. Mother, I said, you're talking about a tubby high-up civil servant in a cushy lifetime's job who is free to follow wherever his heart leads, not some neglected kid the NSPCC has got its eyes on but she would not be consoled.

She does not reproach me directly any more, partly because she has seen the dangerous glint in my eyeballs and partly because she realises that her daughter must be coaxed towards mental health by caring people like herself but she still goes on a lot about the frightful havoc being wrought in Jane, Ben and the baby. One good thing, though. She has stopped saying 'poor little thing' every time she passes him. The last time she said it, he quite rightly charged her, knocked a loose leg off her chair and got her in a rugby tackle on the floor.

Yours, cheering from the sidelines.

Martha

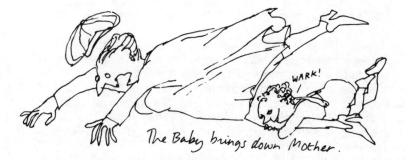

The Baby brings down Mother.

Dear Mary

I cannot quite understand why you and Mo are so churned up about the advent of cable TV. You haven't got electricity, a telephone or even a crystal set. Indeed, so far as I am aware, no cables of any kind connect you to the outside world. The two of you float as in outer space, unpolluted by a single invention of the twentieth century — the *Mary Rose* is probably equipped with more technology than Numero Uno Sebastopol Terrace — so why the sudden desire to team up with Mrs Whitehouse in her banning fits? Besides, you won't get anywhere with her. One foot in her door and she'll ban you both on sight. Specially Mo, with her shaved head and her ears that look like Mr Spock's. Beam that one out, Scottie, for a start.

At the moment I'm looking after two parrots for a neighbour who's evidently heard I run a lodging house. They sit gloomily beside each other on their perches and spend most of their time pecking viciously at each other, squawking loudly and scattering seed. Just like married folk. As a single parent myself, I've rather given up rows. When I hit Josh now, I'm no longer in screaming hysterics like I used to be. I hit him quite slowly and purposefully, like you hit a machine that's broken down and the hit is anyway more like a hard pat.

He's always here, you see, and it drives me up the wall. Extraordinary that I had to leave him in order to see him — he's here at least three afternoons a week these days, yet when we were living together he was so often late home that I almost forgot what he looked like. He spends most of his time wandering about the house peering at things like an auctioneer, with me behind him saying 'half of that Goblin Teasmaid is mine'.

I'm certain he's having an affair with Irene. She's always calling in nowadays, probably after a quickie at Josh's love nest. She says she's not one of those people who lose touch with the wife when a couple is divorcing but since we were never in touch, all I can say is plus ça change. That woman has an air of sanity about her that is not at all attractive, not to mention an air of Arpège, which is. Still, as Mother used to say so wisely, you can't hide a bad smell under a bushel.

Having shot off to a squat, Jane has boomeranged back, too. I'm getting her room ready for a second lodger and she's taking it very badly. Look, I said, they cut the umbilical cord some twenty-one summers ago, my darling, and your womb is now for went. I mean rent. She keeps sitting in there holding an old teddy, looking as pathetic as the Little Match Girl. The only time she disappears is when Mother comes in and says poor thing, there's always room for you with Granny.

Am I being intolerably cruel or frightfully sensible? I've always found the two virtually indistinguishable. My Number One lodger, Judas, has been out a lot lately, which is nice. I know where he goes, too. I was standing opposite our local bookshop and I saw him just inside the window, looking craftier than usual. He takes a quick shufti round, sticks something in the window display and scarpers. And when I go over, I see it's a copy of his own book, *The Gut-Busters*. Charming. So I suppose that's what he's doing at every bookshop in town.

Do you think crime writers are entirely normal? I can hear him creeping about upstairs in his room in a very sinister way. Last time I said how's the book going he bared his teeth at me and said who wants to know? I don't think I'll ask him again. Something might snap.

Must dash — there's a terrible noise upstairs.

Yes, just as I feared. The cat had discovered the parrots. She was standing there gargling at them, with saliva dribbling all down her mouth, while the parrots screamed Pretty Polly at her over and over again. I shall have to get the baby to knock her down, she's getting quite out of hand. I wake up in the middle of the night thinking Judas is torturing someone to death and it's the cat in the garden chewing her way through another cat.

The vet's given me female sex hormone pills for her, says they should calm her down. I put one in Studs' tea but it seemed to have little effect. Did I tell you Studs had reappeared? The doorbell rings and he lifts his beer belly in and stands there with his arms open saying whaddya know, poor little Martha, you're all on your owny-oh now, why dincha call?

I said Studs, honey, it just slipped mah little ole mind but I should have said on your bike. Before I could rinse the suds off my hands he had me locked in a bear hug or, rather, a beer hug. Me and the belly wrestled for a while and I won, but, unfortunately, while I was winning, Josh leapt into the room like the SAS, shouted Stand aside, Martha, and laid into Studs with his brolly. It was all quite ludicrous, them galumphing about banging into things, Josh bawling get out of my house and me screeching get out of *my* house. Eventually, they stood still and said which one of us do you want to leave and I said both of you, now, so they did. It took me half-an-hour to clear up the mess while they stood outside getting more and more friendly and then sauntering off up the pub, with Studs' arm draped across Josh's shoulders. They'll have to stop meeting like this.

Yours, out for the count,

Martha

Dear Mary

I am about to commit to paper some harrowing details of my private life so please, friend of my bust, do not show this letter to Mo. She will only jeer. You, on the other hand, will not *only* jeer and what more can one ask of a friend in this vale of jeers?

The problem is this new hat I'm wearing, the one labelled Single Parent. Sociologists, politicians, Inland Revenue persons, bishops, journalists and other white-collar riff-raff are programmed to pick up only the word Parent whereas I, who must live the label, can hear reverberating in my eardrums only the word Single. Which is my roundabout way of shouting help, what do I do about sex? The above-mentioned riff-raff do not address themselves to this problem, though I once met a man on Hackney Council who arranged wife-swapping parties. Unfortunately, I don't have a wife to swap.

I can cope without sex perfectly well, naturally. What is it, after all? At best a four-star meal, at worst a rotten oyster. Nevertheless, I do not wish to spend the second half of my fourscore years and ten merely coping. I get these wash-day images of sleeves rolled up and cross-over pinnies and stiff upper lips when it was not upper lips I had in mind.

Sure, sure, said Judas, skulking in the kitchen. You wanna live life to the hilt, right? Well, an inch or two up the blade let's say, I said, averting my eyes from the bread knife waving about in his hand. I do not completely trust that man, he has criminal ears. At the moment I'm taking rather a lot of vitamin pills to compensate but I find even large doses of A, C and the B Complex are not an entirely satisfactory substitute for S, E and the X Complex.

I am not, though I say it myself, absolutely at a loss for co-operative partners. There is Josh for instance. There is always Josh for instance. His views on the subject are straightforward — whom God has joined together, let no man put asunder. Women may; even me, Martha, can have a bash, just let no *man*. So Josh continues to regard himself as the only legitimate outlet for my earthier desires.

The odd part is that when we were living together as man and wife under the same sheets, he considered my sexual needs as a mere rivulet, a babbling brook whose ebbs and flows were well within his control. But the moment we separated, those same needs swelled in his mind to horrific proportions, an immense tidal wave that constantly threatened to spill over and engulf any male passerby, to be held at bay only by his heroic presence, his devotion to duty, his courageous finger in the cracking dyke if you'll excuse the expression.

I will admit here and now that on exactly five occasions I have 'gone the whole hog' with Josh (as we doctors say) but the ensuing complications were too much. The way Josh sees it, one glimpse of him in bed automatically quells the storm while, at the same time, solving every one of my marital problems. He lies down a lover and arises a born-again husband, rejoicing to the Lord that his days at the laundrette and the fast-food emporium are over and complaining about his shirts. The change in him is dramatic, immediate and, given half a chance, permanent. This forces me to stage the whole Dear John charade all over again, like some fading actress who keeps arranging comebacks. Listen, darling, they're playing our song, I have to say. Fare thee well for I must leave thee do not let the parting grieve thee etc, etc.

It's awful, Mary. He puts on his Patience On a Monument expression and I can hear him thinking oh no, not the harp on the willow tree *again*. Each time, I'm cast in the eternal role of the Wicked Wife who wilfully refuses to forgive and forget and get on with washing his socks. The mental and physical energy I have to expend just heaving his head off the pillow leaves me limp for the rest of the day.

Besides, this is a crowded lodging house. Last time my weakness overcame me we emerged from the bedroom to find Judas at the bottom of the stairs saying who's been murdered I heard them scream? And Ben was loping about saying what were you *doing* in there and the baby was gathering its strength to knock Josh down. V. embarrassing it was for all concerned.

So far, I haven't succumbed to Studs as an alternative, though I must say that his cheerful willingness to strip off at any time of the day and take on all comers, irrespective of looks, size, age, sex or even species, is very winning. It would not make the slightest difference to him if he bounced into bed with me, Mother, the parrots or Josh. Studs is your true Homo Omniverus and why is that a drawback? I do not know, but suspect there is something twisted in me. If the man said he loved me, I wouldn't give him house room, so it isn't that.

Sometimes I feel like Tigger, remember Tigger? Tiggers don't want Josh and they don't want Studs but what *do* they want? Perhaps a spot of Roo's medicine, sexually speaking, and where in the world do you get hold of that? There's an amazingly good-looking man repairing the road outside at the moment, a sort of cross between Robert Redford and Arnold Schwarzenegger with the merest touch of the David Owens around the steely eyes. Every time I see him, I am shaken to the marrow of my bones. Is this true lust or simply his pneumatic drill?

Yours, throbbing with something,

Martha

Dear Mary

Judas is sulking about the place and when Judas sulks, *everybody* sulks. His book isn't going well — it's dying on him, he says — and he's put out because he's glimpsed the woolly mite and it isn't Raquel Welch. I'm not in the business of providing you with girlfriends I said, and he said no, but did I have to rent my upstairs front to a brillo pad on legs? If you can call those two cloth protuberances legs, he added kindly. I thought Judas was a disaster until she arrived but she's a disaster's disaster. It's been two weeks now and I still don't know her name, leaving aside the matter of her gender. I phoned Mother but all she had to contribute was that the friend from Spain whose son's fiancée's brother's granny I have living overhead is a good Christian woman. Never mind her, I moaned. What's the name of the lodger you've burdened me with? I don't know, said Mother snappily, go and ask her. But I can't can I? What kind of a twit will I look, after a fortnight, saying by the way, lovey, what's your name. Oh dear, said Mother, I think it's Nicholas, or is it Nicola? You mean you don't know the *sex*, I shrieked. Well no, said Mother, but what does that matter, if you do. On my knees by now, I begged her to phone her friend. Mother said I can't, she's in Spain again.

There's nothing for it but to break my iron rule, sneak into her room and search for clues so I can say, casually, next time I see her, how's every little thing Angela. Or Nigel, depending. Josh is a great comfort in this time of trial. He says this would not have happened if we lived together and I said too true, Josho, nothing ever happened when we lived together, which led to cross words. We've been having cross words all week, on account of I got a letter from Tom asking could he stay for a couple of nights. I didn't move out, Josh squawked, so that your first husband could move in. He's not moving in, I said, it's just two nights. That's what they all say, said Josh. You realise what you're doing, Martha, you're husband-swapping. It's time Jane and Ben saw their father again, I said briskly. They won't go down to Mousehole, they don't like his girlfriend. Is he bringing her, asked Josh, brightening considerably. Over my dead body, I said. Oho, aha, you see he chortled and I said what about Irene and get knotted and other witticisms.

None of this improves my temper and Judas is no fit companion, a crime-writer is not fun to live with, almost worse than marriage. When I tell him something, he always interrupts me, coming on like Knacker of the Yard. Guess what happened to me this morning, I say brightly. I jumped on a bus outside the Plaza and inside . . . What bus? says Judas. What do you mean, what bus? I say. *A* bus. There is no bus that passes the Plaza, he says triumphantly. Okay, okay, it was some kind of Red Arrow. The 246? asks Judas. *I* don't know, I say, what on earth does it matter. It matters to *me*, he says smugly, it's my business to get these details right. How would you like it, Martha, reading a murder story and the killer makes his escape on a non-existent bus? I wouldn't give a hoot, I say, I wouldn't even notice. That depressed him. What's the use, my doing all this research, if my readers don't notice? Well, don't do it, I told him cheerfully. Just have this hideous nameless faceless beast lurking about in the bushes somewhere, that'll do me. I don't care what bus he catches to do his fell deeds. Writers are weird. I expect he's got an Arts Council grant so's he can rush about London checking on the 503 from Fulham.

The woolly mite isn't easy, either. I said to it the other day, would you like a tomato salad tonight and it said I'm game, I'll try anything once. I mean, tomato salad. Not ivy stew or pickled ants or snake sauté. The mystery deepens. Where has it been living, what has it been eating? Ben thinks it's been on an oilrig stuck out in the North Atlantic, as a diver. They don't make wet suits in Extra-Large, I said, and besides, it would float. Actually, I believe it's a woman, it's got a woman's voice. They can do that with hormones these days, Studs says, that's part of their trial, passing as a woman before they have the op. But I'm not bothered really. Someone, somewhere, must be thinking of writing her a letter soon and then I'll know. Or the cheque from the Trust will reveal all, at the end of the month. Judas says the suspense is killing him. Suits me.

Oh, I almost forgot. Thanks for the apples your friend delivered, it's nice of you to worry about our vitamin intake, here in The Smoke. It's been a good year for apples. A very, very, very, very good year. Mother brought me some apples last week, too, eight pounds of them. I've made apple snow, apple fool, apple pie, apple crumble, baked apples, apple turnovers, apple chutney and apple juice. Any further suggestions for recipes gratefully received before we all go down with terminal apple blight.

I was also sorry to hear that Mrs Thatcher's cuts are affecting you and Mo. It's obvious to me that we're spending so much on the rehabilitation of the Falkland Islands that next year they'll have to send their gunboats in to rescue us. I hear they've already kitted up the penguins with brandy flasks, so they can succour victims buried under bills.

But I don't quite see how Mrs T. can slash at your lifestyle. I'd have thought you were so cut back already there was nothing left to snip. Do you fear a means test for customers of Oxfam or have you suddenly noticed that the prices of everything you shoplift have doubled?

Yours, falling off a lorry,

Martha

Nameless beast in the bushes.

Dear Mary

I have never been so insulted in my life as I was this morning by my own husband on his-and-my doorstep. I got up early to clean this and that before Tom arrived from Mousehole and there came a knock on the door. In my dressing gown, cigarette dangling, I peered out, thinking it was the milkman come for his pay-off or possibly the dustmen rehearsing a spot of intimidation, and there was Josh on the steps. Pinstriped Burberry draped elegantly over shoulders. Umbrella under arm. Hanky in pocket. The Immaculate Deception. Compared to him, I was not a pretty sight.

Morning, morning, said Josh with hideous brightness. Glumph, I said back, my tongue not having woken yet. Ah, said Josh, Martha. Under this hair it is I, I said. Tom coming today? he said, smiling like a crocodile. It is on the cards, I said. Yes well, well yes, said Josh. I felt I must pass by and warn you, Martha. For your own good, because I am your husband and therefore have your welfare at heart. Then he lifted his brolly, pointed it at my cardiac regions and said, like a man announcing the end of the world, Remember Herpes, Martha.

Herpes who? I said. In my dazed state I thought he was referring to some forgotten mutual friend who had passed on and required my presence at his formal interment. Herpes, said Josh, you know, Martha. The incurable sexual disease. Then he launched into several thousand colourful details of Herpes symptoms. Josh, I said I haven't had breakfast yet and fascinating though I find this recitation from Black's Medical Dictionary, could you put it off to some more appropriate time? As a Single Parent, I am not currently into sexual diseases. My lifestyle is not conducive to them. Then I'm just in time, said Josh.

Upon which he leaned forward and hissed 'Tom' at me. The gist of what followed was that Tom, my ex-husband, was in Josh's eyes Mr Promiscuity himself, therefore in the grip of terminal Herpes, therefore about to have his wicked way with me. I would then pass on the dread disease, via towels, to Jane, Ben, the baby, the cat and the parrots and we would all spend the rest of our lives scratching ourselves in lonely isolation, unable to go out due to looking too hideously leprous for human consumption.

Having delivered this apocalyptic message, he waved his umbrella, said must be off now, awfully late, and leapt away down the pavement in an access of high spirits, leaving me stunned with outrage. How dared he, Mary? The assumption! I fell back into the kitchen quivering all over.

I was still twitching slightly two hours later when Tom arrived. The Oldest Hippie in the World erupted through the front door clutching several noxious canvas bags in the last stages of decay and gripped me in his arms. Then he pushed me away to have a good look and said hey, Martha, wonderful, chick. What's so wonderful, I asked, already simpering. And Tom said sweetie, you look so *young*. A double blow and the clock not yet at noon.

When someone says you look so young you can only be sure of one thing — you look pretty damn old. Okay, you've cheated Nature and bravely hung on to most of your hair and some of your teeth and a small portion of your ankles still look sixteen but on the whole, tragic.

Tom doesn't look so young, I'll say that for him. He still wears his hair to his shoulders but a goodly lot of it has emigrated from his scalp and taken up permanent residence down his back. He also sports many chains and badges and flowered shirts and velvet waistcoats, à la heyday of the Sixties. It's like he went into a time warp when he left me for Mousehole. He clicks his fingers and says groovy a lot and can't wait to stick a joint in his mouth. In the hall, Jane sniffed at the exotic fumes, said wow, Dad's here, and threw herself into his arms, which was nice. Then Ben ambled in, tripping over his long black coat, and bent his totally bald head to kiss his father's tresses, shouldn't that be the other way round? And before I knew it, Tom had stalled the baby in mid-charge and swung it on to his knee, where it sat in an attitude of foolish adoration and it isn't even his.

Tom then waxed tearfully eloquent. You're all wonderful, he said several times. I love you all, you're the greatest. He hugged us over and over, including me, and much as I tried to disassociate myself from this orgy of Sixties sentimentality and put on the proper Eighties frown, my heart melted. Tom could always melt my heart. Just as well, since it was him who froze it in the first place.

At this point, the Woolly Mite strode upon the heap of coiled and grinning human beings, took one look at Tom and joined in, with many a glad cry of Tom you old villain, you old slag, you. Within seconds she was pushing for first place on his knee and Tom was saying Tich you old reprobate, you old scum-bag, and beating her about the back. May I interrupt these touching endearments for a moment, I said, seizing my chance. You know each other, Tom, Tich? Know each other, said Tom. Me and Tich here are mates from way back. Before your time, Martha. We were up in Nova Scotia together, eh Tich? Remember the camp, Tich? Remember Red-Eye Robinson, Four Finger Fagan, King Kowalski? Then they commenced to sway together in the most maudlin way. I left them to it. I can't bear to see strong men cry.

Yours, out in the cold,

Martha

Tom.

Dear Mary

Absolutely. I agree one hundred and fifty per cent with every word in your last letter and for us that must be some kind of record. Like you I went up in smoke when I heard about the Greenham Common women being sent to prison. I was so furious my eyes went all bloodshot and I howled out loud. Tom said I looked like the Hound of the Baskervilles and I dare say I did. I was *luminous* with outrage. If you'd dumped that judge at my paws I'd have scrunched him to pieces in my fangs and buried the bones.

The whole thing is a farce or would be, if it weren't literally dead serious. They invoke a law of the 1300s, when people had nothing but bows and arrows, to put away women in 1982 who're protesting about the kind of weapons that could blow us all to Kingdom Come. Then they drone on about breaches of the peace when they've got enough nukes up their jumpers to breach the peace of the entire planet a hundred times over. And the place where it happens is called Greenham Common. Common to whom, I'd like to know. Not British peace women, that's for sure. Only the American military with their lethal toys are allowed to play there. Some of those men are Justices of the Peace — what justice? What peace? As you said, it make you feel that words have lost all meaning.

On top of that the IBA tries to keep the Truth Game film off our television screen, just as the BBC did with The War Game. When they find they can't get away with that they say that the film has got to be 'balanced' by another film, presumably telling us that war is fun. Who put the boot into the IBA, I wonder? No, I don't wonder, it's crystal clear. And if this is the extent of our precious freedom we're already behind bars, whether we can see them or not. Sometimes I think I wouldn't mind so much if it was only Them who risked getting nuked but it isn't, it's us. I can see it all. They'll come out of their cosy bunkers and look around at our fried corpses and say fancy that, those disarmers were right after all. Dead right.

I'm still shook up, the whole crazed business has done my

temper no good at all. This morning Ben decided it was time he learned to drive, pinched the car keys from my handbag, got into the car and drove it straight into two metal dustbins. When I head the bang, my nerves went on final alert. Then he comes in, announces that both headlights are smashed and says 'Sorry, Mum' in an extremely unsorry way. You don't *sound* sorry, I shout. It's no good saying sorry unless you *sound* sorry. So he says 'Sorry, Mum' again in a sorry voice and I shout what's the good of saying sorry, you can't buy new headlights with sorry and Ben clumps off.

One thing about Ben, though, he isn't a sulker. He clumped in again five minutes later, stood looking at me while I cut up carrots (viciously), cleared his throat, said, 'Mum, what is your opinion about Andropov?' and waited politely, eyebrows raised. I was touched. After all, no one else in the world wants to hear my opinion of Andropov and, besides, one should keep one's children informed on current affairs. I'm glad you asked me that, Ben, I said. In my opinion, Andropov is quite likely to be umm. Or to put it another way, he could well be er. On the other hand, some people maintain that he's er-um. Oh Ben I don't know about Andropov, what do you think? Nothing, said Ben. End of current affairs lesson.

I told Tom about Ben's car accident, well Ben's his son. The stupid boy has muffed up the tiddley-pushes and I can't get the thingummy going, I said, but Tom was no use. He just shrugged his hippie shoulders and said my language was too technical for him. Honestly, how we ever managed to have two children together I'll never know. I suppose we just muffed up the tiddley-pushes and, lo, the thingummy got going. At least he's put me straight on the Woolly Mite. They met in this lumber camp in wildest Canada but my lodger isn't the smallest logger in the West because he's a she after all and was there cooking the chow. No wonder she didn't know a tomato salad when she saw it, all they ever ate in the camp was beans and sour-dough. Tom calls her Tich but her real name is Pauline and she's terribly posh, some sort of rogue Duke's daughter who kicked over the traces like those nineteenth-century Victorian women who trekked about the world quelling the natives with their lorgnettes.

That was all right. What wasn't was her room. I snuck into it while she was cooking up a baked bean storm in the kitchen with her old cobber Tom. My pretty pink carpet was entirely covered with motorbike pieces wall to wall. She must have smuggled them up bit by bit while my back was turned. And I was just sneaking out again to do my indignant landlady act when I heard a snuffly noise. It came from under the bed so I looked and there, amongst the fluff, was a large animated rug with two rug attachments. The Woolly Mite had smuggled up a doggy, too, and the doggy had puppies.

Right, I said to myself, she'll have to go. This is a room, not a motorbike repair yard or a kennel for canines. But, Martha, you couldn't chuck a mother and her babies out on the street, could you? Couldn't I just. Watch me. Martha. Unfortunately, the wretched dog put out a long pink tongue and licked the hand that was trying to evict her so I told her the House Rules — no pets and no radios after midnight — and left.

Yours, in low dudgeon,

Martha

A Flashback to Tom's paella.

Dear Mary

I am in a most peculiar situation. Both my husbands are fighting over me as if I were a bone. (I wish I *were* a bone, what I actually am is a lump of lard, a nasty high-cholesterol diet for two gents going on middle-aged.) No, I must be accurate. The real set-up is that they are the dogs and I am the manger — I don't believe either of them really wants me, they just don't want the other to have me. Rotten for the old self-esteem, being a manger, but horribly apt. A messy sort of heap for the top dog to sleep on.

Everything's friendly enough on the surface. They both manage the odd bevvy in the pub together without war breaking out, but if I go with them the white flag begins to look alarmingly like a red rag. It is all quite absurd and the worst of it is that their courting techniques invariably clash and give me one of my headaches. The other evening, for instance, Tom had a sudden fit of the Old Dependables and insisted I lie on the sofa with my feet up while he cooked one of his curries especially for me.

It was an unnerving experience, lying there acting relaxed while I watched my kitchen explode. By the time Tom had got it together, everything else had come apart. Curried cooker, curried floor, curried ceiling. Even the cat was having hot flushes and dropping from its perch like a winged pheasant.

I was reminded of a truly dreadful event that took place when Tom and I were camping in Spain. While he was making a vast paella out of every sort of meat and poultry and seafood, I wandered off along some cliffs and found a nest of baby birds that had obviously been deserted by their mamma. It broke my heart to see them there with their little yellow beaks hopelessly agape and I pointed them out to Tom and tried to feed them with passing flies.

Over the paella, which was quite delicious, I gloomed on to him about their inevitable demise. And when I went back after the meal, no chicks. The nest was bare. A frightful suspicion hit me. Tom, I said, the chicks have vanished and Tom said che sarà sarà and looked transparently innocent so I knew he was guilty. The monster had dumped them in the paella. He never admitted it, mind you, just went on about the virtues of instant over slow death and the hypocrisy of wimps like me. From then on I kept a very beady eye on Jane and Ben, chicks themselves at the time and clearly at risk.

Anyway, back at the ranch the curry was nearing its apogee and Tom was sitting opposite me with an expression on his mug that said oh foolish Martha, see what you've been missing, when the doorbell rang. Upon the mat stood Josh. He entered with great flourishes of brolly and briefcase and said Martha, you're coming out to dinner. You need a treat and a treat you shall have. I've booked a table at the Connaught so put on your prettiest frock and we'll paint the town. Then he smiled like a head waiter and waited for me to fall upon his chest.

To make things worse Ben, Jane, and the baby were all there, mouths ajar, on tenterhooks to see which of their fathers I would choose. The anguish of it! Especially as I'd never been to the Connaught and Tom's curries were deeply familiar, not to mention ingrained.

But children's feelings are not to be trifled with. At enormous self-sacrifice I settled for the eat-up-think-of-the-Chinese excuse, which pleased nobody, since Tom was offended at hearing his precious curry described as something that shouldn't be wasted and Josh was offended that I didn't behave like a grateful girl on her first date.

Things got so fraught that in the end I crept out and went over the road to Lorna's where she kindly fed me one of her vegan dishes, Sawdust a la Reine with Latex Vinaigrette. Meanwhile, Josh and Tom ate the curry with gusto and washed it down with a great deal of wine. When I got back, Josh was saying to Tom in a rather slurred voice: 'It's about time you got Martha out of your cistern.' I hope he meant system. Otherwise, he must regard me as some form of pernicious deposit, like the grey flakes that gather at the bottom of kettles, and he and Tom need descaling. Of me.

To change the subject, I meant to tell you that if you had a television, you'd approve of Channel 4. There are a lot of women on it. Well, there are a lot more men, of course, but we must give thanks for small mercies. One documentary programme a week is entirely composed of women. The reviewers keep calling it 'an all-woman team.' They do not call other programmes 'all-man'. For 'all-man', read 'all human beings'. Women, as S. de Beauvoir said so long ago, are still The Other, as in A Bit of The Other.

The not-Channel 4 prog that would have given you the terminal sweats was an all-woman yakarama called The C(h) at Show. Mary. Mary? You can't pass out yet, dear, that's only the title. Well, haven't I always said the Women's Movement was altogether too high-minded about our sex? Out there in the real world, there are still enough feather-headed females to stuff a duvet factory.

Shriek, cackle, screech they went, wittering endlessly on about frocks and sex and boys and boys' naughty bits, tee hee, pardon me, oo you are a card. A spectacle that would have had you booked into the nearest sex-change clinic before they could say Street-Porter — she's the one who does for women what Lenny Henry does for blacks. Such fun, said the gu'er press. Fun? Even my leg-warmers froze over. Tom and Josh were thrilled. every one of their prejudices was confirmed without them having to lift a finger.

Yours,

Martha

Dear Mary

Sticks and stones may break my bones but words will never hurt me is one of the dafter sayings I ever heard said. In my fragile state, a feather would lay me flat and your few cruel words have already brought me out in a rash, so kindly restrain yourself on both counts or I'll come round and shout 'Sun reader' through your letter-box. I am *not* behaving like some Mills and Boon hussy, I am *not* man-crazy and don't tell me to grow up when I'm already spending a small fortune covering the grey bits with Autumn Sludge Home Tint. (Once you start that, how do you ever come out of the closet? You'd have to emigrate until you're one colour again.) I have noticed that whenever people tell other people to grow up, they mean the other people are having altogether too good a time and should stop it and be miserable, like them. What incentive is that? The obnoxious Peter Pan had a lot more fun than Mrs Darling, even though he was a lost boy of restricted growth.

The fact is, you won't think I've achieved emotional maturity until I've given up men entirely and settled down with a good woman, the way magistrates hope the criminal classes will. And in my case that's about as likely to happen as multi-lateral disarmament. Of course, you never much liked Josh or Tom, did you? Come to that, I never much liked them either but I quite loved them and there's no use throwing everything out with the bathwater. We must make do with what we have and, apart from them, my heart is fancy-free. I don't reckon on moving in with the Woolly Mite and, anyway, she's already engaged to her motorbike. Now *there's* a happy couple.

You say it's society that has conditioned me to love men and shamed me out of loving women and, thinking about it, I expect you're right. But had you thought that without this brainwashing the species would have died out long ago? I mean, women are so obviously more attractive than men in every way that unless there was a lot of shoving in men's direction, who but their mothers would choose them?

If I had to make a list of Josh's natural assets I could do it on the back of a small box of matches so he'd *need* conditioning to work in his favour wouldn't he, poor lamb? Actually, I believe it all boils down to the fact of motherhood. The difference between us is that I have maternal feelings for men and you don't. Perhaps women loving men is our form of incest, displaced. We really fancy our sons, but that's not allowed so we make out with other women's sons. Besides, sons have protective colouration, like dirty necks and nails and other filthy habits to keep them undefiled by lust-crazed mums.

Talking about men, Lorna's husband has left her. You remember my neighbour Lorna, the mortician technician? I was amazed when she told me. He was such a mild man, wouldn't say boo to his goose and yet he upped and left one weekend without even leaving her a Dear Lorna letter and hasn't been seen since. She was always outspoken, was Lorna, never put up with any bossing from her old man and she's paid the price now. Not that it's been high. She didn't notice he'd gone for two days and then only because the leftovers didn't get eaten.

I'm not surprised. Lorna is quite heroically bad at cooking. Her meals are triumphs of Cuisine Minceur — you'd rather starve than eat them. Well, in these days of obsessive Foodies you have to admire her detachment, the only effort she ever puts into her various dishes is to burn them. She always referred to her husband as 'that boring old fart' and as I said to her, no wonder. Boring he may be, Lorna, but the rest is down to beans. Cut them out and you've got a perfectly normal man.

She's got Queenie in with her now, that's Lorna's mum the music-hall star, but it's driving Lorna batty. Queenie is even more unreconstructed than your friend Martha — at seventy-odd she's still besotted about men. She totters out of a morning to buy her fags, face weighed down with a ton of make-up (Cupid never had lips like our Queenie) and drives all the local octogenarians wild with desire. There are always gentlemen callers on her doorstep waiting to escort her to the pub and one of them regularly calls with a huge bunch of parsley which he presents to her as if she were Nellie Melba making her last farewells.

How does Queenie do it? — I'll tell you how. She ladles out flattery with a trowel and if that doesn't work, she slings on three more trowelfuls and the old boys go under, smiling. I heard her at it with Josh, who considers himself a very cool customer. He managed his ironic you-can't-kid-me expression while she told him he was the finest figure of a man she'd seen since Lorna's Dad passed away, God rest his soul, but when she added that he beat Mr Rudolf Valentino and that lovely Mr Cooper into a cocked hat, his face went all wobbly with suppressed glee and he skipped up the road carrying both Queenie's giant bags of shopping and whistling 'I Enjoy Being A Girl'. Lorna disapproves, I disapprove, you'd disapprove. Meanwhile whatever Queenie wants, Queenie gets.

Yours, with a face like a liberated lemon,

Martha

13 December

Dear Mary

I've been seeing rather a lot of one of our Senior Citizens lately. Give us the lend of an egg dearie, said Queenie, popping her henna'd coiffure round the door last Tuesday breakfast. She stayed, on and off, till Friday dinner.

Look at me, skin and bone, only fit for the knacker's yard, pitiful eh? she said and smacked her hips, causing them to tremble for several seconds. In Queenie's view, her daughter has got some plot afoot to starve her out. All our Lorna cooks is that foreign muck, she complains. It's not foreign, Queenie, I explained, it's vegetarian. She took no notice. She seems to think there's a Third World country somewhere called Vegetaria where the natives live on turnip rinds and smelly cheese.

Suppose there was, I said. Imagine how nice it would be — all those little lambs and piglets and chickie-poos bouncing about in the fields, happily baaing and oinking and cheeping in glorious freedom. Wouldn't that warm your cockles? Not mine, said Queenie. What and leave us OAPs without a steak to our names? Force poor old grannies like me who need our vitamins to limp about with our bones showing? I tell you, if it was me, those baa-lambs would soon change their tune. I'd be after them with a toasting fork before you could say chop.

Queenie is a very unregenerate old phoenix, I've come to see. Those rheumy eyes under the layers of mascara are focused on nothing but her own survival, not unlike my own dear Mother, though being middle-class, Ma manages to put it in ways that make you feel guilty.

You can't only think about yourself in this world, Queenie, I said in my sanctimonious voice. Try me, said Queenie, and her Cupid's bow went all thin. But next minute she was saying she didn't, anyway. I've spent quite a lot of my time thinking about you, gel, as it happens, she said. Oh? I said, stuffing a toffee in her mouth to keep it shut, but she wouldn't have it. Me teeth, she said, tapping them, they won't take the toffees. They'd be out and dancing on the table in a trice. Whereupon she ate three bananas and began a week-long lecture on my marital state.

It turns out that in Queenie's book, me leaving Josh is like someone finding the pot of gold at the end of the rainbow and wilfully refusing to dig it up. That man, she says, is a treasure. That man has a brain like your Leonardo da Vincent. He does, Martha. You give him a question, his mind closes on it like a steel trap. In two seconds flat, he's got the answer, just like in that Blankety Blank they do on television. I don't know how he does it. How does he know it all, Martha? Well, he does, I said, *my* Cupid's bow thin this time. Josh knows it all, Queenie. You're right, she said, it's a wonder. Of course, he's a reader isn't he? He gets it from the reading. And men like your hubby, they move in Circles, do you get my meaning? Yes, I said, I agree. I'll give you a for instance, said Queenie, your hubby is on intimate terms with Lords. Did you know that, Martha? No, I said. Well, there you are then.

And another thing, Martha, your Josh is a marvel on how we got here. Got where? I asked. Here, she said, on this earth. We all come from mud, did you know *that*? I've often thought so, Queenie, I said, Josh has often made me think so. Wonderful, isn't it? said Queenie. Wonderful, I said.

Poor Queenie. Just like my Mother, she can't figure out why I'm not blissfully happy with Josh and to tell you the truth, Mary, their combined harangues have left me feeling a bit rocky. What they're really saying is that I don't know how awful men can be and if I want to be with a man at all, I should count my blessings it's Josh. Which is not unlike what you're saying, except you leave out Josh and substitute a woman, which does me no good.

Queenie puts it like this: you shouldn't run yourself down, Martha. You're a very nice type of a girl and a man like your hubby hasn't got no cause to feel ashamed of you, just because you don't know as much as him about Art and Music and that. *And* mud, I reminded her. *And* mud, she said. Think of the kiddies, they need their Dad, even if you don't. That rocked me even more. Maybe old Queenie is right and I hadn't thought of the kiddies. Perhaps at seventeen, what Ben needs is a father (the baby is too busy charging at people's legs to care).

Tell the truth, Ben, I said, when he dropped in on Thursday to ask for money, do you think me and Josh should get together again? You and who? he said. Well, I tried not to take too much notice of that, seeing as how Josh isn't his real father anyway. So I started on Jane who has Tom as a father, like Ben.

What would you say if me and Tom got together again,

Jane? I asked. You and who? she said. I couldn't believe it. In total confusion, I turned to the baby. What about me and your Dad? I said, but he only dribbled. I can't help feeling that my marriage counsellors are of very low quality and lack all sympathetic training. Which means that it's up to me, in the end.

Josh came just in time for dinner yesterday. What would you say, Josh, I said, if me and Tom got together again? I'd kill him, said Josh. D'you know, Mary, I think Queenie is right. That man's brain is a marvel. Leonardo da Vincent has got nothing on him.

Yours, with roses in her cheeks,

Martha

She would not show her bus pass.

Dear Mary

We saw you on telly, we saw you on telly! There you were, you and Mo, large as life and twice as peaceful, pinning dear little babies' leggings on the wire at Greenham Common and singing fit to bust. My heart leapt up, Josh's leapt down. He flipped his lid. Look at your friends, he shouted, index finger quivering at the box like Lord Kitchener recruiting for World War Three. Those two wouldn't know a human infant from a Sainsbury's Christmas cracker until they pulled it and no funny hats fell out. Where did they find those woolly things? Stole them from the local Oxfam depot, I shouldn't wonder. Women like Mo and Mary, he yelled, make me see red. A colour easily seen in your case, I said. Under the bed, in the TUC, on the left of the Tory Party . . .

But he only blew another fuse. Call themselves a peace demonstration, he snarled, when they won't let men in? All that twaddle about mankind being on the brink, yet these females exclude us. It's men at the top of the CND and the Pentagon and the Kremlin, we're the ones with power, how dare women keep us out? Pretending we'd cause violence, huh. Personally, I'd shoot them all, bang bang bang.

Well, Mary, I couldn't disentangle that lot. I tried but I couldn't. Think about what you've just said, Josh, I said. Mankind, men, power, shoot. Doesn't that give you some message? Can't you understand that's what the women mean? I don't have to understand anything, he said sulkily, unless they let me in. But Josh, I argued, you wouldn't have gone to Greenham Common if they'd *paid* you, not if they'd booked you into a first-class suite at the Newbury Hilton. That's not the point, he said.

Awful, really. Put me right off him again. There I was thinking we might just get together again at Christmas and he comes on like Ronald Reagan in wolf's clothing. I was aghast. This man who mongs war is the father of my child. I reckon they should do some tests on expectant dads as well. Oh dear, the doctor might say, I'm afraid we've come across a very nasty X-chromosome here. Tut tut, I have no alternative but to advise an immediate termination. Of the Father, I mean. As we medicos say, *he* may be viable, but while he's around, no one else is. Sign here please and we'll take him out.

Honestly, Mary, what is love all about? Any kind of love. Mother phoned up on Tuesday, her old friend Jeannie had just died. Ma was very fond of her, supposedly, but what does she say? Martha, it was for the best. You see, Jeannie wasn't attuned to age, she hadn't come to terms with Senior Citizenry, she was secretive about The Pension, she would not show her bus pass. So it was a happy release really, said Ma. Well obviously I didn't comment at the time but I was quite shaken. Next thing we know, *I'll* pass on and Josh will shake his head and say it was for the best, really. Poor Martha, she had two whole days of washing-up ahead and she'd never come to terms with the colour of the kichen walls. A happy release, on the whole. Come to think of it, perhaps Josh would be right.

And then awful Irene popped in, hair sprayed with Wonda-Glu, to sing the praises of her dear old Dad. Wonderful person, she said in a treacly voice, now *there* was a man who cared, a truly loving man. Do you know, Martha, on his wedding night he stood in front of my mother in their Torquay bridal suite and he cleared his throat in that sweet way he had and he said, my dear wife, I am now going to take out my insurance and put it in your name. They don't make men like that any more, Martha.

Good heavens, I thought, with sex education the way it was then, I bet the old boy imagined that was the act that consummated marriage. Please, Mr Pope, I want an annulment. My husband never took out his insurance in the whole of our intimate married life, not once, I swear. In my humble opinion it was a pity Irene's Dad ever lapsed from his high standards and fathered Irene. She only comes here to stand perfectly coiffed beside me, so Josh can compare her with me and see what he is missing by not making her the third Mrs Josh. They'd make the perfect couple. Together, they'd constitute a critical mass and trigger the nuclear holocaust.

And so to Christmas, which is going to be an extremely confusing exercise this year. If I come out of it without succumbing to a lethal identity crisis I'll be lucky. What Christmas proves is not who you are but *whose* you are. Whose wife, whose mother, whose daughter, whose employee, whose friend, whose loved one, if anybody's. (What an odd word 'whose' is, like something you find in a haberdashery department.) We go in for the ritual of gift-giving to make our bondage clear — you're mine and you and you and you but not you and *certainly* not you. It's the Family Mafia in action, obligations are laid on you once a year so you're primed to do someone else's dirty work the rest of the year.

Will Josh eat my turkey on the 25th and prove whose he is? Will Ben and Jane come and show they're mine? Will Judas and the Woolly Mite? All will be revealed shortly but I can only be sure I own the baby and he'll probably spit my turkey out in a grand and definitive exhibition of his essential independence from me.

Yours, in the lull before the storm,

Martha

Dear Mary

Thank you for your New Year card. At first I thought that one of your loved ones had passed away but then I realised the black border symbolised the demise of all hope for 1983. Dead, dead and never called you Mother. I see your point but surely you're jumping the gun a little (unfortunate phrase, that). To put it another way, not a lot of us are leaping with joy at the thought of another year looming, but there is a silver lining, Mary. If you think about it, the nicest thing that can happen to us in 1983 is getting one year older. A positive bonus.

I can't say I actually relish the advancing years but it quite cheers me up to think they have acquired a meaning over and above false teeth, creaking joints and general geriatric disarray. Because all these drawbacks also signify that we are still here upon this earth and *that* signifies the earth is still here to be upon. If you and I get to be octogenarians we will have accomplished something much more important than our own survival. We will have ensured that the planet and its sitting tenants have survived along with us. The Bomb will not have dropped, hallelujah. And at eighty-plus we will have out-lived a lot of nasties: the Board of the Kremlin, Ronnie Reagan and most of the Moral Majority, the Ayatollah and Son of Ayatollah, Mrs T. and a lot of her Dries, Mr Begin and even, with any luck, Cliff Richard.

We'll be old enough to have witnessed the bucket-kicking of all our bêtes noires and too old to know which members of the younger generations bode us illest. We can kick our heels in senile glee and screech We're the queens of the castle and you're a dirty rascal in our little-old-lady falsettos. Can't wait.

My Christmas was on the tacky side. The turkey hadn't quite managed to get itself defrosted, so that it more or less died of a thousand cuts, weeping pale pink blood. The only food that was really cooked was Ben's tiny free-range chicken. The sight of this midget sacrifice aroused an irrational fury in Mother's bosom. I cannot understand why a Christian woman, as she keeps saying she is, should get so cross when her grandchild explains his virtuous objections to eating a turkey that has had no Quality of Life. He's just picky, Martha, she said several times round the edge of her huge drumstick. All these Animal Liberationists are nothing but picky eaters and ought to be smacked.

The other event that caused an upheaval out of all proportion to its genesis was the Dash to Freedom of Ben's mice. No one would have noticed this if he hadn't announced it casually as we began the opening-presents ceremony but, once made public, Mother refused to put foot to ground for the rest of the day. She sat cross-legged and cross on the sofa like a crimplene Buddha — not an easy position to maintain for a woman of her girth — and occasionally toppled over on to the cushions with her eyes closed, something she explained by saying the thought of rampaging mice made her faint and I explained by the rapid emptying of the gin.

The mice were eventually traced to an improvised nest in Ben's laundry and encaged again. They looked distinctly baggy-eyed and out of puff due, I am sure, to Ben having bought them for Christmas a complete mouse gym: ladders, wheels, balls and a sort of spiralling tube within which they were required to heave themselves into yet another rodent penthouse. Ben, I said, the poor creatures are simply exhausted, they have vacated their premises for a little rest. Exercise is good for them said Ben sternly. I pointed out to him that he hadn't done anything more energetic than watch James Bond on telly for the past three weeks but he was not abashed.

Nothing much improved with my New Year's resolution: to tell the truth. I am amply cognisant of the fact that such a project carries with it heavy responsibilities. One cannot just tell the truth; one must examine oneself scrupulously in order to make sure that one has no hidden and inglorious motives for causing the concomitant pain and distress to others. One must also meticulously search for the mote in one's own eye.

This means that by the time the truth comes to be told, the person to whom it is to be told has left on a trip to the Costa Brava or possibly died of old age. But I did manage one truth. Josh got me alone in the paper-strewn sitting room and asked me if I loved him. I thought for a long time and then said yes, Josh, I love you but I don't like you. For reasons best known to himself, this seemed to stimulate him no end and led to an unseemly scuffle around the tree. In Josh's case, at least, truth-telling appears to have unexpected aphrodisiac effects.

We are about to go off to a party given by Josh's ex-wife, a woman called Mimsie. She lived in the depths of the country until a few weeks ago, when she untactfully moved to within four streets of us and clearly made a New Year's Resolution to love her enemies, woe is me. Mimsie wears her hair in plaits round her ears and gives Musical Evenings, in which various wispy young men play medieval instruments whose forlorn noises arouse a deep compassion in my bosom for medieval folk. How Dark were their Ages.

Josh has got himself into a most unbecoming flap about the way I should present myself at this Evening. I must look sexier than Mimsie (not a difficult task) yet not, as he puts it, bezonkers. I must also look more Earth Mother than Mimsie, which is harder because she has the most enormous boobs. I pointed out to him that I was also an ex-wife in a manner of speaking and therefore had a perfect right to go to Mimsie's party in a candlewick dressing gown if I so desired but he took no notice. I think I shall wear a little black number with a Plant a Tree for 1983 badge nestling in my bosom and play Diamonds Are a Girl's Best Friend on Ben's pocket mouth organ. That should confuse the various issues.

Yours, putting on the thermal undies,

Martha

Everybody must do what they want.

10 January

Dear Mary

I cannot believe it. I can *not* believe it. Not a dickie bird from Tom to his kids over Christmas or the New Year, not a card or a phone call or a gift-wrapped sausage. And then, first post after the hols, a scrawled note to Ben and Jane (not from their father but from Polly, his teenage bedwarmer) saying sorry Daddy had not had time to write or send prezzies or anything, but he had been ever so busy joining an ashram. Collapse in apoplectic rage of this stout party.

An ashram, Mary. How is it *possible*? Ever since we parted, he has not contributed so much as a grain of brown rice towards the support of his flesh and blood nor vouchsafed them the slightest sign of paternal love, yet now he is hell-bent on the ultimate self-indulgence: scratching away at the hard withered prune that constitutes his soul under the doubtless extremely expensive guidance of a tinted twit no self-respecting Asian would look at sideways and in the sort of squalid haunt of geriatric hippies the Beatles resigned from two decades ago. Where, I dare say, he will be encouraged to babble on about Cosmic Love when he has not enough ordinary affection to attach his signature to a missive to his kids. The great bald toothless middle-aged ijit. My only hope is that he'll learn to levitate himself right off this planet, never to be seen by human eye again.

I elected Tom the recipient of my first Christmas bread-and-butter letter. Dear T, I wrote, I hereby nominate you Worst Father in the Western World. I went on to inform him, as a matter of interest, that though not one of Jane or Ben's friends had a father living with them, all of them bar Tom had managed to maintain some sort of contact with their offspring, be it only a card at Christmas or the occasional fiver.

Only you, I said, have managed to scale the peaks of total failure. You would never see your kids at all unless I sent them down to Mousehole or provided you with a convenient roost in London where you could down a few Real Ales. Well, mate, that's it. Don't ever darken my doors again or I'll kick you from here to Hanging Rock. Rage, rage.

Also depression. What fatal flaw in me drove me so unerringly to pick out the Worst Father in the West to sire my children? It makes nonsense of eugenics, the maternal instinct and most of the theories of women's liberation. Shackled as I was, pre-Women's Movement, I should at least have felt impelled by my conditioning and my financial dependence to pool my genes with a Captain of Industry or some other real go-getter, thus submitting to the blind drive for the children's best survival. Instead, I chose Tom, a Failure's failure, a man who couldn't support a heavy moustache never mind children. Compared with Tom, Josh comes on like the Rock of Ages. Even Studs looks sturdy.

I was sounding off to Queenie about this woe and she struck her henna'd head on one side and said trouble with you, lovey, you haven't taken in nothing about men yet. All you got to know is one thing. They're not quite right in the bonce. Once you got that straight, you're laughing.

But Queenie, I said, what about Lorna's Dad, your sainted hubby who has passed to his reward? You can't say enough good things about him. You're right I can't, said Queenie, my lips is sealed about the Dear Departed. But if ever they was to come unsealed, I could tell you things about my old man would make your hair fall out, God rest his soul. See, Martha, you expect things of the poor buggers. I never. I had my Lorna because I wanted a kid. It never crossed my mind her Dad would do a hand's turn for her or me and I wasn't disappointed. That's the difference between you and me. Expectations.

Oh yes? I said, and what was all that you said to Josh, about him having a brain like Leonardo da Vinci and looking like Gary Cooper and that? She had the grace to turn a trifle pink then. Well dear, she said, that's es ee ex, isn't it? Very nice in its place, is es ee ex, but it never buttered no parsnips as I know of and you're daft if you thought it would. Cheer up, my gel, men is only the marzipan on the cake. I don't like marzipan, I said. Well there you are, said Queenie, count your blessings.

That made me cross. I got a lot crosser when I told Jane about her father and his ashram. That's fine, she said. So I had my second apoplectic fit of the day. Your Dad has turned his back on you and your brother and thrown in his lot with an effing guru and you say that's fine?

People must do what they want, she said. Oh *must* they? I shrieked. And supposing I'd done what *I* wanted? Supposing I'd gone off to chant mantras in Mousehole and left you and Ben to be brought up by Doctor Barnardo? Did you want to?

asked Jane. No, I yelled, I did not want to, mutton-head. Well there you are, she said.

They've all ganged up on me. There's a flaw in their logic somewhere, if only I could see it. What's the point of having a sense of duty and putting your children's well-being first and sacrificing your own desires if everyone from Queenie the one-time vaudeville star to your own daughter tells you all you are is Unenlightened and Unliberated and out of touch with reality? I tell you, Mary, if you write back and say the same thing, I'll cash in my engagement ring and go up the Amazon in a kayak. *That's* what I've always wanted to do.

Yours, taking the malaria tablets,

Martha

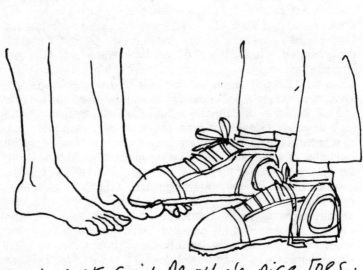

Ben's feet spoil Martha's nice toes.

17 January

Dear Mary

I suppose I must be grateful that you didn't actually join with the rest of my loved ones in their whole-hearted attempts to reduce me to pulp for the New Year. But did you have to confine your comments on my positive assets to saying (and I quote), 'Cheer up, Martha. After all, you've got quite nice toes and now that's enough about you, let's talk about me . . .' Quite nice toes? Thanks a million, friend. Now *there's* a solid achievement upon which to build a life. I can just see strong men fighting to the death to possess my quite nice toes. And what a trump card to wave before prospective employers. Wait now, Sir or Madam, while I take off my shoes and show you what no other employee can offer: ten quite nice toes. If you'd ever looked at me properly, Mary, you'd know I have quite nice hands, too, nice and strong and positively itching to fasten themselves round several people's necks.

Well, let it pass, other things press more urgently upon me. Had you noticed that the capacity of this generation not to enjoy themselves is truly phenomenal? Someone should do a thesis on it. Someone probably is. We ancient left-overs from the Swinging Sixties did at least know how to give ourselves a roaring good time on nothing more than some sprouted beans, a sack of lentils and a few sticks of Acapulco Gold. You could stuff the kids today with Beluga caviar and magnums of champagne and they wouldn't crack a smile. Perhaps it's that glue they sniff — it's cemented their faces straight forever.

Take Ben. That boy hasn't moved a feature so's you'd notice since Josh fell over the baby's wooden duck and concussed himself. When his lips do begin to split, it's like a natural disaster and those in the neighbourhood run screaming for cover. Jane's no barrel of fun, either. Her hair may be gold but all that's gold does not glister. Both of them stand rooted to spots around the room like conifers the Forestry Commission has planted for quick growth and all about them withers and no birds sing. Lorna says it's the Bomb but that's contrary to all previous human behaviour. Usually, when there's a threat to the race, people throw themselves into orgies of drink and sex. Ben won't drink anything but water and informed me yesterday that he'd given up sex. At sixteen.

He also informed me (well, Queenie, actually — I merely overheard) that he'd left school. I was stunned. When I left school, it was a real occasion. First exam results, then cheers and tears, then Speech Day and prizes and farewell parties and a mass of other ceremonies that mark a rite of passage. All Ben did was cease to walk schoolwards and begin to walk Flaganwards instead, a rite of passage that remained unmarked even by me, his mother, since he didn't tell me until it was too late. Breathing fire, I rushed off to see his teacher who said oh yes, Ben did seem to have left and oh no, she didn't think he ought to come back. Not really. Faced with this new low in permissiveness, every authoritarian bone in my body stood to attention and saluted. You should *make* him come back. I screeched at the unfortunate woman, but she only shook her head mildly and stared at her toes. Quite nasty toes.

One good thing at least — all that awful getting-on-with teacher is over. I never did it well. One time, I dropped into Ben's classroom and there he was, playing snooker. The teacher said it was the children's Relating Hour. I said I didn't want Ben to relate, I wanted him to spell and add and subtract and other abstruse academic things. She looked at me sadly and said it was all very well for Ben but did I realise how many other children had terrible *problems* relating? Whereupon I said I didn't *care* about other children and immediately felt like something rude she'd have to wipe off the blackboard. But, rotten with guilt though I was, I did notice she was knitting ever such a complicated jumper for some lucky man while the kids related (pompous word for hitting each other over the head with snooker cues).

The trouble is, who cares about Ben but me? His father's in an ashram, all's right with *his* world and Josh, his step-father-as-was, isn't interested. Well, he pretends to be but it isn't convincing. He'll be all right, Josh said. Give him a while and he'll find his feet. Find his feet? Ben's so huge he hasn't even seen his feet for three years. They could have trekked off to Katmandu without him knowing. The only definite response I got out of Josh was when I asked would the Department give Ben a job and Josh said no.

What do you want to do? I asked Ben. Ride my bike, he said. For a *living*, I said trying not to box his silly ears. Play the bongos, he said. So, grabbing at straws, I rang the local sound shop for someone to teach Ben the bongos. No, they said, no one was teaching the bongos, that was Latin percussion, see, and there wasn't a lot of call for Latin percussion these days. Perhaps, I said to Ben, you could learn to play the bongos while riding your bike and then join a circus. *Yeah,* he said, his face very nearly brightening. So I did box his silly ears. Who wants a sixteen-year-old with boxed ears and a forty-year-old with quite nice toes? All offers gratefully received.

Yours, dolefully,

Martha

Martha
rescuing Iris
Murdoch from
flames

Dear Mary

New and ever more crippling blows to the self-esteem continue to rain down upon me. I have recently filled in and posted ten job application forms. Encapsulated in them was every last bit of my wit, wisdom and life experience and, though I say it myself, they were pretty impressive: fluent, informative and transparently honest, revealing just the sort of person perceptive employers would give their eye teeth to hire. So far, the response has been zilch. What makes this particularly depressing is that I was asking for any sort of work at all — shelf-stacker, crate-heaver, tea-maker, sweeper-upper, bottle-washer, dogsbody — and asking for it under Ben's name. So not only do they not want an incredibly mature boy they have rejected *me* into the bargain.

After a discreet interval, I rang the various Personnel Managers. Each time the Personnel Manager turned out to be a woman. Each time she said oh dear, very sorry, we've had ten trillion young lads applying, no chance I'm afraid. Each time I said I hope you don't mind my ringing but one must do what one can for one's son in these hard times, mustn't one? And each time Madame Personnel Manager said oh absolutely, I do so understand, I have a young son myself you see. I see, all right. Just guess whose son gets the job, eh? This women's liberation has gone too far, Mary. Finding one's path blocked at every turn is a frustrating experience in itself but when it comes to being blocked by another unscrupulous mother — I mean, another mother unscrupulously promoting her quite inadequate offspring — well, all I can say is, well.

In despair, I cornered the manager of the local cinema who happens to be married to Mrs Next-Door. Yes, he said, backing away and banging his shin badly on the local skip, he did have a part-time job for an usher and yes, ouch, ouch, he'd consider Ben. £1.50 hourly, now and again, he said as he hobbled away. Triumph! There, I said to Ben, I've got you a job. Usher in a cinema. My goodness, you might meet anyone, doing that. Like who? said Ben. Umm, errr, I said, Lord Goodman, perhaps. Richard Burton, Vanessa Redgrave, Iris

Murdoch, Frankie Vaughan. Who? said Ben.

Then he flatly refused to have anything to do with it, just flatly refused. In vain I sketched out various tempting scenarios for him. Usher Saves Life of Film-fan Millionaire in Cinema Fire, Is Named Heir to Fortune. Usher Takes Over When Projectionist Dies of Heart Attack, Now Heads Chain of Cinemas. Usher Steals Heart of Famous Sex Symbol on First Night, Weds Her and Stars in Her Next Film. How about that, Ben? I said. No chance, he said. In vain I screeched that he'd end up on the streets like a bag lady — bag boy — but he wouldn't budge.

So I turned for help to his nearest and dearest. Ring your father, I told him, see what he says. I should have known that was a non-starter. Ben got through to Tom in his ashram while I listened on the extension. First, it took Ben four minutes to explain to Tom what a job was. Then all Tom said was don't do it, boy, it's exploitation, no good papering up the cracks, better swell the ranks of Maggie's unemployed like your old Dad's doing and so on. That man is hideously predictable.

Then Josh came in and said of course Ben should take the job. I was very encouraged. I was very soon discouraged. A young man must expect to start at the bottom of the heap, said Josh, with a certain vindictive gloom. He droned on. If Ben worked very hard, in a year or two he might be promoted to ticket-collector. If he really slogged his guts out, in another year or two he might get into the box-office.

By the time Josh was finished, he'd got Ben as far as his eightieth birthday and a job as head usher at anything up to £60 a week plus luncheon vouchers and a free seat at the cinema for his starving seventy-year-old wife. Thanks but no thanks, said Ben and who could blame him.

Jane was useless, too. All she contributed was a long and dreary argument about why the cinema wanted ushers and not usherettes and she had a good mind to report the owner to the Equal Opportunities Commission and what kind of a wally would Ben look in black trousers and a bow tie and, anyway, he couldn't usher his feet into his socks, never mind . . . Could, said Ben. Couldn't, said Jane. Next thing, these two uniquely talented job-seekers were scuffling like kinder-garten entrants on the floor.

And I was left stranded as usual, with only my fantasies to keep me warm. This is one of them. I put on black trousers and a bow tie and I'm the new usher. The manager doesn't recognise me because his eyes are still full of tears, due to his barked shin. On my first day's ushering I meet Richard

Burton who has come to see the film with Lord Goodman, Vanessa Redgrave, Iris Murdoch, and Frankie Vaughan. The cinema catches fire and I rescue them all.

In gratitude Lord Goodman gets me a divorce, Frankie includes Ben in his work with delinquent boys, Vanessa makes Jane her P.A., and Richard Burton marries me, stars me opposite him in his next film and names me heir to his fortune. Only Iris Murdoch does nothing for me, because she is jealous.

Yours, blowing pretty bubbles,

Martha

Dear Mary

Josh took me out to dinner yesterday. I didn't much want to go: what with one thing and another I've rather given up food. All that fuss seems so dated — fine in the Sixties, okay in the Seventies but definitely passé in the Eighties. I'm simply not into the cookety-cook lark any more, nor into the noshety-nosh neither. Besides, watching the baby apply food to his person like a hot poultice three times daily is enough to take the edge off Nero's appetite, never mind mine. That infant works as a sort of symbolic vomitorium: one look in his direction and whatever you've just swallowed is making its exit again.

I'm taking vitamin pills instead and even that seems too much effort. What I'd really like is a nice restful intravenous feed administered in beddy-byes by an apple-cheeked district nurse or, possibly, a sort of food pill that acts like that contraceptive: a nutritionist inserts it under your skin and it leaks meals into your bloodstream at appropriate moments throughout the month. Think of it. No more shopping or banging about with saucepans or washing up. Just occasional small surges of taste-bud sensation and the odd psychic burp.

So when Josh suggested eating out, I said why not order a takeaway kebab and have it here instead? But he looked in a shifty manner at Ben, Jane, the baby, Judas and the Woolly Mite milling about and said with unnecessary fervour no no no no. Then he went on about this marvellous little place he'd discovered, really Martha you'll love it, it'll remind you (and here, I swear, his eyes went misty) of Our Very Own Perigord caff, remember Martha, remember? So, sighing, I put on my wellies and we sloshed off into the rain.

Why do the English look down on everything French and then go bonkers when they find they can cook a perfectly ordinary French dish? The place was one of those hysterically casual little bistros called something studiedly unchic like Service Non Compris where the owner puts you through an exam in Food Appreciation and you can't crumble a piece of bread without him springing from the wings for a round of applause. So tiring.

For Josh's sake I did my best to live up to the demanding role of four-star gourmet, smiling myself silly and saying très bien at every bite to the boring patron, who was no more French than I am, under his quivering moustache. Anyway, at last we reached the coffee stage (beam beam, clap clap, c'est formidable Monsieur Fred) and were finally left in peace as Monsieur Fred darted off to knot his cordon bleu round another customer's jugular. And then Josh leaned towards me, cleared his throat and said Martha, I need your advice. It is a problem of Sexual Harassment in the Workplace, will you help? Oh Josh, of course, I said. Mary, I was really moved. All those years of talking were not wasted on him, after all. Josh had understood. At last he empathises with the woman's dilemma. Whose sexual harassment? I said in a low and caring voice. Mine, he said. Me. I'm being touched up at work, Martha, and I don't know what to do.

Well you could have knocked me down with a rogon de veau au vin blanc avec herbes de Provence. You, I said, staring. Yes, he said, miffed. And who's the lucky lady, I said. Martha, he said, with that remark you reveal a deeply sexist attitude that I would not have expected of you. Irene, he said. Irene? I shrieked quietly, scalding my tongue with le demitasse. A short interlude followed in which I rolled in the aisles. What does she do, Josh? Run her fingers round your turn-ups? Tweak your braces? Get you behind the filing cabinet and loosen your cuff-links? For heaven's sake, you're a foot taller than Irene even counting her bee-hive. What are you a man or a Mickey Mouse?

I see you have not grasped the implications, he said coldly. Irene is my boss. She can make or break me at the Department. There is no fury, Martha, like a woman scorned. Laugh if you will but when I get fired, you'll be laughing in a caravan park in Neasden, how does that grab you? An icy hand clutched at my heart as I wiped away the tears and saw a bleak future. Me and the baby reduced to penury, our little blue chilblains throbbing, our little tummies empty of even a draught of Vitamin C, all because of a sex-crazed harpy storming down the corridors of power after my poor Josh.

Then the voice of Josh said it's all your fault, Martha. None of this would have happened if you hadn't left me. A man in my position needs a woman to protect him. Irene thinks I'm fair game and without you, Martha, I am. Complain to the boss, I said. She is the boss, he said. Well, the Minister, go to the Minister, Josh. Sir John? he said. Sir John becomes sexually over-heated if he reads the word 'she' in a brief. The word 'brief' is almost too much for him. If I complain to him he'll think I'm gay and have me followed. There'll be security checks, confidential files will be withdrawn, men will edge away as I unzip, your letters to Mary will be opened and possibly leaked to the *Guardian*. I shall end up wishing I *were* homosexual — at least, then, I'd have *some* friends in high places. Oh Martha, I beg you, make an honest man of me or we are all undone!

Or words to that effect, Mary, which went through me like a knife. What am I to do? Where is the Sex Discrimination Act, now that I need it? Write with advice immediately, in the old school code.

Oursay,

Thaymar

Joan of Arc

7 February

Dear Mary

I feel chastened by your last letter. You've got things into proportion and I haven't. Of *course* the Peace Movement is more important than Josh having his bottom pinched or the baby's filthy eating habits or Ben not getting a job or Tom going into an ashram or any other thing at all that only concerns one individual: in this case your myopic friend Marth. You are entirely right to devote your energies to that good work.

Sometimes I wish I was childless or, at least, a childfree grannie so that I could join those amazing mothers who, unlike me, seem able to raise their kids and sit down outside nuclear bases all at the same time. Soon, when people ask 'Where were you educated?' the status answer will not be Roedean and Girton but Greenham Common. What I wonder is if it's ever occurred to Mrs Thatcher that a lot of the Peace People she so distrusts are not financed, as she seems to think, from Moscow by the KGB but by her own purpose-built mass unemployment? All the real activists in our local group are on the dole and busy turning the sow's ear she's handed them into a silk purse, like you. Nice one, Maggie.

Part of my trouble — besides sloth, that is — stems from the low level of thought around here. Ben got a wad of paper stuck in his ear the other day and when I'd finally managed to tweak it out, he solemnly said did I realise that after a nuclear war there'd be nobody about to tweak paper out of his ear? I tried to convey to him that such a war might have rather more serious consequences than one Ben with a slightly blocked ear drum and I think I succeeded: he is now sporting a CND badge. A small conversion but mine own.

Jane is a harder case. She is saving to go to Australia on the grounds that nothing nastier will happen to her there than being called a Pommie sheila. I asked how would she feel, knowing that of all her loved ones, only *she* had survived and she said, with an actressy gesture towards her tearless eyes, 'The show must go on.' I blame that theatre group she's just joined. Still, you've got the politicians worried, Mary. Now they're all pretending disarmament was *their* idea and if we're going to have any last laugh, that's it.

In view of all this I hesitate to bring up Josh and his sexual harassment again, but you did give me your advice and the least I could do was follow it up. Which I have done. I rang Irene at the office. It wasn't easy. Each time, the switchboard girl said 'Hold on, please' and then emigrated — probably to Australia, like Jane. I wouldn't be surprised if half that continent isn't populated by switchboard girls whose callers are still hanging on at the end of English telephones.

Anyway, I finally got through and asked Her Highness to drop by. She dropped. And I said with a suitably grave expression that an anonymous mole at the Department had leaked to me (and possibly to others) the patently false and slanderous allegation that she was molesting men at her work place, including, of all people, Josh. I added, with many a casual shrug, that none of it was my business but I thought it my duty to put her in the picture, woman to woman. I am acutely aware, I said, that there are those who will stop at nothing to blacken the name of outstandingly successful women such as yourself, Irene, and I, Martha, cannot stand by and see that happen. No way.

She gave me a couple of beady looks but I stood my ground like Joan of Arc, radiating innocence and a modest strength, and she crumbled. I have, she said, more than enough on my mind sorting out the problems of this country without running after men. Isn't it typical of them, Martha, to spread such lies just because they can't bear to see a woman in a position of (and here she lowered her lashless eyes) Power. We agreed that it was, indeed, dastardly, caddish, and disgusting behaviour and all we could say was thank heavens for the natural solidarity between women. Anything I can do, I said as we parted, and Irene said you're a true friend, Martha.

So Josh now goes unmolested about his business, cuff-links unloosened, lapels unrumpled. I detect a faint aroma of disappointment in his bearing. Could it be, I ask myself, that he made the whole thing up to lure me back, green-eyed? Naming no names, I related the story to Judas, who said he'd use it in his next thriller. Very trendy plot, he said. And who would get the old dagger in the back? I asked. Oh, he said. I think the woman who passed the information on don't you? No, I said.

Actually, I'm rather cheered by the episode, so much so that I've stopped taking the vitamins. Well, I nearly choked to death on a large B-complex pill yesterday, which would have been a macabre way to go. Body in fine fettle, announced the Coroner, only a mite short of breath.

The other cheering thing is the standpipe down our road. We ran out of water two days ago and I've met more neighbours since then than in the whole five years before. It is *awful*, of course, but I like it. Old Queenie is having a whale of a time, making assignations at the well and getting strong young lads to hoist up her buckets, and even Lorna has had to come out of seculsion, looking like a widow spider on the prowl. If she wasn't a vegetarian and men weren't meat, she'd have had the two boys next door for breakfast. It's an ill water hole that blows no one any good, I say.

Yours, boiling away,

Martha

Martha, you can't go on like this.

Dear Mary

Mother descended upon us this week, to give us a good talking-to. She claims she is all of a doodah due to our antics and hasn't had a wink of sleep since I 'deserted' Josh. I know Mother's winkless sleeps. I shared a bedroom with her once, when we were staying with an aunt. She kept me awake with her snores all night and then complained she'd tossed and turned till dawn. Beside that woman, Rip van Winkle was an insomniac. Anyway, winks or no, she was wakeful enough when she arrived — she burst into the house with her eyes out on stalks, probing every corner as if there were terrorists concealed behind the saucepans. Then she sat down, loosened her corsets and began to sort us out.

You can't go on like this, she said. Like what? I said. Like *this*, she said, waving vaguely about the kitchen. Without a man, Martha. It isn't right. Hang about a bit, Mother, and I'll *get* a man, I said, there's plenty of pebbles on the beach. I am not interested in pebbles, she said, I am referring to your lawful wedded husband, father of your child. Look at you, Martha, you're a shadow of your former self. I know Ma, I said, isn't it wonderful, I'm down to nearly ten stone. When a woman of your age starts losing weight, said Mother, it is the beginning of the end. In Mother's book, marriage is an inflationary device — the more respectably wedded you are, the fatter. She hasn't caught a glimpse of Father over her mammary shelf since 1952.

After that, she droned on about the ghastly fate of children from broken homes. Look at him, she said, jerking her head towards the cooker, where Ben was stirring up a mess of pottage laced with lentils. That poor boy is well on the way to becoming a vegetarian. He *is* a vegetarian, Mother, I said. Not a glue-sniffer or a mugger or a heroin addict, just a vegetarian. One who eats two or more veg. Humph, said Mother. Clearly, to her, a leguminous diet is half-way to damnation.

And has he got a job, Martha? she asked. It does speak Mother, I said. In spite of being a vegetarian it speaks all by itself. Well Ben? she said. No, said Ben. There you are, said Mother. Gran, said Ben, there are over three million people unemployed. Oh *them*, she said, they're pickers and choosers, they only want to do what *they* want to do. (And that from a woman who has made a life's work of only doing what *she* wants to do.) You, Ben, she said, must be prepared to take *any* job. I am, said Ben, I can't get any job. Rubbish, said Mother. I can't get that either, said Ben, I've tried. There's a waiting list for rubbish.

So she started on Jane. Had she got a job? Yes, said Jane, I'm an actress. Ho, said Mother. I don't call *that* a job. What do you call it then? said Jane, but her grandmother merely pursed her lips and said, as her final threat, next thing you'll be reading the *Guardian*. The Yorkshire Ripper is a *Guardian* reader, Ben said informatively. I'm not surprised, said Mother, that Woman's Page is enough to drive any decent man to murder. Well, I couldn't let that pass. Ma, I said, I forgive you for you know not what you say but if you don't stop saying it I'll put you on the next train back to Father. That shut her up.

For two minutes. Then she was on to Nesta. Nesta is 72, her next-door neighbour and life-long enemy. Do you know what that woman did last week? she said. That woman baked a dozen lemon tarts and brought them round to give to me. Oh heavens, Mother, I said, I don't know how you stand it, does Nesta's wickedness know no bounds? Mother went on. If that woman thinks she can buy her way into my house with twelve lemon tarts, she's got another think coming. I had friends in, Martha, you see. I *have* friends. And no sooner does that woman see them coming than she's round like a flash with her baking tray, worming her way into their affections with her horrible confectionaries. I told her straight. I said Nesta, I was baking tarts before you'd got round to boiling an egg and I'll thank you to confine your culinary disasters to your own four walls, *if* you don't mind. I'm a long-suffering person, Martha, and a good Christian but there are some things at which even I draw the line and that woman is all of them.

Poor Nesta, my heart goes out to her. As far as Mother's concerned she can do no right. But then, who can? Dad's been trying for forty years but his original sin was fathering me. I was thirty hours in labour with you, Ma frequently says, sighing deeply. You'll never know what your birth cost me, Martha. Once I made the mistake of saying perhaps I did, since I'd had three children myself. Some women, she said gimlet-eyed, squeeze them out like toothpaste but I was not made for reproduction, I hadn't got the hips. I said to your

Father at the time, George, I haven't got the hips, but he took no notice. Men are animals, Martha, and that's a fact. Well, I've got rid of mine, I said, you should be pleased. She isn't, of course. Only death must us part — anything else is for weaklings and sinners.

Oh Mary, I must tell you. I was dusting the telly the other morning and switched it on by mistake. I *did* get a fright. There were all sorts of people on it that I'd almost forgotten, like Frostie and Parky and Angela Rippon, drinking bottles of champagne. Have they been there long? And if so, why? I think we should be told.

Yours, righteously indignant,

Martha

I laugh at my own jokes —

Dear Mary

I visited Friz-Chops on Wednesday. You remember old Friz-Chops, now Auriol August. Famous Feminist Writer and Reliquary for many furred and feathered friends? I haven't seen her since she popped in this time last Candlemas for a cup of tea and condescension . . . you'll recall she took an A in condescension. Anyway, last Monday the telephone rang and it was she, or rather She. Would I come and see her? The address was appropriately posh: Binden Old Hall, Binden-in-the-Mould, that sort of thing. So propelled by the urge for a few dry martinis and a small but perfect luncheon I put the baby in charge of Ben, and set off in my best frock, reeking of alcohol (I've had that scent for far too many years).

Binden Hall, it turned out, is not where Auriol lives but one of those incredibly luxurious places where the rich go to have their nervous breakdowns and people like me have to be smuggled in with the grapes. Brideshead Bin for Very Wealthy Loonies, all fountains and croquet lawns and Capability Brown tree-arrangements, with starched white minions pushing Fabergé wheelchairs about.

The inmates lay on chaise longues propped up by wads of banknotes, pressing bells for drinkie-poos and having little turns. Auriol received me in the kind of bedroom the Sun King had his levées in, her limbs extended upon a goose-down sofa, her feet warmed by various Endangered Species and a small French vineyard by her side in crystal decanters. She looked in tip-top condition, which made me feel extraordinarily unwell.

Martha, she said on a dying fall, how kind of you to come. Then she put out a pale hand sparkling with diamonds and downed the contents of a vintage Bordeaux. I adopted my sickroom voice — brisk, with a sadistic edge — and said goodness me what have we here, fancy being in on a lovely day like this and other jarring remarks calculated to make any but the terminally ill arise and walk and place their hands about my throat. Auriol merely sighed forgivingly. I am, she said, very low, Martha, very low indeed. Well, I said brightly, a couple more drags at the old plonk and you'll be very high indeed, so I shouldn't worry. Then two silver-plated tears emerged from her shining eyes and I felt a moment of remorse.

The rich also fall, I told myself and patted the corpse of an ocelot that lay across her legs. This was the signal for a marathon moan-in. Auriol, it appears, has unaccountably lost her taste for Swiss bank deposits, the flavour of Krugerrands no longer pleases her palate, she has no appetite for stocks and shares, she is suffering from anorexia dollarosa, she has a bad case of best-selleritis.

It's all very well for you, Martha, she wailed, you're not lonely, you've got a man. I am not a one-night-stand person, I want a *home*. You have a home, Auriol, I said. Not to put too fine a point on it, you have four homes. London, Cannes, New York and Ireland-for-tax-purposes. Auriol was uncomforted. She squeezed out another silvery tear and mopped at it with a piece of antique Honiton lace. Martha, a home is not a home without a man, she said. A strong, loyal, devoted and protective man. Perhaps you mean a dog, I said helpfully. That's how they make dogs, not men. I'll take you to this marvellous kennels when you're better and you can pick out the strongest, loyalest, and most devoted Standard Apricot Poodle you could ever . . .

But it didn't work. Auriol turned her face to the flocked wallpaper and I tried again. Auriol, I said, I no longer have a man and look at me. She looked. Well, I said, I was always chubby and I never could do a thing with my hair. Then I told her I'd left Josh. I expected, from the author of *Twenty Ways to Skin a Man*, some mild praise. Instead, a distinctly furtive expression hit her enamelled face. Where did you leave him? she asked.

That is the wrong question, I said. I didn't pawn him or drop him down a drain. The question is *why* or possibly, *when* or even *what* for. Then I told her why and when and what for, at some length, while her eyes wandered about the room as if searching for flies. Finally ending the list of Josh's faults, I paused with my sure sense of drama and said I left him, Auriol, on principle. On feminist principle, like you said I should in *Ten Good Reasons for Dumping Your Man*. Uh-huh, said Auriol. What do you mean, uh-huh? I said. I am now leading an independent life. I lean no more. I repair my own fuses. I laugh at my own jokes. It is not uh-huh, it is three cheers. Three cheers for me.

I must say, my stirring speech did cheer her. She became distinctly more upright and her cheeks took on a healthy glow. No honestly, she said, I admire you, Martha. You've done the right thing. I only met Josh once but I could see immediately that he was a totally unreconstructed male. I expect, she continued, toying with her lace hankie, he's taken up with a silly blonde half our age, the way these chauvinists do? No, I said. No. As a matter of fact, he's living alone at the moment and brooding, I hope, on his sins. If he comes to understand the women's movement and the desirability of sharing life's chores with a liberated partner such as myself, I may — just may — take him back.

Clearly, these sentiments invigorated her. She was on her feet in a trice and gazing into a large gilt mirror, only swaying a little. You've done me a world of good, Martha, she said, pass me my lipstick, I'm leaving here tonight. Mary, caring for one's friends in their hour of need is what friends are for.

Yours, the lady with the lamp,

Martha

— Die for Thatcher!

Dear Mary

I was ever so taken aback by your latest news — you and Mo have had a dog. I mean, got a dog. Evidently you were led to confess this lapse in taste because of the remarks I made in my last letter about apricot standard poodles. Mary, in my experience of the world, the acquisition of a dog or dogs is a most virulent symptom of incipient character rot, especially in women. Men's characters already suffer from endemic gangrene, so they don't count.

In the first place, dogs are clearly anti everything feminism stands for. I cannot say exactly why, they just are. Men call women they don't like 'dogs', which ought to be a dreadful warning. There is something about a dog's way of life or (to be fair to the beasts) a dog *owner's* way of life that is entirely incompatible with the women's struggle. It may be the overtones of Hitler Youth. All those walks, all that rushing about on command. Those leads and studded collars, the Obedience Classes, the Die-For-Your-Country, Salute-The-Flag, Sit-Up-And-Beg bag of tricks. All that meat they eat, torn from the limbs of weaker species. All that burying of bones. I get goose pimples just thinking about it.

You must ask yourself, Mary, what having a dog reveals about your inner drives. What hitherto unsung ego-deficiency impelled you towards this sad choice of pet? Dogs are heavily dependent creatures — why do you need to be needed so, why do you wish to be worshipped by this hairy acolyte? You will have to come to terms with the hierarchical demands of dogdom, too. Any owner will frequently tell you that dogs must know who is their Master. Or, more gruesomely, their Mistress. Do you yearn for this basically jackboot relationship? Or is your dog a child-substitute? I could make a good case for the harmlessness of that, except that dogs aren't child-substitutes, they are Little Lord Fauntleroy-substitutes and thus a very poor preparation for parenthood. Dogs always love you, never willingly leave you, are grateful for everything you give them, think you omnipotent, do not smoke or drink or watch too much television and can be got rid of if they are bad, none of which applies to children, who will, therefore, come as a severe disappointment to the conditioned dog-lover.

Also, dogs are politically unsound. The very essence of their nature is Tory. They are inherently High Church, deeply class-conscious, profoundly xenophobic, and like nothing better than a good snap at the heels of the unemployed. If they got suffrage they'd vote for savaging the homeless, slaughtering more baby seals, sending the gunboats into Hong Kong (where the Chinese wisely eat them), and increasing the power of the Royal corgis. They'd be against working women, peace people, vegetarians, noise abatement, and shopping on Sundays. They are Thatcherites to a dog and the Species that Supports Our Boys. It would be nice to think that getting a dog is a cry for help but Mother has dogs, so it isn't.

What's more, it has frequently come to my attention that dumping the family canine is many an oppressed wife's first step to freedom. When I was thinking of leaving Tom, I kept saying I'm going to leave you, Tom, and he kept saying oh and don't be daft and who for, Robert Redford? It was only when the dog went that he sat up and took notice. You shouldn't have done that, Martha, he said, I liked that dog, that was my dog. Tom, I said, that dog's legs would be stumps by now if I hadn't walked it. That dog would be pushing up the daisies if I hadn't fed it. That dog would be yapping at its Maker if I hadn't deflea'd and dewormed and demanged it through the years, so don't give me your dog, please. Then I departed because he never once said I like that Martha, that is my Martha, here Martha, walkies.

Think on these things, Mary. Meanwhile, I've got other things on my mind. I knocked on Josh's door yesterday evening — we don't need marriage guidance, our bills bring us together — and he took a very long time answering. I would have given up, except his car was outside. When he finally appeared he was much the worse for wear: hair up in tufts, collar awry, and a very informal look about the flies. 'Aren't you going to ask me in?' I said in my pretty way. Not now, Martha, he gasped, not at this minute, I have to see a man about a dog. 'You too?' I cried hoarsely, the disease is contagious, we're in the grip of an epidemic, have the authorities been informed? Cut it out, dear one, Josh said, so I reminded him that it was Ben's birthday on Sunday 'What does he want?' asked Josh. Ten pounds, I replied. My boy has simple tastes and gift-wrapping is not obligatory. Fine, said Josh, and shut the door.

What does this mean? Is he holed up in there with a rabid

Doberman Pinscher — female, of course, nothing queer about our Josh. Or, the thought strikes cold, has Ms Auriol August flown from her sickbed to nestle by his side? Auriol is the proud mother of no fewer than three giant-size boxers so I put nothing past her. At least Irene, for all her sexual harassment of Josh, possesses nothing more ideologically suspect than an old and unbalanced canary.

As for me, as you know, I have a cat. The fact that this cat is overweight, clumsy, given to fainting at moments of stress and utterly devoted to me is neither here nor there. She makes up for these small shortcomings by stealing everything edible in the kitchen, frightening the life out of inoffensive rodents and being sick on the cushions. Now that's what I *call* a cat.

Yours, barking,

Martha

Ben with fresh hairstyle and liver.

115

Dear Mary

The baby scoots about all day long now bleating da da da da da. Mrs Next-Door, who wanders in occasionally 'to cheer herself up' (I don't much care for the implications of that) said aaah, the poor dear, he's missing his Dad. That might have touched my heart a bit more if only his Dad was actually missing. In fact, Josh is here most of the time, staring at me. He stares at me the way men stare at barometers on the wall. Once he even leaned forward and tapped me, so I said I predicted squally showers with tempests by nightfall and he said Martha, why do you talk such utter rubbish? As if he expected an answer. Tempestuously I said I don't have to sit in my own house and be insulted and he said it's my house too. From then on, we were into the old 'mine, no *mine*' genre of conversation, over which I will draw seven veils.

But it's not my imagination, he does look at me a lot. Lorna noticed it and asked what I made of it. I said that, to tell her the truth, Josh had probably discovered, rather late in the day, my resemblance to that wonder of the ancient world, the Sphinx. D'you mean, said Lorna, that you're getting on a bit? No, Lorna, I said patiently. I mean I'm a bit of an enigma to him, the Eternal Female, that's me. You? snorted Lorna. Martha, you're about as enigmatic as a dishcloth. That Lorna can be very uncouth when she lets herself go which is, regrettably, most of the time and what does *she* know about the essential mystery of womankind? It takes a man to appreciate that, when all's said and done. I've forgiven Lorna now because I realise she was prompted by envy. Her husband hasn't stared at her since she set the chip pan on fire and tried to put it out with lighter fluid.

Come to think of it, quite a lot of the women I know (excepting poor Lorna) have men staring at them now. Perhaps there's Spring in the air. Even Jane has got a boyfriend. I mean, so has my dear daughter Jane. Not that I knew. Queenie brought the matter up at the pub on Sunday. She stuck her pinkie in her mouth, cocked her head like a very old squirrel and said your Jane's courting, then. Courting what, I said, alarmed. Disaster? German measles?

She's *had* German measles.

A beau, said Queenie, Jane's got a beau. I was just trying to think my way through the tip in Jane's bedroom she calls her wardrobe (a *bow?*) when Queenie patted my hand. There'll be wedding bells soon, she whispered beerily, but never mind lovey — you won't lose a daughter, you'll gain a son. I don't *want* a son, I said crossly, I've got enough of my own. What I *want* is to lose a daughter. Then, of course, I had to buy Queenie three more halves of best bitter to put the stars back in her eyes.

Later on, tanked to the gills on True Romance, she poked me in the ribs and said you'll be back with your old man before I'm much older. Restraining the impulse to tell Queenie I didn't think she could *get* much older, I said come off it. No, she said, wagging her wig (red this time, in a very pert Afro). Queenie knows about these things, Queenie's never wrong. You mark my words, Martha, there'll be a new baby for you this time next year. Well, I leapt back from the bar as if my round had come. I don't mind a bit of neighbourhood gossip but this was too much. Queenie, I said, you couldn't be wronger. I can't see Josh reproducing again, except by Xerox. Oh dear, is that what I really think about my ex or was it the best bitter talking? Who can tell.

Compared to all this billing and cooing, Ben comes as a real rest. He and his geriatric friend Linda split up a year ago and since then I haven't seen hide nor hair of the fairer sex around him. Maybe because he looks so odd. I'm quite nostalgic now for his punk days — all that electric hair was rather stylish. The only trace of punkdom left is the one ear-ring he wears and all that does is remind me of when I decided to wear one ear-ring, like all the kids. A depressing experience, that was. I kept getting stopped in the street by passers-by saying excuse me but you've lost an ear-ring. So much for trying to bridge the generation gap. Anyway, now Ben has his hair short back and sides with a terrible sort of furry lid on top that extends over his forehead like a handle and makes him look like a Toby jug. I have to resist the temptation to lift it up and say 'is anybody there?' Well, *is* anybody there? And if so, what age is he and when's he in?

The other day I cooked that boy a nice plate of liver and bacon. For a while he poked silently at the liver and then said what's liver made of, Mum? Ben, I said, you'll *never* get a job if you go around asking employers what liver's made of. I'm not asking employers, Ben said, there aren't any employers. I'm asking *you*, Mum. To be frank with you, Ben, I said, — or to be ben with you, Frank — I haven't the faintest idea what liver's made of. And I poured myself another drink. To which my own son said, most hurtfully, *your* liver, Mum, is made of beer.

Yours, still reeling,

Martha

Dear Mary

How strange, you writing to me about Arthur Koestler. I was just going to write to you about the same thing only I remembered how much you admired him and I thought you'd think it in the worst *possible* taste, as K. Everett wouldn't say. Besides, I admired him too. But that didn't stop me from thinking what you thought when I read about him and his wife. I suppose it was because she was so much younger than him and not ill and also the funny feeling I got when I read the long obituaries about him and nothing about her, not a dickie-bird, which left me a bit goose-pimpled.

You're right, of course, we know nothing about the Koestlers and therefore our thoughts aren't really connected to them. They did what they did for their own forever private reasons, and that's that. But it does raise a few rather anxious-making questions for others, doesn't it? Very faintly on the horizon looms the ancient spectre of suttee, like you write, where wives were expected to throw themselves on the husband's funeral pyres and were given discreet but determined shoves in that direction if they showed any impolite signs of wanting to hang about. Or those old Sultans whose concubines were instantly disposed of when their Husband passed away. Most of these women were young enough to be their husband's daughters — like Mrs Koestler — which makes it that little bit harder to believe that they couldn't wait to join their old men in the sky.

What worries me is the example it sets to the rest of us. If mutual suicide pacts caught on, I can just imagine Josh's reaction if I said I didn't want to go with him. Oh ho, Martha, so there's another man is there, I can hear him say and he'd likely refuse to believe me if I said no, Josh, it's just that I quite like being alive. Because then he'd have to come to terms with the unspoken end to that sentence — *even without you.* That's the crunch, isn't it?

All this only makes me realise what a very peculiar thing love is, particularly *in extremis.* When Josh was first in love with me he went on a lot, in a very romantic vein, about what I meant to him and how life would be meaningless without me and how perfect I was and how wonderful and all that — which I enjoyed no end. But just once I said to him, Josh, would you love me if I had a beard? And to cut a long and rather dismal story short, the answer came loud and clear. Not on his nellie.

Well, you see? He couldn't imagine life without me, I was his ideal woman in every way and the thought that I might become his wife was Paradise Enow. Yet he was prepared to ditch all this on the instant if I remained adorable me in every adorable ingredient except for the small matter of growing several hundred hairs upon my chin. Which, given a sneaky dose of rogue hormones, could even happen. It was a sort of a joke at the time but I kept thinking about it because I don't know what it means. I could shave, I said to Josh then, and you'd never know, but that didn't make him rally. So it's all very well, the marriage vows, with their 'in sickness and in health' business but let them add 'in a beard' and the whole sacred structure comes tumbling down. Talk about hanging on by a hair. But that's what it comes down to and we'd better face it.

Mrs Thatcher hasn't got a beard but that's all that she hasn't got — she is in every other way a male and an unreconstructed one, at that. Have you noticed that it's only her who constantly uses the male pronoun to include females? It is Mrs T. who says 'he' and 'his' and 'men' when she means 'she' and 'hers' and 'women' as well? Whereas Michael Foot and even Denis Healey both carefully say 'he or she' and use nice open-ended nouns like 'human beings' where Mrs T say 'mankind'. And I don't have to tell you, Mary, how revealing that is. The lady is like the ducklings who fell in love with Konrad Lorenz and thought they were him and quacked at other ducks, like Maggie quacks at women. I am a housewife and mother, so I ought to be pleased when our PM says others should join me in the ranks. But I'm not, because I know *she* thinks she's Josh, poor benighted her. Even Josh thinks she's Josh.

I'm sorry to say that Mother feels the same. She sees everything from the male point of view and has much more contempt for women than men do, presumably because (a) she doesn't get the rewards men get from women and (b) every now and then she has to admit she's a women herself, which makes her extremely tetchy. Of course she's been brainwashed and should therefore be pitied but that doesn't make my life any easier, raised by her as a Living Reproach who let her unforgivably down by being a girl. Mother would be pleased if I grew a beard. She'd see it as a noble effort to overcome congenital weakness.

Mary, sometimes I think that turning women into surrogate men is the worst sin the opposite sex commits against us — and their most successful weapon. They can sit back and let these man-made androids hit us over the head while busily washing their hands of it all, like Pontius Pilate. It's about time they made a sci-fi film about the real fear — not Creatures From Another World taking over human beings but men in this world taking over women.

Yours, aargh,

Martha

A Fresh Tragedy .

Dear Mary

Josh came in with a bunch of daffodillies wilting in his hand. 'For you, for Mothering Sunday,' he announced. I said: 'I'm not your mother and it's Tuesday.' He took the news badly, said my remarks were ungracious and perhaps they were. But there isn't much room in the nuclear family, and if you don't keep relationships carefully labelled you'll find you're committing verbal incest. Once upon a time you had all your relatives under one roof or in the close neighbourhood, and it was easy to render unto Auntie that which was Auntie's, etcetera. Now there are so few people imprisoned within the same four walls that each incumbent has to stand in for a host of others. If your Daddy's in Australia, your brother's gone for a sailor, and you haven't got a son, then your husband has to play them all. Likewise the wife, only more so. We have to understudy for a cast of thousands — mum, sister, daughter, nanny, skivvy, cook and, all too frequently, the missing domestic animals that used to share the agricultural residence. Cow, workhorse, sheep, cat, retriever, old boiler, and, if you were lucky, a bird in a gilded cage.

No wonder we get confused. A man leaves his mother for a woman who turns into a wife and then into his mother, so he leaves mother again for another woman who turns into a wife and then into his mother and so on, theoretically, at least, till death doth him in. And we do the same, all in an attempt to escape the emotions (if not the reality) of incest. Perhaps an older generation was wiser. They accepted this as inevitable and called each other Mother and Father and no fooling about. I realise now that this is why I'm increasingly keen on seeing Ben and Jane married. Not for any of the conventional reasons but because when Jane has a new Daddy and Ben a new Mum, they'll be off my mind for the first time since they were born and someone else can worry when they're looking peaky. PS. Ben bought some Kitty-Chocs for the cat on Mothering Sunday. I do not care to think what this means.

Anyway, to get back to Josh and his daffs. After the official presentation of the bouquet, he cornered me on the upstairs landing and said we ought to have a serious talk about getting together again for the sake of the children. Jane, Ben and the baby immediately gathered round and Josh immediately bellowed naff off, which did not exactly strengthen his argument. I mentioned that in my opinion the children were managing frightfully well in the circs and there a pregnant pause. During it the Woolly Mite struggled past us clutching the spare parts from a small motorbike factory and Judas addressed us from above upon his intention instantly to strangle his publisher and decapitate his agent since neither of these benighted persons had the wit to recognise a best-selling whodunnit when it was stuffed up their jumpers.

Then came a cry of despair from Ben's room. One of his goldfish had departed for the Great Fishtank in the Sky. I couldn't leave my son alone with his grief so it was some while before I could rejoin Josh, who by that time was the worse for several ounces of cooking sherry. I said I'm sorry, Josh, but you'd have liked that fish if you'd known him, he was a very out-going sort of fish, always ready for a bit of a gurgle and a good friend to Ben but Josh only retorted, in his cold-hearted way, that he didn't know that fish, thank God, so he couldn't like that fish and did I intend to put a dead fish before a declaration of love from my husband?

Before I had time to respond, the phone rang. It was Lorna. She said she'd been to a clairvoyant a week ago and he'd seen a wreath on her front door and did I think that meant her old man was on his way out? I told her I'd seen him down the High Street yesterday and he looked in the pink and she said 'pity' and rang off. Next thing, it was Queenie on the line going on about Lorna and wreaths and how things had come to a pretty pass when your own daughter, what you'd worked your fingers to the bone for, kept talking about wreaths and buying black. Black shoes, black cardy, black skirt, all in the same week, Queenie said. Well, Lorna does work at an undertaker's, I said. No wonder, said Queenie. One look at her and you'd go under. Six feet under.

When I was finally through, Josh had gone. I felt rather bad but a man's got to realise there are other people in the world. If I do go back to him I'm not going to drop all my friends and ignore my children for his satisfaction. I did that before, and where was he when I needed him? Working late at the office is where, or that was the story. To tell you the truth, Mary, I'd like him back. Well, what I mean is I'd like a man with Josh's face and Josh's hair and Josh's cute little dimple but sans le vrai Josh. Do you think that inside him there's a whole other man struggling to get out? There's certainly a whole other woman hatching from the shell of me. Perhaps we could be a born-again couple. I, not-Martha, take thee, not-Josh, to be . . .

Ah well, as Jane always says, while there's life there's dope.

Yours, flying highish,

Martha

Dear Mary

Please, I beg you, don't ever be tempted to write a lonely-hearts column in a women's magazine — the circulation would hit rock bottom as fast, if not as messily, as the readers. Talk about depressing. If the sash cords on my windows weren't broken so the frames stick, I might be half-way to the ground right now. I mean, I tell you Josh and me have changed and that I think we have a future together and what do you say? That every silver lining has a big black cloud, that walking into the sunset means things are getting very dark, that mosquitoes and toads are born again·as well as pretty chicks and butterflies and that the phoenix doesn't exist. Oh and I forgot — most little acorns don't turn into tall oaks, they just rot where they fall. Charming. Excuse me a moment while I stick my head in the oven.

No, I know you mean well and you may be right about Josh, though I think it was the *leopard* that couldn't change his spots, jackals don't have them. Ben does, of course, but that's another story and besides, his are zits. Anyway, none of this makes any difference now because, Mary, the fact is that Josh has moved in again and we are once more a couple. A right couple. Tea for two and he for you and me for who and he for two and all that jazz. Okay, let's hear it for Josh and Martha. Three cheers. Two, then? Ah, so *that's* the sound of one hand clapping.

Well, since you ask, what happened was this. A knock at the door, I open it, Josh looms in the twilight with the terrible smile of a man who has just heard the four-minute warning. He appears concussed, he trembles, he prepares to give the pavement a big kiss. So I fetch him rapidly in (Queenie's curtains are already on the twitch) and he says in a voice like a gong in a cave: 'The Department's been axed.' He says he's been made redundant. He says he's got the chop. Then he sits down on the cat. Two more deflated objects you never saw. And I tell you, Mary, I was marvellous. I bit off the words 'so much for your precious Mrs T,' from the end of my tongue and stuffed them back down my throat. I gave Josh a hug and a swig of the old mother's ruin. I had one myself. So did the cat. I don't remember too much more except that Josh was in my bed in the morning. In case you're wondering, so was the cat.

A little time has passed since those moving moments and we have talked a lot. Or rather, Josh has talked and I have said mmm and, later, huh. Well obviously I can't sit around being supported by a redundant male, can I? And I quite see we'll do better if we pool our resources. On the other hand, Josh's idea of a solution is that he will stay at home looking after the house and the baby and Ben and the lodgers and I will rush out and get a job. Good heavens, Martha, he says, it's the chance you've always wanted. Mmm, I say. You won't recognise this place, he says, I'll have everything ship-shape in a jiffy and in between I'll write a book. Huh, I say.

That's how it goes around here now. Him, gabble, gabble. Me, mmm. Gabble gabble gabble. Huh. For two days he's been following me around with a clip-board, making horrid little notes. I said to him Josh, if I catch you with a hand-held camera concealed about your person I'll inform Equity and down tools but he only scribbled some more. He says he's familiarising himself with departmental routine. He says he's doing a Time and Motion study on me. Huh, I said. Martha, he said, can't you say anything more constructive than huh? Uh-huh, I said.

Where will it end? Even the baby's looking slightly tense. Josh put his nappies on for the first time yesterday and when he tried to stand up I thought for one awful moment that he'd lost a leg. It was all right, of course, we found it doubled up in a corner of the terry but it gave me quite a turn. Only one of many that lie ahead, I fear. Already I can't put a cigarette down without a husbandly tutting and a quick dart with the ashtray to the sink. You ought to give up smoking, Martha, Josh said, it creates unnecessary Motion. Next thing, he'll be complaining about dishpan hands.

What's more, I have to listen to him going on endlessly about how lovely it will be to relax a bit and be his own master after all those years at someone else's beck and call. The baby becks, I said. He becks a lot *and* he calls. Some would say bawls. Now Martha, *language*, he said. I don't want to hear language in *my* house. I think he was joking, but I'm not sure enough. *His* house, indeed.

You can see my problem can't you, Mary? It's one thing to consider launching myself on to an unsuspecting world in my own good time, but being booted out is quite another. Do you know, last night he actually asked me to show him how pastry was made. Have you no sense of decency, Josh? I said.

Is nothing sacred? What would mother say if she knew I had passed on such Eleusinian Mysteries? There is something called the Feminine Mystique, my man, and I'll thank you not to forget it.

Yes yes, I know, Betty Freidan didn't mean it like that — but I do. Honestly, this week I've felt like a veiled woman who's having her chador ripped off by some fearful First World reformer. I'm hanging on grimly to the last shreds because. Because. Because they're *mine*, that's why, and they might be all I've got for all I know. Surely that shove I feel between my shoulder blades isn't liberation?

Yours, only asking,

Martha

The Third World War in its honeymoon period.